ADDITIONA[...]

# TRUE B[...]

═══ ★ ═══

"Marton tells the incredible true story of Field's fanaticism with Communism and Stalinism. Marton's own parents were the only Western journalists to ever interview Field and his wife, Herta. . . . The conspiracy, subterfuge, and cataclysmic destruction of Field's family and friends are all addressed in this well-researched book."

—*Library Journal*

"Riveting page-turner."

—*National Review*

"This is more than just a spy story of white hats versus black hats. Kati Marton has written a gripping but nuanced account of the fanaticism and betrayal by one of the most notorious American traitors in Cold War history."
—Amanda Foreman, author of *A World on Fire*

"A riveting account of how fanaticism arises, who's vulnerable to it, and why. A rich portrait of a lost era, with fascinating implications for our own."
—Cass R. Sunstein, Robert Walmsley University Professor, Harvard University, and author of *Going to Extremes*

"At a time when violent extremism and fanaticism seem automatically to have an Islamic prefix, *True Believer* reminds us of equally brutal causes that swept up deluded young men and women, shattered families, and destroyed lives. Kati Marton gives us a gripping story with a timely moral."
—Anne-Marie Slaughter, president and CEO, New America, and author of *Unfinished Business: Women Men Work Family*

"In the name of justice and socialist revolution, Noel Field lost his own humanity. His story is a chilling piece of history but also a timeless moral lesson about how unmoored idealism can abet murderous evil. Kati Marton tel[...] [...]logy as well as the politic[...] *the Egalitarians*

"In this original and gripping real-life thriller, Kati Marton brings a lost chapter of the Cold War back to vivid life. In telling the story of Noel Field, Marton—a distinguished chronicler of the vicissitudes of the twentieth century, particularly in Europe—draws on a cast of characters ranging from Alger Hiss to Josef Stalin. This is a terrific piece of history."

—Jon Meacham, author of *Destiny and Power* and *Thomas Jefferson*

"Marton tells Field's story beautifully, reminding readers of the potential horrors of well-meaning but unquestioning idealism."

—*Publishers Weekly* (starred review)

"A true story of intrigue, treachery, murder, torture, fascism, and an unshakable faith in the ideals of Communism . . . Exciting to read, a fresh take on espionage activities from a critical period of history."

—*Washington Independent Review of Books*

"[Noel Field's] sordid story is grippingly related by Kati Marton, whose parents, Hungarian journalists, covered various show trials that resulted in Field and other 'traitors to the cause' being jailed. She also gained access to Field family papers and those of persons brought down with him."

—*The Washington Times*

"Fascinating."

—*The Washington Free Beacon*

"*True Believer* is both thorough and engaging. . . . Every generation has its share of such fanatics, secure in their belief that they are doing good even as they leave chaos and destruction in their wake. This portrait of a monster is an important lesson of what Communism wrought."

—*The Weekly Standard*

"Kati Marton richly documents the story of the Swiss-born, Harvard-educated Noel Field. . . . [Marton] builds a detailed narrative with twists and turns galore."

—*The Daily Gazette*

# STALIN'S
# LAST
# AMERICAN SPY

# TRUE BELIEVER

★

## KATI MARTON

SIMON & SCHUSTER PAPERBACKS

*New York London Toronto Sydney New Delhi*

Simon & Schuster Paperbacks
An Imprint of Simon & Schuster, Inc.
1230 Avenue of the Americas
New York, NY 10020

First Simon & Schuster paperback edition September 2017

SIMON & SCHUSTER PAPERBACKS and colophon are registered trademarks of Simon & Schuster, Inc.

For information about special discounts for bulk purchases, please contact Simon & Schuster Special Sales at 1-866-506-1949 or business@simonandschuster.com.

The Simon & Schuster Speakers Bureau can bring authors to your live event. For more information or to book an event, contact the Simon & Schuster Speakers Bureau at 1-866-248-3049 or visit our website at www.simonspeakers.com.

Book design by Ellen R. Sasahara

Manufactured in the United States of America

1 3 5 7 9 10 8 6 4 2

The Library of Congress has cataloged the hardcover edition as follows:

Names: Marton, Kati.
Title: The true believer : the secret life of Noel Field, Stalin's last American spy / Kati Marton.
Description: First Simon & Schuster hardcover edition. | New York : Simon & Schuster, 2016. | "Simon & Schuster nonfiction original hardcover"—Title page verso. | Includes bibliographical references and index.
Identifiers: LCCN 2015041712 (print) | LCCN 2016006744 (ebook) | ISBN 9781476763767 (hardcover : alkaline paper) | ISBN 9781476763774 (paperback : alkaline paper) | ISBN 9781476763781 ()
Subjects: LCSH: Field, Noel Haviland, 1904–1970. | Spies—United States—Biography. | Communists—United States—Biography. | Stalin, Joseph, 1878–1953—Friends and associates. | Espionage, Soviet—United States—History. | United States—Foreign relations—Soviet Union. | Soviet Union—Foreign relations—United States. | United States—Foreign relations—1933–1945. | BISAC: HISTORY / Europe / Former Soviet Republics. | BIOGRAPHY & AUTOBIOGRAPHY / Historical. | POLITICAL SCIENCE / Political Freedom & Security / Intelligence.
Classification: LCC E743.5.F47 M37 2016 (print) | LCC E743.5.F47 (ebook) | DDC 327.12092—dc23
LC record available at http://lccn.loc.gov/2015041712

ISBN 978-1-4767-6376-7
ISBN 978-1-4767-6377-4 (pbk)
ISBN 978-1-4767-6378-1 (ebook)

*To my children*
*Elizabeth Jennings and Chris Jennings*
*first readers—best companions*

# CONTENTS

# CONTENTS

# TRUE BELIEVER

# THE CAPTURE OF MINDS

*He whom a dream hath possessed knoweth no more of doubting.*

—Shaemas O'Sheel

How DOES AN idealist turn into a willing participant in murder? How does such a person—who is neither poor, nor socially deprived—learn to crush those he loves for the sake of a cause, a promise, and an illusion? Noel Field was such a man—and for that reason his story is relevant for our troubled times. The mystery at the core of Field's life is how an apparently good man, who started out with noble intentions, could sacrifice his own and his family's freedom, a promising career, and his country, all for a fatal myth. His is the story of the sometimes terrible consequence of blind faith.

*

The power of an idea that promises a final correction of all personal, social, and political injustices—be it a holy crusade, fascism, Communism, or radical Islam—can be compulsive. Some movements add the lure of immortality. They prey on questing, restless, dissatisfied youth

1

who are gradually persuaded to surrender their freedom to a higher cause, an all-knowing master. In this submission, there is relief from soul-searching. At last there is an answer to every question. Once he surrenders, the convert feels a rush of relief: his existence now has meaning beyond himself. With the conversion he gains a fraternal comradeship, a family of the like-minded. For this rapture, he yields moral responsibility, the duty to think for himself. The master—be it the führer, the commisar, or the caliph—knows best.

The submission demands service and sacrifice, a willingness to break society's rules and laws for the cause. Human lives must sometimes be sacrificed on the road to the Promised Land. Prison, torture, and the abasement of self: all are explained away as necessary for the cause. One's families are insignificant compared to the new family.

Beyond a certain point, it is hard for the convert to reclaim his moral freedom, his ability to think for himself. Without his faith, life seems empty. Without his comrades, existence looms as a lonely prospect. Then, too, the convert has almost always compromised himself in service to the cause. With the passage of time, return to his old life becomes ever less possible. He also knows that punishment for such defection can be fatal.

Noel Field's betrayal of his country and his family for the promise of Communism was not motivated merely by his deep longing for a life of significance. Like so many children of the Depression, disillusionment with democracy, capitalism, and the West's appeasement of Hitler were strong motivations in signing up with Moscow. For them, the dictatorship of the proletariat seemed to offer the only alternative to the West's breadlines and mass unemployment, as well as the only opposition to the Nazis' aggression and racism.

But Field's conversion was not essentially political. He and thousands of others deserted out of far deeper personal needs than politics. They had no way of knowing that their recruitment was managed and manipulated by hard-boiled cynics skilled at spotting society's vulnerable and promising youth. Nor did they suspect how far the reality of the workers' state would be from the promised utopia.

*

Noel Field, a sensitive, self-absorbed idealist and dreamer, was both an unlikely revolutionary and an ideal target for conversion to a powerful faith. In the 1930s, he joined the secret underground of the international Communist movement. It was a time of national collapse: ten million unemployed, rampant racism, and, before Franklin Delano Roosevelt, a Washington parched of ideas. Communism promised the righting of social and political wrongs. To Field, world revolution and the violent overthrow of his own government seemed a necessary price to pay for the ultimate triumph of the proletariat. Strict discipline and sacrifice for a cause beyond his person were expected of Field and his fellow recruits, as they are of today's Islamist warriors. Noel Field never hoisted an AK-47, or strapped on a suicide vest, because he was never asked to. But his commitment and his submission to his cause were as total, and ultimately as destructive, as those of today's ISIS recruits.

Field was not one of Stalin's master spies. He lacked both the steel and the polished performance skills of Kim Philby or Alger Hiss. Field's betrayals nonetheless led hundreds to the gallows and destroyed scores of lives. Above all, however, Noel Field's story reveals his master's boundless cruelty and sinister disregard for human life—including the life of his own faithful. Like thousands of others, Field was used—then, having served his purpose, he was discarded.

*

Communism tempted many of Field's generation. Most, having observed the chasm between the promise and the brutal reality, eventually moderated or abandoned their early zeal. Not Noel Field. Though the dream of a triumphant working class soured and turned murderous, he stayed locked to his faith. He did not die a martyr in battle, but eventually he embraced a form of the martyrdom of innocents—his own among them—because that is what his master, Stalin, ordained.

Field never publicly spoke or wrote candidly about his terrible choices. His only candor is contained in these pages—from letters never before published. As Hungarian journalists working for American wire services in Budapest in the fifties, my parents covered Field's arrest by Soviet authorities, as well as the show trial that followed. Then my parents were themselves arrested, and my father shared Field's interrogator before his own fake trial for espionage. Moreover, my father was held in the same cell the American had previously occupied; both had been "Prisoner 410" for a period. Later, during the chaos of the Hungarian Revolution of October 1956, my parents located Field and his wife, and conducted the only known press interview with them. Those are the circumstances that led me to this strange and prophetic tale, which begins in Prague in 1949.

History—and a certain human vulnerability toward messiahs of all stripes—make clear that there will be other waves of fanaticism in the future. They may be as dangerous and hard to control as the movement that now captures fighters for militant Islam, or the one that once held Noel Field.

# THE TRAP

*I never knew a man who had better motives for all the trouble he caused.*

—Graham Greene

*Kafka's images are alive in Prague because they anticipate totalitarian society.*

—Milan Kundera

I N MAY 1949 an American of patrician bearing, with the slight stoop of a tall man, walks the streets of Prague. Though Noel Field appears aimless and unhurried, he is not a tourist. Tourists are scarce in Prague during the second year of Soviet rule, and foreigners, especially Americans, even more rare. Czechs passing Field avoid eye contact with a man so obviously from the enemy camp. They have no way of knowing that this elegant man with the long, aquiline features is a Soviet agent. The American is in Prague because he has nowhere else to go. For two decades he has lived a double life. Noel Field is unaware that his life as a traitor is about to be brutally ended—not by the country he betrayed, the United States, but by the one he serves, the Soviet Union.

As always in his life replete with terrible choices, Field is focused on the rightness of the one he has just made. He has come East to escape an FBI subpoena. Field knows and loves the medieval city on the Vltava River, and tries now to let Prague work its timeless magic on his agitated spirit. On the surface, the quiet streets below the immense Hradčany castle seem unchanged. Prague had been spared the bombing that destroyed so many other ancient European cities during the recent world war. Though the great Baroque and Gothic monuments stand undisturbed, Prague's spirit has been snuffed out. An eerie stillness hangs over the town; people in the streets do their business, then hurry home. No carefree laughter wafts from the cafés off Wenceslas Square to break the quiet. This is not the old Prague. Noel Field, however, has the gift of seeing only what he chooses to see.

As the days pass, Field pays ever less attention to the statues of Baroque saints lined up like sentries on either side of the Charles Bridge. The prematurely gray-haired American shambles unseeing among these architectural wonders. Daily he passes 22 Golden Lane, Franz Kafka's house in the Old Town. Out of habit, he still pauses before the Gothic tower of the Old Town Hall, but he is no longer mesmerized by the hourly appearance of Death clanging its bell to mark the time.

How strange that so many friends—comrades from the Spanish Civil War and the Communist International, whom he had helped in so many ways—were too busy, or out of town. Yet they had encouraged Field to come to Prague, held out the prospect of a teaching job at the famed Charles University. When he hears nothing more about the job offer that lured him here, does he have a premonition? Some sense that he is about to embark on his own Kafkaesque journey? Did the seasoned spy realize that his every step in the Old Town is shadowed?

The American's bland, expressionless features do not quite mask his anxiety. Secrecy—from even friends and family—was hardwired into Field. Recently, Field's secret exploded in articles in his own country's front pages. Whittaker Chambers, a confessed Soviet spy, named Noel Field in his Senate testimony about Communists in the highest reaches of the US government. Chambers shattered Field's meticulously compartmentalized life. The *New York Times* revealed still more details in its coverage of the trial of Noel's friend and fellow Soviet agent Alger Hiss. With dread mounting, Noel had read those accounts in his home in Geneva. He admired his friend Alger's smooth deception under oath, but knew he was incapable of such a performance. One step ahead of an FBI subpoena, Noel fled to the presumed safety of Prague.

Field could not know that the Kremlin had chosen him for a key role in the upcoming purge of Stalin's would-be enemies. The fact that Field was Stalin's loyal foot soldier was irrelevant. Noel Field, who knew all those targeted by Stalin for liquidation—and was a citizen of the new enemy—would make the perfect witness against them. Starting in 1949, the paranoid Soviet leader prescribed a fresh wave of terror and show trials, with Noel Field—his faithful acolyte—at their center.

Field's idle stroll through the ancient city would be his last as a free man for many years.

He had served his masters with unflinching loyalty. In the thirties, as a State Department official and later at the League of Nations, and, recently, as head of an American humanitarian relief agency, Field's loyalty to Moscow never wavered. For a long time, his earnest air of a wide-eyed idealist put most people off the scent.

Five aimless days after checking into the gloomy, tattered splendor of the Palace Hotel near Wenceslas Square, Field got the call he was waiting for. Someone was ready to talk to him about his future. On May 12, 1949, Noel strode calmly through the Palace's revolving doors and did not reappear for six years. He would never see his own country again.

Minutes after leaving the Palace Hotel, rough hands clapped a chloroform-soaked rag on the American's face. When, several hours later, Field regained consciousness, he was handcuffed and blindfolded, his head covered by a sack. At the Czech-Hungarian border town of Bratislava, Czech secret police agents turned him over to his new captors. All Field knew was that he was in the hands of people who spoke a language he did not understand. Noel Field's life as prisoner of the AVO—the Hungarian secret police—had begun. The stage manager of the Hungarians' every brutal step, however, was the man Field most revered: Josef Stalin. A decade and a half after his conversion to Communism, Field had become Stalin's latest victim.

★

This is the astonishing tale of an American's journey from pacifist idealist to hard-core Stalinist. The stage, however, is much wider. In the late twenties and early thirties, a disillusioned generation despaired at America's ability to solve its own problems. Before FDR's transformative, optimistic activism, the country was on its knees. In the 1930s America stood for hunger, unemployment, broken promises, and smashed hopes. With eleven million Americans out of work, it was a failed state. Capitalism—indeed, democracy—seemed to have run out of new ideas. The national mood was sour and self-absorbed. The 1927 executions of Italian immigrants Nicolo Sacco and Bartolomeo Vanzetti revealed corrosive social injustice at the nation's heart.

A continent away, fascism was surging. Many wondered if the American system was even worth saving. Appalled by the injustices, thirsting to make a difference, they were drawn to a radical ideology that left no room for doubt or skepticism. Communism shone bright in the aftermath of the successful Russian Revolution. Its dogma offered answers to social, political, and personal problems, and promised a radiant future for humanity. To echo Abraham Lincoln's words, it appeared to many of Field's generation as "the last best hope of earth."

It was more than the Depression, and more than Washington's passivity in the face of fascism that fueled Field's alienation and led him to work actively for the overthrow of his own government. His was a quest for a life of meaning that went horribly wrong. Such was Communism's power over him that not even Moscow's admission that Field's hero, Stalin, himself betrayed the dream shook his faith.

# CHAPTER 1

# A SWISS CHILDHOOD

*I went to Communism, as one goes to a spring of fresh water.*

—Arthur Koestler

NOEL HAVILAND FIELD spent his first eighteen years in the Swiss lakeside town of Zurich. It was a tidy if dull place, where money, science, and Christian values commingled. Here Noel's father, Dr. Herbert Haviland Field, a Harvard-trained biologist and Quaker pacifist, set up his research and documentation institute. Switzerland, then as now, cherished its neutrality in a sea of fractious neighbors. Beneath its tranquil surface, however, Zurich was a listening post for both sides during the first and second world wars. Both the elder Field and his son Noel would be swept up in Zurich's web of intrigue—the son more lethally than the father.

A burly, bushy-bearded Victorian paterfamilias, Noel's father built the Field family's massive stone house—the very embodiment of their solid, New England values. In the Harvard alumni newsletter of 1938, the elder Field was described by a classmate as "one of the most high minded and pure minded men I have ever known, and I doubt that the

Quaker spirit ever produced a finer specimen of mentality or character." Field family life revolved around this intimidating and remote figure. All Fields addressed each other in the Quaker manner as "Thee" and "Thou." This earnest, rather austere family was singularly ill prepared for the intrigue in which they would soon be enmeshed.

The Fields first settled in Boston, Massachusetts, in 1644. They were proud of their sturdy Yorkshire roots, and their political nonconformism. Even during the Revolutionary War, the Quaker Fields, referred to as "between the lines," supported neither colonists nor the colonial power, and were thus harassed by both. Pacifism and service were the family's core values and, in quest of both, the Fields gradually migrated from Boston to Brooklyn over the next hundred years. In keeping with their Quaker faith during the Civil War, the family actively supported and sheltered slaves in flight from Southern states.

Much later, Noel described himself as a "dreamy, feminine, and withdrawn child, shunning interaction with peers." From early childhood, Noel was an outsider: an American in a Swiss school; taller, more awkward, and more earnest than other children. Emulating his father's air of moral superiority did not win him playmates. The boy preferred long, solitary Alpine rambles to the rough-and-tumble of the schoolyard. He had one companion, a classmate, Herta Vieser. The plump, blond daughter of a German civil servant, she, too, was an outsider. With her long blond braids and full figure, Herta was in sharp contrast to the gangly Noel. But in her eyes, the bookish, wistful Noel could do no wrong. Herta's unshakeable devotion eased the awkward youth's loneliness—and would for a lifetime.

For the rest of his life, Noel would recall a single childhood event more vividly than any other. Shortly after the end of World War I, Dr. Field took Noel, his eldest child, on a tour of the battlefields. The trip was of such importance to his father that he ordered a car from America to make the drive to the recent killing fields of Verdun and the Marne. The still-smoldering battlefields where not a living thing stirred made a powerful impression on the young Noel. He never forgot the landscape of blackened tree trunks and lunar craters full of stagnant water, where hundreds of thousands of the Continent's youth had recently been slaughtered—and for what? A few miles of territory. They rested under mounds of still-fresh earth—and left a searing memory. Thanks to the machine gun, automatic rifle, poison gas, airplane, and tank, a thousand soldiers died per square meter in Verdun, Dr. Field explained to his son. And what was achieved by four and a half years of carnage? The trauma suffered by the eleven million soldiers who returned from the front—having experienced poison gas, exploding grenades, and artillery barrages, as well as the deaths of their comrades—was beyond compensation. Noel took his father's unspoken message to heart: *Do something to prevent the next one.*

"A Call to the Young Throughout the World" by N. Field, founder of the "Peace League of Youth," was the young man's first political engagement and a direct result of that shattering battlefield expedition. "We must not wait any longer," Noel wrote in a tract that his mother typed and that he distributed to his classmates at his Swiss *gymnasium.* "If the rising generation of the whole world were to cry with one voice: Enough of slaughter and murder! From now on let there be peace! If they were to set to work and start a real crusade against war, then a world peace will no longer be an idle dream."

Noel then outlined a ten-part program for the youth of the world, including abolishing war propaganda and military training in schools. "So come and lend a hand!" Noel urged his classmates. "Forget the barriers of country, race, and religion, show that we are brothers! We will not confront might with might, but with *the persuasive power of a great idea, the firm conviction of a divine ideal."*

Within a decade, the young man would find both the divine ideal and the brotherhood he hungered for.

"My high school days in Switzerland during World War I," Noel wrote, "were the determining factor in the choice of my subsequent life. They set up my dual interest . . . to work for international peace, and to help improve the social conditions of my fellow being." He might have added that they also laid the groundwork for his dual life.

\*

Wedged among France, Germany, and Italy, Switzerland, haven to fleeing European radicals, was the ideal spot for Allen W. Dulles, a spy operating under diplomatic cover, to set up shop in Berne, the Swiss capital. Shortly after Noel's field trip with his father in 1918, he met Dulles, whose name would be like a curse on Field's future. Dulles, two decades from becoming the first director of the Central Intelligence Agency, the brother of future secretary of state John Foster Dulles, was in search of local "assets."

Dr. Field, who straddled the expatriate and Swiss communities, was known to keep his ear to the ground, a good man to know. During World War I, the elder Field routinely shared high-level local gossip with US officials. In fact, his meddling nearly ruined the career of American consul James C. McNally. Field complained to the State Department about McNally's too "pro German" attitude. McNally never forgave him, though others admired Field's zealous patriotism. Another Swiss-based American diplomat, Hugh Wilson, described Noel's father as having "the gentlest, bluest, most candid pair of eyes that I ever saw on an adult man. They were the eyes of an unsophisticated and lovable child." His son inherited that candid, childlike aspect and used it to great advantage.

In early 1918, Allen Dulles joined the Field family for lunch in their spacious lakeside home. "What do you plan to do with your life?" Dulles asked the reedy fourteen-year-old Noel. "To bring peace to the world," the boy answered without hesitation, making his father beam with pride. The lesson of the battlefield had hit its mark. Dulles and Noel Field would meet again, two decades later, and cause each other great trouble.

\*

On the morning of April 5, 1921, everything changed for the Field family. Fifty-three-year-old Herbert Field suddenly suffered a massive heart attack and died. The peaceful, well-ordered family life presided over by the aloof father was shattered. The eldest of four children, Noel—the focus of his father's attention—was hardest hit. Moreover, he felt a personal responsibility for his father's death. The night before his fatal attack, Dr. Field had fulfilled one of his dreams. A passionate admirer of Richard Wagner, he had talked for years of taking Noel to the first Swiss performance of *Parsifal*. "In the months and years after his death," Noel later wrote, "I built up a guilt complex, believing that I had caused [Father's] death by hurrying him up the stairs at the opera performance to which we arrived late."

His father had high hopes for his bright, sensitive son. But he left the job unfinished. Noel, emotionally immature and highly sensitive, was suddenly unmoored. Full of outrage at the world's cruelties and guilt at his privileged status, he was now without direction or guidance. Years later, he wrote his younger brother, Hermann:

> You ask for my memories of our beloved father. . . . I loved, revered and stood in awe of him, almost as a distant, unknown and unknowable *god*. He was often absent and even when at home, always so busy that I was afraid to approach him (I can still hear Mother's "Hush, Father is busy, don't disturb him!").
>
> [After his death] I began a pathological hero worship in which I pictured him as one of the greatest saints of modern times and swore to imitate him as a means of relieving my guilt.
>
> Of one thing I am certain: had he lived longer, there would have been growing conflict between him and his elder son—unless I had simply taken over his ideals and sought to adapt my thinking to his. This I know: his socialism was of the *religious* kind and in his diary he expressed hostility to the more militant variety that I ultimately found my way to.

At age seventeen, Noel lost the powerful figure who might have moderated his dreams of changing the world. How differently might Field's tragic life have turned out had his father lived long enough to harness his son's idealism to a milder faith?

"Not long before his death," Noel wrote his brother, "Father had a serious talk with me about my future. . . . It was, as I remember, mainly a question of his desire that I should . . . go to America, to study at his beloved Harvard."

Reeling from the sudden loss of their patriarch, his widow, Nina, and her four children set off for Herbert Haviland Field's cherished homeland. There, too, Noel Field would be a stranger.

# CHAPTER 2

# AMERICA

*I can sum up the United States in two words:*
*Prohibition and Lindbergh!*

—Benito Mussolini

NOEL'S FANTASY AMERICA was a land of boundless opportunity, free from the Old World's stagnant class system and its savage wars. All Noel knew of this distant land he had heard from his father.

Harvard in September 1922 was a shock to the young man. The most privileged sanctuary of American higher learning, it did not match Noel's fantasies.

Many undergraduates in those days arrived with trunks containing dinner jackets, tennis rackets, golf clubs, and the swagger of those born to privilege. The sons of the nouveau riche shunned Harvard Yard for the more opulent new dormitories on the "Gold Coast," Mount Auburn Street. In their sophomore year, the social clubs picked the brightest stars from the new crop—the *Crimson*'s editors, the *Lampoon*'s wits, and the man who might score the final, memorable touchdown against Yale. There were still other Harvards—for scholars, for carousers, for those already decided on a Wall Street career. Noel did not fit in with any of these Harvards.

Instead of a dorm, Noel lived at home, in the faded gentility of a Berkeley Street row house. With three younger siblings, and a matriarch presiding, this was not a place the freshman would bring new friends. Filial obligation had brought him to Harvard; he treated it as a place to get through honorably, but as fast as possible. Taking twice as many courses as required, he earned his BA with highest honors in two years.

As awkward outsider in the hail-fellow world of the Yard, Noel's social conscience deepened. In a 1923 term paper entitled "On the Present Distribution of Property" he submitted for his Social Ethics course, the nineteen-year-old raised issues that still seem strikingly relevant. "There are two very dark spots . . . in the existing system . . . which have led to the *crying injustice* of the present distribution of wealth. It is not right to pass on to the heir enormous wealth without the latter's moving a finger for it. Inheritance of property seems to be as old as mankind; and yet I think it is a great evil and *must* be changed if social injustice is to stop.

"And as for interest on capital," he wrote, "its injustice appears to me self-evident. If a man can live off this interest, while his capital is increasing without his doing any work, while millions of others have to work for every crumb, it is clear that the fundamental justification of property is completely disregarded."

Later, he would regret his Harvard years as a missed opportunity. Four years after graduating, he wrote Hermann, "Nobody has ever been interested in the fact that I graduated with distinction . . . whereas the fact that I raced through college without mixing in its life and without learning its practical life lessons has caused me endless embarrassment." Social embarrassment fueled Noel Field's alienation from American life.

★

Noel's deepest estrangement from his country occurred outside the classroom. Nicola Sacco and Bartolomeo Vanzetti, rarely recalled today, in the 1920s came to symbolize the political volatility of the Depression. A shoemaker and a fish peddler, the pair of Italian immigrants were charged with robbery and murder in a Braintree, Massachusetts, payroll holdup in a case that grew from local crime story to an international cri de coeur. Sacco and Vanzetti—names redolent of ethnicity and the immigrant experience—turned into a chant that galvanized the Depression era.

Class resentments that normally simmer below America's surface exploded in the trial of the two self-declared anarchists. In the witness box, the two immigrants mangled their English and reeked of stubborn unassimilation, a couple of "greasy wops," in the era's ugly vernacular. Facing an all-Anglo-Saxon jury and a judge who freely declared his hatred of radicals, Sacco and Vanzetti never had a chance at a fair trial. ("Did you see what I did with those anarchist bastards the other day?" Judge Webster Thayer was heard to remark at a Dartmouth football game, after he had turned down a defense motion for a new trial. "That will hold them for a while!")

The Boston trial became one of those not-to-be-missed events, a magnet for the day's celebrities, pundits, poets, and radicals of all shades, some of whom were actually interested in getting Bartolomeo Vanzetti and Nicola Sacco a fair hearing. For much of the population, one and a half years after World War I, pumped by patriotic fever and growing isolationism, love of country was on trial.

"Did you love this country in the last week of May, 1917?" the prosecutor asked Sacco, referring to the week of the crime.

"That is pretty hard for me to say in one word," the shoemaker answered, sealing his fate. The prosecution never established a motive, nor was the stolen money ever found. A jury not of their peers sentenced the accused to die in the electric chair. The case took seven agonizing years to resolve—seven years during which Sacco and Vanzetti languished in prison and young idealists like Noel Field grew more estranged from their country.

On August 23, 1927, far from the searchlights and machine-gun-wielding guards of Boston's Charlestown State Prison, Noel huddled by his shortwave radio and waited for the announcement of Sacco and Vanzetti's death by electrocution. Then he wept.

Field later recalled the moment—and its impact on his life. "From that midnight of the two martyrs in a Boston jail, there is a chain of events leading in an almost straight line to the present," Field wrote. "I am no Sacco, no Vanzetti. . . . But in my own much smaller way I have remained true to the beliefs that began to take shape . . . during the ghastly wake, when hope changed to despair."

In 1977, to mark the fiftieth anniversary of their executions, Massachusetts governor Michael S. Dukakis ordered a reexamination of the Sacco and Vanzetti trial. "It is my conclusion," the governor's chief legal counsel, Daniel A. Taylor, wrote, "that there are substantial, indeed compelling, grounds for believing that the Sacco and Vanzetti legal proceedings were permeated with unfairness, and that a proclamation issued by you would be appropriate."

The governor obliged, but no proclamation fifty years later could heal the terrible injury done to America, or its devastating impact on Noel Field's generation. "America our nation," wrote John Dos Passos, "has been beaten by strangers who have turned our language inside out who have taken the clean words our fathers spoke and made them slimy and foul."

For Field, the fact that the president of his own university, A. Lawrence Lowell, was head of a commission to review the death sentence, and affirmed it, made the case even more personal and more deeply disillusioning.

★

Across the Atlantic, in Berlin, Willi Münzenberg, a rumpled but brilliant agent of Lenin, the father of the Russian Revolution, saw opportunity and hatched his plan. The Sacco and Vanzetti case was Münzenberg's unexpected gift from a land he barely knew. Münzenberg—electric with ideas for manipulating global public opinion—had been chosen by Lenin to spread the message of Marxism to Western intellectuals.

Arthur Koestler, the future author of *Darkness at Noon*, the work that did much to unmask Stalinism's sinister face, worked for Münzenberg's Paris-based agitprop machine, and recalled Münzenberg as "short and stocky, a man of proletarian origin, magnetic personality of immense driving power and a hard, seductive charm." Known as the Red Eminence of the international anti-fascist movement, Münzenberg swiftly organized international committees, congresses, and movements to protest Sacco and Vanzetti's executions. Though Münzenberg's name or actual affiliation never appeared anywhere, his was the invisible director's hand that exploded Sacco and Vanzetti's executions into a global cause.

For Communism to flourish outside Russia, "the myth of America"—land of opportunity, final sanctuary for the world's hopeless—had to be destroyed. Supported by a web of agents, Münzenberg's Comintern—the Communist International—organized "Sacco and Vanzetti Defense Committees" in world capitals. Even before the executions, crowds surged down Paris's great boulevards, tore lampposts from sidewalks, and hurled them through shop windows. For the first time in history, tanks ringed the American embassy in Paris. Sixty policemen were injured by an angry mob of protesters. Similar scenes played out all over Europe and Asia. None of this was spontaneous. Münzenberg choreographed it all. Blessed with a dream cast of Yankee villains, led by the arch-WASP judge Webster Thayer, Münzenberg galvanized idealists worldwide. Co-opting such Western celebrity intellectuals as Ernest Hemingway, John Dos Passos, Arthur

Koestler, Lillian Hellman, and Dorothy Parker, Münzenberg more or less invented the art of the ideological spin. Noel Field may not have heard of Münzenberg, but he made an ideal target for the latter's campaign.

The executions of Sacco and Vanzetti sparked a generational revulsion, stoked by Münzenberg. With Noel, alienation grew in step with his romantic yearning for a radical transformation of society. He was not alone. Lincoln Steffens, Malcolm Cowley, and Upton Sinclair agreed with Edmund Wilson, who declared that Russia "is the moral top of the world where the light really never goes out." The lure of a distant and mysterious land that had recently cleansed itself of a tired, corrupt tyranny was powerful. In the Russian Revolution's aftermath, disaffected youth like Noel Field wondered why their own country couldn't cast down capitalism and militarism as easily as the Soviets had. Communism seemed on the brink of a worldwide explosion. Russian literature, Russian music, and the Russian sages Lenin and Trotsky were all the rage among liberal intellectuals. Few were aware of the human cost of the "cleansing" that brought the Communists to power, and kept them there.

CHAPTER 3

# THE MAKING OF A RADICAL

*It is already very hard to remember that, only a generation ago, there were . . . Americans who believed our society was not merely doomed, but undeserving of survival . . . crying out to be exterminated.*

—Murray Kempton

G RADUATING FROM HARVARD with full honors after only two years, it was natural for Noel, an international-minded idealist, to take the Foreign Service exam. The written part he passed with flying colors—one of eighteen young men (they were all men) chosen, out of three hundred candidates. The judges of his oral examination, however, found the bright, multilingual youth emotionally immature and not ready for overseas assignment. "Lacking in social experience," they wrote, "he has good breeding and is distinctly a gentleman."

On September 1, 1926, the excited newlyweds, Noel and Herta— for she had followed him from Zurich to Cambridge three years earlier—boarded a Washington-bound train. To mark the day, and following the tradition of the times, Noel posed for a formal photograph by a prominent Washington photographer. The handsome young man is looking directly into the camera, a serene smile on his lips, eyes wide with anticipation, eager to begin his life of service.

★

In the late 1920s, Washington, DC, kept an unhurried pace. Lights in government offices rarely burned into the night. Seven hundred clanging streetcars ferried Washingtonians from the distant suburbs of Chevy Chase and Silver Spring to the Pennsylvania Avenue hub. Most passengers—gentlemen in straw boaters and ladies in the loose frocks of the Jazz Age—were there because the government was. Foggy Bottom, where the State Department stands today, was a "Negro" slum, and Georgetown had not yet been discovered as a picturesque enclave for the wealthy. Over one-quarter of Washington's population was black, but African Americans were barred from most department stores, movies, and government cafeterias.

In those pre-air-conditioning days, Washington's climate was officially deemed "subtropical," particularly interesting for the study of insects. The Lincoln Memorial and the Washington Monument drew sparse clusters of wilting tourists; there was no Jefferson Memorial, or yet a Supreme Court building. Security was virtually nonexistent in the nation's capital. The State Department occupied part, not all, of a sprawling architectural monstrosity next door to the White House, sharing space with the War and Navy Departments. During the summer, President Calvin Coolidge—who did not have a telephone on his desk—usually called it a day at lunchtime. The four-hour day was Coolidge's notion of an effective presidency.

Washington—a provincial outpost in a continent-size country—felt remote from foreign crises. What difference did Japanese aggression against China really make to *us*? The capital was also cut off from its own nation's growing distress. News came slowly, mostly on the radio, and the newspapers were largely Republican owned and sluggish in reporting the bad news seeping from the heartland. The town—for it could hardly be called a city—was decades from becoming capital of a world power.

Coolidge—a pro-business, pro–tax cuts, laissez-faire executive—presided over a prosperous, self-satisfied, and self-absorbed nation. The twenties still roared. Coolidge disdained market regulation, almost as much as he discouraged American membership in the League of Nations. "The business of America," he famously intoned, "is business." He sought to be and succeeded in being the *least* interventionist president in American history. When he spoke—a rare event—it was to urge Americans to pour their lifetime savings into the bottomless pit of the stock market. The day his own Treasury Department urged him to take control of the investment market, he turned away and retreated to the White House basement to admire apples sent him by a Vermont farmer. To Will Rogers's question of how the president kept so fit in a job that had broken Woodrow Wilson, Coolidge answered, "By avoiding the big problems."

When Wall Street crashed in 1929, "Silent Cal" was as astonished as anyone, but by then he was enjoying a peaceful retirement in Northampton, Massachusetts. His punishment for driving his nation into an iceberg was to witness the closing of his hometown bank, the Northampton Savings Bank—and the daily sight of neighbors, homeless and jobless as local factories, one after another, shuttered.

★

For Noel Field, however, the world was still a place of promise. Inside the State Department's gleaming marble corridors and mahogany-paneled chambers, he shared space with some of his generation's brightest and most ambitious young men. State was a gentlemen's club of Ivy League graduates. Having secured a coveted spot in the West European Division, Field quickly earned a reputation as a talented researcher and drafter. "Field was one of the most brilliant men we have ever had in this Division," wrote one of his superiors. Soon, he was charged with helping prepare for the upcoming naval disarmament conference in London.

Despite his success, Noel still felt an outsider looking in, still in search of a deeper fulfillment than any bureaucracy could offer. "I have been a pacifist," he wrote his mother on December 19, 1926, "I have been a socialist, I have been a liberal, I have been an atheist—I have espoused many a cause . . . but what do I *do*? I have believed that I could stand firm to my ideals in the diplomatic service. But can I?" he asked. "Unless I ground myself firmly in *some deep and lasting foundation*, I will be torn loose and drift in the stream instead of battling with it and guiding its course. I must base my life on an inner, spiritual plan, grounded in high ideals." Of his job at State, he wrote, "I am dissatisfied. It's so very different from what I dreamed of as a boy." Noel still missed and was obsessed with his father. "I know that Father would not be pleased if he saw deep into me. He would find that I am wasting energies." He yearned for a deeper reward. "If I can't be a guiding star, a leader of men, as I once dreamed, at least I will try to be a light which will brighten the path for others."

Noel and Herta settled into a shabby two-story walkup near Union Station, in a seedy neighborhood deemed unsuitable for a State Department official. The Fields liked it that way. They did not join the socially ambitious, young diplomatic set. "We had neither servants, nor even a car," Noel recalled, "and when we invited colleagues for dinner, my wife was the cook, the maid and the hostess all in one." They also liked having "Negro" neighbors, with whom they socialized. This, too, was radical behavior for the times. The only African Americans Noel encountered at State were messengers and the waiters who served the secretary of state in his private dining room.

"The race problem interests me more and more," Noel wrote his mother in the spring of 1927. "It may be my undoing so far as my career is concerned, for it is a crime for a man of my position to talk with colored people more often than with whites. My most pleasant evenings here in Washington have been in their midst."

Field's humanitarian instincts were real and ran deep. In 1927, he wrote his mother pleading with her to help save "the great Negro college down South," Fisk University, from bankruptcy.

On the way to his office each morning, Field passed men in business suits lined up for a handful of menial day jobs. Noel did what he could for the hungry huddled in church doorways. Sometimes he invited "hoboes"—as they were called during the Depression—home for a meal. By night, he found solace and inspiration in John Reed's account of the Russian Revolution, *Ten Days That Shook the World*; Karl Marx's *Das Kapital*; and Lenin's *The State and Revolution*.

Allen Dulles—who had last seen Noel at his father's home in Zurich—ran into Noel demonstrating with a group of his black friends against a segregated Washington theater. "Come join us, Allen," Noel urged his friend. Dulles and his wife, Clover, politely declined. They had tickets to the performance Noel was picketing.

"Mother," Field wrote, "if I don't make a success in the Foreign Service—don't be too surprised or too pained," he said, as if preparing her for his future. "It's a brilliant career and all that—but brilliant things often have no soul. I remember Father's admonition . . . not to be deterred from doing what was right simply for fear of what those around me would say. . . . If I lose my job it will be because of my beliefs, and these, I know, Thee would not want me to sacrifice."

Noel assured his mother, however, that he was no longer that anguished, vacillating youth. "I was different," he wrote her on January 8, 1927, "when I spent day and night groveling and worrying and self-torturing; that was wrong and useless and there's no danger of my doing that again. It's so different now. There's no self-torturing, no long introspection." Noel was silent about the source of his new peace of mind. He was clear, however, regarding the government he still served. "I am being rent asunder between loyalty and deep conviction that this same government is wrong, wrong, wrong in its dealings with other nations." He does not elaborate why Washington was wrong, wrong, wrong.

Though by 1927 Noel had begun to explore a radical new faith, bursts of youthful exuberance—and pride—still occasionally broke through his discontent. "I wish I could send Thee some of the crocuses," Noel wrote his mother, on March 14, 1927, "that dot the White House lawn," unmistakably proud of his proximity to the presidential garden—and the seat of power. "A year or two ago," he wrote, "I would have thought myself a lunatic even to have dreamt of someday being in a position to observe the secret weaving of history while sitting at a desk of the Division of Western European Affairs. . . . It's rather a nice feeling to see how indispensable I've become in the Department and to hear them worrying about what will happen while I'm away at Xmas," he boasted. "My chief told me I'd probably find my desk snowed under with documents when I get back, because everybody will say, 'Oh, let's leave this til Field gets back, he knows all about it anyway.' "

In the same letter to his mother, Noel casually mentions, "Sunday night, after the picnic, several of us went to hear William Foster, the Communist candidate for President, speak."

The secret radical was nonetheless dazzled by a visit from the greatest hero of the day. On June 23, 1927, aviator Charles Lindbergh, "Lucky Lindy," brought his magic to the State Department and revived Noel's flagging dreams of greatness. "This morning," Noel exulted, "when Lindbergh visited the State Department, I stood right next to him—and all I saw was a tired, lovable boy, with bloodshot, exhausted eyes, absolutely unaffected, without a trace of the pride which the spectacular triumphs from city to city would surely have created in most men. . . . Nothing that has happened in recent years has again given me as much faith in humanity and revived my belief that fundamentally every man is good at heart. Napoleon is called great because he slaughtered millions. Pershing is honored because he smashed the Huns. But has the world ever before witnessed mankind worshipping a hero not of war, but of peace—not a bombastic, triumphant giant, but a simple-minded, pure-hearted young boy, who in his whole character represents the very best that is America—to see not only this country but all mankind rejoicing in this symbol of youth and courage and simplicity, is in itself, one of the most marvelous wonders I have experienced."

In two decades, Charles Lindbergh, like the young man who gushed about him, would make a terrible choice: the former chose friendship with Hitler; the latter, with Stalin.

★

Noel Field's path to an alternate faith was gradual, and tortured. He yearned for a life of *meaning*—undergirded by a belief system that as-suaged all his self-doubt, in ways that his Quaker belief did not. His after hours were spent reading tomes that confirmed his growing dis-satisfaction with America. Charles Beard's sharply critical *Rise of Amer-ican Civilization* "is by far the greatest history book I've come across," Noel wrote his brother, Hermann, in early 1927 after reading Beard's work, which posits economic self-interest as the primary driver in American history. "It's completely changed my view on this country's background." On November 14, 1927, he asked his mother to send him the following books:

*The New Theatre and Cinema of Soviet Russia* by Huntley Carter
*Chains* by Henri Barbusse
*Karl Marx and Friedrich Engels* by David Riazanov
*The Economic Theory of the Leisure Class* by Nikolai Bukharin

He also began to subscribe (secretly) to the *Daily Worker*, the Amer-ican Communist Party organ.

"My real life," Noel wrote his brother, Hermann, on October 23, 1928, "begins in my free hours—in the evenings and in the early morning hours—studying, writing little essays . . . trying to understand the reality behind the mask of things."

To his mother, who must have complained about all the books he was asking her to send him, in an undated letter from the same period, he wrote, "A number of the works I am studying I can get in the Library; but most of them are *socialistic* and I therefore prefer *not to compromise myself by borrowing them*; that is why I want them to keep." Then, more poignantly, he adds, "Thee sees, Mother dear, I can't go on indefinitely not knowing exactly where I stand in this world—whether I am a Socialist, or a Liberal, or a Radical or a Democrat—these are all questions that bother me ever stronger, and I'm determined to make up my mind soon; but I can't do that until I know something definite about all these movements—and my aim is to gain this knowledge before next summer. I think this will explain to Thee the general trend of the books I am seeking."

It is remarkable that in his midtwenties, Noel still put almost total faith in books. He had lived a sheltered, family-centered life. Herta was an extension of his childhood; they had been together since they met in grade school. A romantic, idealistic young man, Noel shied away from real life experience in favor of dusty tomes by largely failed revolutionaries. There was one exception: Vladimir Ilyich Lenin, whose revolution appeared a shining success. Noel devoured Lenin's *What Is to Be Done?*.

"Last week we saw 'the Fall of St. Petersburg,' " Noel wrote his brother in late 1927, "a Bolshevik film which is as great if not greater than *Potemkin*, in fact I sat through three performances and might have seen a fourth if I had time." Noel's fantasy of the workers' paradise was shaped partly by the same public relations genius who mobilized world outrage after the Sacco and Vanzetti executions. Willi Münzenberg, still operating under cover, mass-produced articles, newsreels, and bestselling books about the rising Soviet phoenix, side by side with "exposés" of capitalism's decay. Everything beamed to the West about the Soviet state was triumphant: the willing collectivization of the peasantry; five-year plans ahead of schedule; smiling, muscular workers parading beneath the heroic portraits of the icons Marx, Lenin, and Stalin.

It wasn't only Soviet propaganda that gushed disinformation. The *New York Times* correspondent in Moscow, Walter Duranty, also spun a pro-Stalinist line. "It is better, no doubt," Duranty wrote in his arrogantly titled memoir, *I Write as I Please*, "for a foreign correspondent to stick to the facts as far as he can, and allow the interpretation to be provided editorially by his home office, but *if the latter lacks sufficient information*, as was the case about Russia . . . it is the duty of the correspondent to fill the gap where he can." "Fill the gap" the *Times*man did, writing with pride, "Stalin himself expressed my attitude rather neatly the last time I saw him. . . . He said, 'You have done a good job in your reporting of the USSR, although you are not a Marxist, because you tried to tell the truth about our country and to understand it and explain it to your readers.' " Rare praise, indeed, from one of the twentieth century's bloodiest tyrants, who dispatched most of his own country's truth tellers to the Gulag or to oblivion.

On the eve of 1928, Noel wrote his resolutions for the coming year:

Remember that self-control is the first requisite for self-fulfillment. Practice self-control of the body as well as of thought and emotion.

How unworthy that wish not to meet your colored friends while walking along with your business colleagues. And you a socialist!

Have the courage to be yourself. There is no need to flaunt your views to those who do not understand.

Let your voice express the harmony of personality toward which you are striving; let it be quiet, gentle, slow, expressive, confidence awakening—like Father's.

*If you must wear a mask to the world* remove it at least to your wife. Let her know the truth about you.

The days' events continued to fuel Field's radicalization. Following the 1928 election of Herbert Hoover, he wrote his mother, "I was thoroughly disappointed with the result. But there is one good thing in it: the breaking up of the 'Solid South'—and I'm hoping that it will mean the end of the Democratic Party—founded on race hatred—and the formation of a new, progressive party to oppose the present dictatorship of Big Business—for Hoover means little else, to my mind."

By July 18, 1929, his dissatisfaction with the lack of real reform had hardened into cynicism.

"I have lying before me on my desk," he wrote his mother, "a voluminous letter to Hoover from Paul Otlet, seeking support for his perennial World City Scheme. The poor old man, if he only realized the guffaws such a letter must cause here. Naturally, the answer is in the most routine form, drafted by one of the clerks in our office and all the many documents he sent will never get anywhere near Mr. Hoover. It make me heartsick to think of all these idealists riding their own particular little hobby to salvation and believing that someday surely the world must recognize them for their great ideas. *And to think that once I was on the way to becoming one of them!* Every day I get more impressed with the immeasurable and yet inevitable cruelty of the world."

The young idealist who, seven years earlier, founded the "Peace League of Youth," calling for "young men and women of every land to make a new beginning," now discovered that the world was a colder, tougher place than the one for which his father had prepared him. In 1929, the rest of the country, too, was stripped of its optimism.

★

They were called Hoovervilles: corrugated tin, cardboard, discarded oil barrels, and scraps of lumber rigged up to shelter humans who had hit rock bottom, shrines to another failed president. In New York City, a Hooverville stretched along Riverside Drive's magnificent mansions. Yet Herbert Hoover had a proud record for humanitarian intervention and was credited with the rescue of starving Belgians in the aftermath of World War I. But now, with factories quiet and banks closing, eleven million of his countrymen were out of work as the Depression blazed across the land. Hoover was as parched of fresh ideas as the Dust Bowl of rain.

During the last months of 1929, the crash wiped out forty billion dollars in stocks. The bankers and businessmen recently admired by Americans were now themselves lining up at soup kitchens. Author Thomas Wolfe described the new nomads—bankers and grocers the week before—lining up to use the public latrines in front of New York's City Hall. "Just flotsam of the general ruin of the time—honest, decent, middle-aged men with faces seamed by toil and want, and young men, many of them boys in their teens, with thick unkempt hair. These were the wanderers from town to town, riders of the freight trains, the thumbers of rides on the highways, the uprooted, unwanted male population of America . . . hungry, defeated, empty, hopeless, restless, driven by they knew not what, always on the move, looking everywhere for work, for the bare crumbs to support their miserable lives, and finding neither work nor crumbs."

Eric Sevareid, the future network news correspondent, was one of the twenty-year-old wanderers in the early 1930s. He recalled that "cities were judged and rated on the basis of their citizens' generosity with handouts." "You did not," Sevareid recalled, "attempt to travel to Cheyenne, Wyoming if you had any alternative. You were apt to be chased from the yards there not only with clubs, which was fairly common, but with revolver shots, and it was a long walk to the next station."

Across the country, farmers with World War I rifles formed gangs to stop banks from foreclosing their mortgages. Farmers had never shared the rest of the nation's prosperity and, after 1929, when the bottom dropped out of food prices, they staggered under debts they had incurred when crops were worth four times as much. Washington, DC, the last to feel what ailed the rest of the country, finally felt the Depression's concussive force in the summer of 1932.

They were the Bonus Army: twenty-five thousand destitute veterans of World War I who turned every patch of green space in the capital into a disheveled campground, and waited in vain for Congress to pay them their promised bonus. The vets couldn't wait until 1945, when their bonuses were due. Like millions of other Americans, they were out of work and impatient for relief promised them by the country they had served. Their mortgages were due and their children were hungry. In the wilting heat of Washington's summer, the vets, medals pinned on their faded uniforms, drilled and sang old war songs as they marched down Pennsylvania Avenue, where they had marched in a Victory Day parade not long before.

Many of the capital's residents tried to avert their gaze from the grim, unwashed, unshaven faces. Noel Field did not look away. He joined the marchers. A colleague spotted Field and remarked how proud he looked marching with those sad, tired men; how his eyes shone; and how shocked he was that the Bonus Army's leaders could not get a hearing from President Hoover. Indeed, for the first time since the end of the world war, the White House gates were chained shut. The marchers, who had traveled such a long way to claim their last hope, had nowhere to go.

The deadlock between the vets and the White House grew long and bitter. As the city's orderly routine unraveled into mayhem, its grand boulevards littered, its parks spoiled, Hoover ordered the army to act. On July 28, 1932, a force of tanks and cavalry under the command of General Douglas MacArthur stormed the Hoovervilles. Soldiers torched the vets' camps, shooting giant flames into the scorching Washington night. A young aide to General MacArthur, Major Dwight

D. Eisenhower, later recalled, "The whole scene was pitiful. The veterans, whether or not they were mistaken in marching on Washington, were ragged, ill fed, and felt themselves badly abused. To suddenly see the whole encampment going up in flames just added to the pity one had to feel for them."

In full regimentals, saber drawn, Eisenhower's commander felt no such pity as he rode his troops into the bivouacked vets, driving them across the Anacostia River, a tributary of the Potomac. The air over the capital was thick with smoke and the acrid odor of burning trash. A vet and a baby were killed in the melee, many others injured.

Worn out, hungry, and defeated, the vets soon joined the two million Americans roaming the country in search of work.

Noel Field had seen his country at its most heartless. For a young man with a powerful urge to ease suffering, the sight of the general on horseback driving the pathetic marchers—veterans!—across the Potomac was an indelible image. A government that had no better way to deal with its most vulnerable population did not deserve support. President Hoover, like President Coolidge before him, was obdurate before the crisis that overwhelmed capitalism and democracy. Field wanted a country that was better than the one he found, one that would feed and educate its most oppressed. He was not alone.

"Moneymaking," Edmund Wilson wrote, capturing Noel's distress, "and the kind of advantages which a moneymaking society provides . . . are not enough to satisfy humanity—neither is a system like ours, in which everyone is out for himself, and the devil take the hindmost." Wilson urged that old institutions "should be dynamited . . . and new ones . . . substituted." Wilson seemed to be calling for revolution.

The thrill of a secret life—as well as his father's continued influence—shine through a letter Noel wrote his mother on November 7, 1929. "I'm having the most interesting days of my life in the State Department," he wrote Nina Field, "working on the [London] Disarmament Conference. The meager accounts appearing in the press

don't give the faintest hint of how thrilling it is to be on the inside of
these events. I'm beginning to realize what Father must have felt like
when he was admitted into secret events at the end of the War—about
which everybody else was in the dark."

★

A decade later, J. B. Matthews, a former Communist Party member,
testified under oath to the House Un-American Activities Committee,
a subcommittee investigating Communists in the government. "I had
lived in Washington one year in 1928," Matthews told the committee,
"and knew one of the younger men on the Department of State staff
who was a Communist."

"Who was that man?" Chairman Martin Dies asked.

"Noel Field," Matthews answered.

★

The nation, however, chose elections over revolution. The American
Communist Party always had more support from intellectuals than
from workers. On March 4, 1933, Americans chose a jaunty, optimistic
man who declared, "We have nothing to fear but fear itself." Two days
earlier, in Berlin, Adolf Hitler had seized power from a deadlocked
legislature and a dying executive. It was, in Eleanor Roosevelt's later
words, "no ordinary time." Some urged the new president to assume
dictatorial powers. "The situation is critical, Franklin," the premier
columnist Walter Lippmann warned FDR. "You may have no alternative."

Roosevelt resisted that advice. "My aim," the president announced,
"is to obviate revolution. . . . I work in a contrary sense to . . . Moscow."
Instead, he transformed the government into an engine of change. He
decreed a bank holiday, and the same week sent Congress an emergency banking act to reopen the banks, and increased the power of the
Treasury. It did not hurt morale that among the new president's first

acts was to call for the repeal of Prohibition. During his first hundred days he pushed through an avalanche of measures to stabilize the economy and restore the traumatized nation's confidence. Crucially, FDR made relief a federal responsibility, forming the Tennessee Valley Authority and the National Industrial Recovery Act and providing mortgage help for farmers. Most relevant for Field, FDR also established the Agricultural Adjustment Administration.

The rich, mellow, paternal voice of the new president reassured much of the country, but not those whose alienation ran deeper, who craved more certitude; revolution, not reform. To Noel Field, FDR was merely patching up the failed old system. Field wanted to replace it. FDR's cheerful anthem "Happy Days Are Here Again" rang hollow to Noel, who memorized the "Internationale" in Russian. With its rousing summons to "Stand up, stand up, damned of the Earth, Stand Up ye prisoners of starvation," it was an incomparably headier tonic.

All the while, Field's star at the State Department shone ever brighter. His colleagues praised his memoranda on naval disarmament, and on the mounting troubles with Mexico. Whatever the assignment, he seemed up to the task. "When I came to the State Department in 1936," Alger Hiss, Noel's friend and soon-to-be comrade in the Soviet underground, recalled, "I heard people say, We haven't had anybody who could write [Secretary of State Cordell] Hull's speeches since Field left."

# CHAPTER 4

# THE CONVERT

*I had no premonition that the Soviet Union was to become one of the most hideous tyrannies that the world had ever known, and Stalin the most cruel and unscrupulous of the merciless Russian tsars.*

—Edmund Wilson

*The only form of strength in the weak and wavering is fanaticism.*

—Friedrich Nietzsche

F OR TEN YEARS, with declining conviction and growing doubts," as Noel later described his conversion to Communism, "I tried to do my share within the framework of American policy. . . . Many an inner conflict had to be fought out and overcome before the pacifist idealist—a typical middle class intellectual and son of a middle class intellectual—could become the militant communist of later years and the present."

Communism—like his original Quaker faith—eased Field's guilt for his privilege amid so much misery. Like the Quakers, Communists encouraged self-sacrifice on behalf of others. The austere Quakers, however, were no match for the siren song of the Soviet myth: man and society leveled, the promise of a new day for humanity. Communism also offered a tantalizing dream: join us to build a new society, a pure, egalitarian utopia to replace the disintegrating capitalist system, a comradely embrace to replace cutthroat competition. Then, too, in embracing Communism, Noel felt he could deliver on his long-ago promise to his father to work for world peace.

Another convert of the same disillusioned generation, Arthur Koestler, described the process: "To say that one had 'seen the light' is a poor description of the mental rapture which only the convert knows. The new light seems to pour across the skull; the whole universe falls into pattern like the stray pieces of a jigsaw puzzle assembled by magic in one stroke. There is now an answer to every question, doubts and conflicts are a matter of the tortured past—a past already remote, when one had lived in dismal ignorance in the tasteless, colorless world of those who *don't know.*"

"From 1927 onward," Field wrote, "I gradually started to live an illegal life, separate from my official life." It was thrilling to be in on a secret, to fool those smooth careerists rushing past him—thinking they knew Noel Field! They were all wrong. "There were occasionally charges made against me," Noel recalled. "My colleagues smiled at these suspicions, and noted that I was merely a 'naïve ideologue' whose 'youthful indiscretions' should be forgiven."

Noel's friend Ben Gerig recalled a dinner at the Fields' apartment. In the middle of an argument, Noel jumped up from the table to root around a coat closet, where, under a pile of old clothes, he kept back issues of the *Daily Worker.* An amateur's mistake. Eventually, secrecy and duplicity would come as naturally as breathing.

*

"I browsed around the Communist Book Store," he wrote Herta on January 6, 1929, during a trip to New York, "and bought myself a $2.50

ticket for the evening festivity in honor of the 5th anniversary of the *Daily Worker*. . . . I felt thrilled the moment I got in. . . . Every seat and standing space was filled by an eager audience—mostly Jewish workers. W. Z. Foster (Bolshevik candidate for President) sat in my row, just a few seats from me. . . . The revolutionary dancers were inexpressibly beautiful. . . . The audience simply forgot itself and yelled and stamped. . . . For once, I felt myself a 'comrade' among that enthusiastic workers' audience. *I saw visions of Moscow with its peasant worker theaters, and of the future, the distant future which they spoke about in speeches between the dances.* And they say that workers can't appreciate beauty!" Joining with the others, Noel shouted, "Long live the American worker!" in Russian.

For the stiffly self-conscious Noel, melting into an audience of "real workers," joined together in warm, spontaneous fellowship to the thumping beat of Russian revolutionary music and dancing, was rapture akin to what Koestler experienced. Since childhood, Noel had dreamed of being part of the "brotherhood of man." Here, finally, he felt a "comrade."

"Please don't lose the enclosed program," he wrote Herta. "Also, keep this letter!"

George Orwell described a similar enchantment a few years later in Barcelona, in the intoxicated, early days of the Spanish Revolution. "It was the first time I had ever been in a town where the working class was in the saddle," Orwell recalled. "Practically every building of any size had been seized by the workers and was draped with red flags. . . . Every wall was scrawled with the hammer and sickle and with the initials of the revolutionary parties. . . . Nobody said, 'Senor' . . . everyone was called 'Comrade.' "

★

Knowing the atrocities Stalin committed in the name of the people, it is hard for us to fully comprehend what Field experienced. His exposure to Stalin's Russia came entirely from Moscow's propaganda. America's economic disintegration and its hateful bigotry Noel observed with his own eyes.

The prospect of being part of the high-voltage, transformative Roosevelt administration drew some of the brightest, most idealistic youth from across the land. Many joined the Department of Agriculture. Under Henry Wallace, the department was on the cutting edge of innovation and the reform of a sector twice pummeled: by the Depression, and by drought. An Iowa farmer-revolutionary named Harold Ware soon arrived to galvanize the bright Ivy Leaguers at the Agriculture Department. Legends swirled around Harold Ware, who, in the twenties, had rounded up a group of midwestern farmers and traveled with them to the Soviet Union. Ware tried and largely failed to instruct Soviet farmers in modern farming methods. The Iowan would prove more adept at organizing the first underground Communist cell in Washington.

"Hal Ware," Hope Hale Davis, a member of the cell, recalled, "with his tanned, lean face, his rolled-up blue shirtsleeves showing the muscles in his forearms, might have been a farmer neighbor out in Iowa." The Ware group—ultimately over forty members—boasted five Harvard graduates, a University of Chicago Phi Beta Kappa, and extreme youth: only one member of the group was over thirty. Electric with plans for a workers' state, New Dealers Alger Hiss, his brother Donald, Nathaniel Weyl, Nat Witt, John Abt, Victor Perlo, Julian Wadleigh, Henry Collins, Hope Hale Davis, and Noel's best friend, Larry Duggan—among others—formed the clandestine underground in the nation's capital.

Ware had chosen them for their intelligence, their seriousness, and their potential entrée into the highest reaches of the Roosevelt administration. When (not if) the Communists took control in America, these revolutionaries-in-the-making felt there would be a need for men and women who knew government and politics. The Communist Party (a legal entity) was unaware of the cell's existence; its members were ordered to have nothing to do with other Communists. Membership in the underground was a secret not to be revealed even to a husband or wife. Once a week, the group gathered in a converted coach house on St. Matthew's Court, near Dupont Circle. Approached by a long, narrow passageway, it seemed to have been designed as a clandestine meeting place. Hung with mirrors, its walls lined with books, the studio belonged to Alger Hiss's former roommate, Henry Collins, another New Deal rising star, employed by the National Industrial Recovery Act.

Ware provided the revolutionary magic, but a much less visible, tougher apparatchik actually ran the group. Known as J. Peters, he had a dozen other names. Born Sándor Goldberger in Hungary, the Moscow-trained Peters was a hardened veteran of Hungary's failed 1918 Communist revolution. From the legal Communist Party USA headquarters on New York City's Union Square, the short, barrel-chested, mustachioed Peters ran the clandestine Ware group. From the same ninth-floor shambles of an office, he also supervised a fake passport operation for Soviet agents. Peters made regular trips to Washington to impose discipline on the aspiring revolutionaries. If questioned or resisted, Peters' jovial mood vanished in a flash. Hope Davis recalled Peters's "thundering accusations" when she asked an innocent question about Moscow's ever-shifting policies. Membership, she realized, made it her duty not to think for herself. Assignments to group members came directly from Moscow, and could not be challenged.

Peters had credentials to impose respect and fear, including being the author of the much-quoted Communist *Manual on Organization*, which, among other things, advocated "the revolutionary overthrow of capitalism, the establishment of the dictatorship of the proletariat, the establishment of a Socialist Soviet Republic in the United States, the complete abolition of classes, the establishment of socialism, and the first stage of the classless Communist society."

The Hungarian revolutionary had two goals for "Apparatus A," as he called the Ware group. First: espionage, the theft of government documents for copying, to be transmitted to Moscow. Second: influencing US policy by infiltrating the so-called old-line agencies of the government: State, War, Treasury, and Interior. Apparatus A was the first of a number of Washington cells and, in terms of talent and access, represented the high-water mark of Soviet infiltration of the US government. "This veritable little intellectual army," Peters's liaison, Whittaker Chambers, boasted, "joined the Communist Party without the Party having to exert any particular effort for their recruitment." Peters had a sharp eye for those poised for rapid career advancement. "Even in Germany," J. Peters said of his Washington cell, "under the Weimar Republic, the Party did not have what we have here."

Recently declassified KGB files spell out the rules of the Ware group: "The secret apparatus created by Peters was financed by people who are *entirely without Party affiliation and hence undercover.*" Paying dues to the party was part of the group's weekly ritual, "a test and a binder of party loyalty," in Lenin's words. Like the income tax, party dues were progressive. Alger Hiss—a respected figure in the group—voluntarily paid more than the others, changing his stepson Timothy's school to a less expensive one so he could contribute more to the party. Named for Horatio Alger, the writer of rags-to-riches fiction, Hiss, with his aristocratic bearing, Ivy League credentials, and winning personality, seemed to embody the American dream. Few of his comrades were aware of the Hiss family's history of loss and suicide.

For members of the Ware group, lying about their true affiliation was a sacred duty. When on August 25, 1948, Hiss swore under oath to a subcommittee of the House of Representatives, "I do not believe in Communism. I believe it is a menace to the United States," he was doing no more than fulfilling his early pledge to his primary loyalty. But, in a way, he was telling the truth too. For Hiss was not formally a party man; he was an agent of the GRU, Soviet military intelligence.

He neither wanted, needed, nor sought party membership. That was for the civilians, the amateurs. Actual truth was reserved for the comrades. As late as 1939, Noel Field, in a notarized letter to the House Committee on Un-American Activities, swore that "I am not and never have been a communist. I am not and never have been a member of the communist party nor of any other radical organization. I have never engaged in any radical activities. By no stretch of the imagination can my brief membership in the Fellowship of Youth for Peace during my student days be considered as a 'radical' activity."

Field, too, embraced unconditional obedience and the distancing of friends who were not comrades. "If a friend ceases to be a comrade," Field said, "he is no longer my friend." The party was the embodiment of the revolutionary idea of history, and could not be wrong. Noel encouraged others in the Field family to strike out on a radical path, though he never revealed to them how far his own radicalism had led him. "Good for thee and thy strike activities, Comrade Nina!" he wrote his mother on May 26, 1933. "Next thee will be setting off bombs on Boston Common!" he wrote, only half in jest.

*

By the midthirties, anti-fascism was as strong a motive in joining the Soviet underground as the original impulse, disillusionment with democracy and capitalism's feebleness. Hope Davis's husband and fellow Ware group member, German economist Hermann Brunck, was ordered to infiltrate the German embassy in Washington to learn Hitler's plans in the coming war. Equally important for Moscow was binding these promising recruits to the cause—partly through faith, partly by compromising them irreversibly. "The underground agents," Weyl recalled, "bound themselves to lives of secrecy and silence. If discovered, they would be deprived even of the small joys of martyrdom for a cause. Their role under such circumstances would be to repudiate any taint of even *sympathy* for Communist ideas."

Similar Communist cells were springing up in Europe too. Koestler was a member of a Berlin cell. "One among several thousand in Berlin," Koestler recalled, "and one among the several hundred thousand basic units of the Communist network in the world. . . . The consciousness of being one unit among millions in an organized, disciplined whole was always present. . . . Half our activities were legal, half illegal."

In the early thirties, Noel was not yet part of any Communist cell. His Communism was based on conviction, not yet action. His closest friend, however, was a member of the Ware group. "My best, almost my only friend," Noel said of Larry Duggan, a fellow State Department official. Duggan was the first person, other than Herta, with whom Noel shared his conversion to Communism. "Later," Field wrote, "Hiss joined [Duggan] in this knowledge."

Duggan and his wife, Helen, lived in the same building as the Fields, at 419 Fourth Street in northwest Washington. The two couples soon discovered shared interests, values, and a mutual disillusionment with their own country. Two gentle idealists—Noel and Larry—resembled each other in background and appearance. Larry, too, was tall, fair-haired, and pedigreed. A graduate of Phillips Exeter Academy and Harvard, Larry was two years Noel's junior, and from a similarly distinguished lineage. In KGB files, Duggan is referred to as "Prince." Like Noel, Duggan, too, was the son of a celebrated academic, and avid for a cause beyond his own advancement. Most important, the two men were enthralled by the example of the distant land that claimed to stand for world peace. "The repeated Soviet proposals for complete disarmament," Noel wrote, "thrilled me. But the Soviet government stood alone and the rest of the world laughed."

★

A former small-time Viennese actress, tall and statuesque, with wavy red hair and flashing red-lacquered nails—a Raymond Chandler heroine—

helped to lure both Duggan and Field into the secret life of a Soviet spy. Working out of Berlin, Vienna, and Paris, Hede Massing had been transformed from so-so actress into seasoned agent by Ignaz Reiss, a legendary Soviet spy. Reiss taught her to have eyes in the back of her head, to *feel* that someone is watching, to *hear* that someone behind you is adjusting his pace. Never be in a rush, the master instructed his protégée; never flustered, never obvious, never self-conscious. Walk slowly into a place of meeting, always with a back exit. (Hede's favorite meeting places in New York were the public library on Forty-Second Street and the lobby of Radio City Music Hall.)

Hede's most important lesson from Reiss was how to exploit the unspoken yearnings of young American idealists and tap their just-below-the-surface rage at their society's injustices, which cohabited alongside their ideals. "Of the conquests I made while a Soviet agent," Hede said, "the one I regret most is Larry Duggan. . . . Larry impressed me as an extremely tense, high strung, intellectual young man. . . . His wife, Helen, was beautiful, well balanced, capable and sure of herself. She was an attentive and loving companion to Larry. They had four young children." Hede's job as KGB recruiter (under the cover of reporter for the German magazine *Die Weltbühne*) was to stoke the intense unhappiness beneath the surface of Larry Duggan's sweet American portrait.

Hede invited Larry to lunch. "Every decent liberal," she told him, "has a duty to participate in the fight against Adolf Hitler." The Soviet agent was on sure ground here. Larry agreed the Nazis were a real threat to peace—and isolationist America had shamefully tuned out the world. Emboldened, Hede soon revealed that she was a Soviet agent. "Much to my surprise," she wrote, "he not only consented to work with us, but developed a complete plan, and explicit details of how he would collaborate with us."

The next step, persuading Larry to steal documents from his own government, would take more lunches, more subtle persuasion. "He was not going to hand over any documents to us," Massing wrote, "that he made clear beyond a doubt. But he was willing to meet me . . . every second week and give me verbal reports on issues of interest." The first step was always the hardest. Hede had done her work exceedingly well. Larry was hooked.

By 1936, when Hede Massing left for Europe, Duggan was regularly turning over State Department documents to a Moscow handler named Boris Bazarov, a veteran Soviet agent newly posted to Washington as a reward for his recent success penetrating the British Foreign Office. "Duggan," Bazarov cabled Moscow, "said that the only thing that kept him at his hateful job in the State Department, where he did not get out of his tuxedo for two weeks, every night attending a reception . . . was the idea of being useful to us."

Another of the Fields' circle of friends, Communist Party supporter and ACLU founder Roger Baldwin, recalled hosting a picnic at his place in New Jersey. Noel and Herta, Alger and Priscilla Hiss, the Duggans, and Henry Collins were all there. "All of them the same young aristocrats," Baldwin said, "polished and athletic and vigorous looking. Real gentlemen, lively and full of interests." Noel's mother, Nina, was also present, "Mama Field looked like everybody's aunt, a wiry, thin, very active woman. She would take a dare on anything. Plunged into the icy water of our pool. She got deference from Noel, who seemed to accept that Mama knows best."

To Alger, Noel "seemed rather British, and that appealed to me." Priscilla and Noel, fellow Quakers, slipped into comfortable "thees" and "thous." "Noel was always inviting me for the weekend," Alger said. "The Fields had this little boat and they liked to drift along the Potomac and laze about. That wasn't my idea of fun. I never went. Noel was rather incompetent with his hands and he was afraid of handling the motorboat for fear it would blow up. I guess that's why he wanted me. Imagine anyone being afraid of such a little thing! . . . Field was a man of real sincerity, spiritual grandeur, but not a brave man."

*

Much of the still ongoing acrimonious dispute regarding core values of American life—from the meaning of patriotism to the role of
elites—can be traced to a fateful meeting arranged by J. Peters in 1934.
That year, Peters introduced to each other two men whose names
would forever be entwined and spark debate and argument well into
the twenty-first century. The case of Whittaker Chambers and Alger
Hiss, pitting two former friends and comrades against each other, has
left a permanent mark on American politics. Hiss's 1948 trial and conviction for perjury (he was tried only for perjury, as the statute of
limitations on espionage had expired) has shadowed liberal and con-
servative discourse for generations. McCarthyism in the 1950s, and
the astonishing rise and spectacular fall of Richard M. Nixon, can both
be traced, in part, to the Hiss trial. The seemingly never-ending saga
began in a cafeteria in the nation's capital. This meeting, in a dimly lit,
forgettable setting, was the decisive encounter of Hiss and Chambers's
lives. Noel Field would be swept up in its wake.

"Peters and I picked up Hal Ware," Chambers remembered. "We
drove his car to a basement cafeteria on Wisconsin Avenue in Georgetown. There we sat talking . . . there I again heard the name . . . of
Alger Hiss. I learned that he was an American, a lawyer, an exceptional
Communist for whom Peters had an unusual regard, and that he was
a member of the Ware group. He was about to leave, or had just left
the AAA [the Agricultural Adjustment Administration], where he had
been assistant general counsel, for the Senate munitions investigating
committee. This change made it important that he should be separated
from the Ware group at once. He would be the first man in the new
apparatus, which I was to organize. . . It was a brief meeting, for the
sake of introducing Hiss and me."

"Hiss began an intensive campaign to recruit Field and Duggan,"
Chambers recalled. "He reached the point of talking very openly to

Noel Field. . . . I was soon to learn just how far the two young State Department men had gone. One night, Alger reported to me that Noel claimed to be connected with 'another apparatus.' 'Is it possible?' Alger asked me in surprise. 'Can there be another apparatus working in Washington?' " Chambers asked Peters what he knew of this "other apparatus." "It's probably Hede's," Peters answered. "Leave Noel Field alone," Peters told him. "But Alger's spirit was up," Chambers said. "He was determined to recruit Noel Field."

The "other apparatus," was, indeed, Hede Massing's NKVD— predecessor to the KGB—charged with political espionage. Chambers and Hiss worked for the GRU, Moscow's military intelligence agency.

In 1935, Hal Ware was killed in a car crash while visiting Pennsylvania mines. "Each comrade," Hope Davis recalled, "felt a personal devastation." Peters now took charge of the entire Washington underground. The Hungarian ruled more by Soviet-style discipline than charisma.

In retrospect, Peters's plan to infiltrate the highest reaches of the US government seems grandiose and almost delusional. But in the thirties—the peak period of Soviet infiltration of the upper reaches of both the US and British governments—security was lax, to put it mildly. The FBI took little notice of Peters. Its chief, J. Edgar Hoover, dismissed Peters's activities as uninteresting "Communistic inner circles." As the world edged toward war, Hitler and fascism were the immediate menace. Communists, in those days, were seen as just a bunch of youthful radicals posing no danger to anyone at home or abroad. By the decade's end, Hoover bitterly regretted his early nonchalance. Partly to compensate for his prior negligence, Hoover ignited a witch hunt long past when the witches were dead.

In the early to midthirties, however, they were very much alive.

# CHAPTER 5

# SPY GAMES

*The Revolution—we loved it so much!*

—Daniel Cohn-Bendit, leader of the 1968
French student revolts

I N THE DUSTY and cluttered Union Square offices of the Communist Party USA, in New York City, J. Peters was hearing glowing reports about a young Foreign Service officer at the State Department's West European Division. Peters's agents observed Noel Field and noted his promise, his alienation from his country, and the fact that Field was not a man to be rushed. "He was a soul-searching, uncertain person," Alger Hiss recalled. "Noel was a worrier."

In 1934, Hede Massing was dispatched to the capital for the express purpose of meeting Noel Field. "Field was important enough to warrant such a trip," Massing said. "He was rated among the rising young men in the State Department." The timing was urgent.

The Treaty of Versailles had made a mockery of Woodrow Wilson's Fourteen Points, which promised the removal of economic barriers, the reduction of national armaments, and diplomatic openness. Seventeen million people had died in World War I, and France and Britain, in particular, demanded revenge. Versailles assigned sole blame and punitive reparations for the war to Germany—uniting that country in a blanket denial of any guilt whatsoever. That left the door wide open to the Nazi Party to proclaim Germany's absolute innocence. Hitler, one year in power, promised to restore national pride. Flagrantly defying Versailles, he was gearing up for war. Europe, its industries struggling to recover, its male populations tragically depleted, was in no mood to mobilize for more bloodletting. How would the United States—the sole power strengthened, not depleted, by the Great War—react to Nazi aggression? On this crucial matter, the Soviets were looking for hard intelligence.

Noel Field's perch at State's West European Division made him an ideal target for recruitment. Moreover, J. Peters preferred tall, pedigreed WASPs. Who would ever believe a well-mannered young man with deep New England roots and immaculate appearance such as Noel Field could betray his country?

A *Daily Worker* correspondent named Marguerite Young, who socialized with the Fields, introduced the couple to Hede. She addressed Noel in German, the language of his childhood. In the hands of such a pro, conversation flowed easily for the normally awkward Field. Hede spoke of her husband, a hero to Noel. Paul Massing had recently escaped from a Nazi concentration camp at Oranienburg and published *Fatherland*, the first exposé of life behind Hitler's barbed wire. With such solid anti-fascist credentials, and under J. Peters's careful manipulation, Hede and soon Paul Massing were in business with Noel Field.

Hede was beguiled by the "tall, long limbed, lanky Noel, with a mane of soft, slightly wavy brown hair and wide, beautiful, intelligent eyes." Herta Field she described as "attractive . . . a Nordic-looking woman with a full-busted figure and golden spun hair," her beauty marred by slightly protruding teeth. But it was Herta's utter devotion to her husband that struck Hede as extraordinary. "Herta would have followed Noel," Hede said, "if he had been a Fascist or a Tibetan monk."

It was a gentle courtship. The Massings knew better than to rush Noel, who liked nothing better than arguing the fine points of Marxism with Paul and Hede all night. In those days, the Massings recalled, Field was opposed to Stalin's official policy of socialism in one country, and in favor of Trotsky's concept of a permanent revolution. "Noel was a profoundly moral person," Paul Massing recalled. "Nazism was gaining strength. Brutality was increasing. Noel felt strongly that it wouldn't do, just to sit around and watch. He yearned to *do* something about it." Strangely, Noel never raised the possibility of using his official position to rouse Americans to oppose Hitler. By the thirties, Field was too deeply enraptured by Communism to compromise. The times demanded radical action and he did not see America moving in that direction. He had given up on his country's will to do the right thing.

Field first of all sought Communist Party membership, an idea Moscow vetoed. "I remember so well," Hede recalled, "how I argued with Noel about his not joining the American Communist Party," Hede wrote. "To convince him that a man of his stature and intellectual capacity would be misplaced in the open Party. . . . It was my job to get him into my apparatus, [the NKVD]." When Noel boasted about marching with the Bonus Army, Massing was appalled. "That Noel would jeopardize his chances of staying in an important government job!" Massing said. But Noel told the story with an indulgent chuckle, as an example of his youthful, pre-Communist recklessness.

At times, Noel's naïveté worried the Massings. "He knew absolutely nothing of practical Communist politics," Paul said. Nor, in those early days, of how to conduct himself as a potential secret agent. One evening, after dinner, Noel told Hede he had a special gift for her. "He drove us all to the Lincoln Memorial," she recalled, "We looked at the Memorial, and then began to walk down the steps toward the car.

As we swung around, we heard Noel's voice singing. Standing tall and straight on the top of the Memorial steps he [sang] the "Internationale" . . . at the top of his voice—in Russian!" The Massings were both touched and terrified. This was indeed reckless behavior for a fledgling spy. "Poor dear Noel!" Hede noted. "My heart went out to him." Hede did not report Noel's violation of clandestine behavior to Moscow.

Gradually, Noel embraced the double life. "He found it very romantic," Paul Massing said. "He almost never slipped up in conversation to reveal his real loyalties. He was a highly disciplined man in that respect. The double life suited him. He was always a selfless, disciplined servant [of Moscow]. Noel could be strong only when he was doing what his superiors told him to do."

Soon the Massings and the Fields—including Noel's mother, Nina—were spending weekends together, listening to Noel's beloved Wagner operas, boating on the Potomac. It was during one such excursion on his little motorboat that Noel brought up the name of his friend Alger Hiss. "I remember that Herta had gone off swimming," Hede said. "Noel said he had this very close friend whom he considered a man of high ethics and moral standards, a trained Marxist . . . whom he admired very greatly." "You know," Field told Hede Massing, "he is trying to win me, as you are, and I am tending to be with him. I've known him so much longer than I know you." "Well," Mrs. Massing replied, "why don't you let me meet this man?"

Noel was torn. Not between loyalty toward his own country and the Soviet Union, but between two spies working for different Soviet agencies: his friends the Massings, and his friend and State Department colleague Alger Hiss. Hiss had by then left the Department of Agriculture—though the AAA was among the capital's most innovative agencies—for the State Department, a far more hidebound bureaucracy. Whether Hiss made the move as a result of Moscow's urging or his personal ambition is a matter of conjecture. There is no question, however, that for the Kremlin, Hiss was of far greater use at State than at Agriculture. The fact that Hiss was in military intelligence likely also pushed Noel—a recent Quaker pacifist—to Hede's political apparatus.

The three unlikely comrades finally did meet at the Fields' apartment, sometime in the fall of 1935. Hede took an immediate liking to the "slender and intelligent-looking" Alger. "I could not keep pace with the cleverness of Hiss and Noel," Hede remembered. "Later, standing by a window . . . Hiss and I had the brief but decisive talk. . . . 'I understand that you are trying to get Noel away from my organization into yours,' I said. Hiss asked, 'What is your apparatus, anyhow?' 'Now, Alger, you should know better than to ask that. I wouldn't ask *you* that question.' 'Well, we will see who is going to win,' Hiss replied."

"Then," Hede Massing recalled, "one of us—I can no longer recall who, but the words are clear in my memory—summed up the argument: 'Well, whoever is going to win, we are working for the same boss.' "

★

What the Massings did not share with their recruit was their growing disillusionment with Stalin. Having recently spent two years in the Soviet Union, Paul and Hede had seen the disturbing new face of the movement to which they had attached their hopes. "Not because of the hardships," Hede noted, "but the pompousness, the hypocrisy, the lack of ethics of the ruling bureaucracy." But, like so many others, their waning enthusiasm for Stalin was given a fresh jolt by the West's passivity in the face of the Nazi threat. "We saw that the West did nothing [to stop Hitler]," Massing recalled. "We all believed that sooner or later the Soviet Union would have to fight Hitler. That it was the only country that would fight. So in serving it, providing it *information*, we were helping the Soviets to prepare for that fight. I tried to convince Noel that with all the stupidity, the ugliness in Moscow, it was a New Society which couldn't live in peace with the Nazis and that it was an obligation to help them fight Nazism, whether you liked them or not."

Their still-vacillating recruit frustrated the Massings. "He couldn't make up his mind," Hede recalled. "It was very important for him that he not work for the [Soviet] apparatus from the State Department."

By the fall of 1935, however, the recruiters had achieved their mission. "Finally," Field recalled, "I succeeded in surmounting my inhibitions and took on espionage for the Soviet intelligence service." Typically, he cast his betrayal in moral terms. "I had become conscious of the fact that the task [of spying] is an honorable duty." Noel Field had been captured and for life.

After the thirties, Noel wrote no more anguished, heartfelt letters to his mother. He had found a new family. Camaraderie and the sense of being part of a historic, clandestine movement filled the emptiness and confusion left by his father's death and the family's sudden uprooting.

Spying on his government turned out to be less hazardous than Field anticipated. "The mentality of the State Department," he recalled, "was rather provincial in my days. . . . This was evident from the careless manner in which state secrets were managed. The most secret documents, sometimes in multiple copies, circulated from hand to hand."

At first, Noel gave the Massings only oral reports—another way to assuage whatever residual guilt still nagged him. Gradually, he overcame those scruples. "I wrote brief bios of my colleagues," he said, "I also got hold of a memo of the American Ambassador in Moscow—William Bullitt—which was sharply anti Soviet." Noel's sources were often his own reports, but he also stole classified documents from the West European Division and turned them over to the Massings.

Most significantly, he reported to the Massings on the State Department's preparations for the upcoming Naval Conference in London in the winter of 1935–36. From December 9, 1935, to March 25, 1936, Noel attended the London conference and regularly passed classified reports to Paul Massing, who came to personally collect them from Field. Intended to limit the rapid growth of naval armaments, submarines, and battleships, the treaty hammered out was soon to be honored in the breach, especially by Japan (which withdrew from the conference) as well as by the rapidly arming German and Italian navies. Field and Massing spent that Christmas together in the Swiss ski resort of Arosa, where Noel drafted a detailed report on the Naval Conference for Paul to pass on to Moscow.

Herta supported her husband in his fateful new mission, as in all things. Sometimes, she transcribed her husband's notes in a code they invented for the Massings. But Herta, intuitive rather than intellectual, was a different personality altogether. "I feel as if . . ." was how she often began sentences. Noel was the opposite. He first read everything he could get his hands on concerning a given subject, studied it, agonized, and wavered. But he trusted and relied on Herta's common sense, something he knew he lacked. Together since early childhood, Noel and Herta generally arrived at the same conclusion. She adored—almost worshiped—him; while he, essentially a loner, was dependent on her as his closest and most trusted human contact. On matters of Communist Party dogma, she matched him in devotion and zeal. It is hard to imagine their marriage surviving had she not.

Noel had made his choice. He would work for the Massings and not Hiss. Still, Alger did not give up on luring him into Soviet military intelligence, which he considered in more urgent need of American agents. Shortly before Noel's departure for the London conference in late 1935, Alger made one more stab at recruiting Noel.

"Our friend [Field]," Hede cabled the KGB the day before Field's trip, "related to me the following incident of which he himself will give a detailed account to our friends overseas. Roughly a week before Noel's departure from Washington," Hede wrote, "Alger Hiss [whose name appears in full here, a rare breach of spy craft as Hiss is normally referred to as "Jurist," as well as by other code names. Massing clearly did not know for certain in which apparatus Hiss served—normal Soviet procedure—or his cover name.] informed him . . . that he has ties to an organization working for the Soviet Union and is aware that

[Noel] has ties as well. However, [Hiss] fears that [Noel's ties] are not robust enough, and that his knowledge is probably being misused," Hede related to Moscow. "Then, he bluntly proposed that [Noel] give him an account of the London Conference. Because they are, as [Noel] put it, close friends, he did not refuse to discuss this topic with him, but he told Alger that he had already delivered a report on that Conference. When Alger, whom as you probably recall I met through [Noel], insisted that he would like to receive that report himself, regardless, [Noel] said he would have to contact his 'connections' and ask for their advice. Within a day, having 'thought it over,' Alger said that he would not insist on receiving the report himself, but that he would ask [Noel] to speak with Larry and Helen [Duggan] about him and tell them who he is [i.e., which apparatus he is spying for] and give him [Alger] access to the Duggans. . . . [Field] spoke with Larry about Alger and of course about himself as well, telling him, 'that their main task at present is the defense of the Soviet Union,' etc., etc. and that 'each of them has to use his advantageous position in order to provide assistance in this matter.' Larry seemed upset and frightened and said that he had not gone so far yet . . . he is still hoping to do some work [for Moscow] of a conventional sort. . . . Alger also asked [Noel] to help him in getting into the State Department [Hiss was then working for Senator Gerald P. Nye, chairman of the Senate Munitions Committee as assistant legal counsel]. Which [Noel] apparently did."

Field, it appears, was an eager but maladroit spy. "When I pointed out to Noel what a terrible lack of discipline he had shown," Hede reported to Moscow, "and what a danger he had created . . . for the whole enterprise by linking three people with each other [i.e., Field, Hiss, and Duggan], he acted as if he did not understand. He believed that 'because Alger had been the first to show his cards' he did not have a reason to keep everything secret. Moreover, because Alger had said that he is 'doing this for us' . . . he thought the best thing would be to establish contact between them."

This long cable from Hede Massing to her control officer is significant in many ways. It unmasks Alger Hiss, who, until the end of his life, denied he was a Soviet spy. It also reveals Hiss, a man of legendary self-control, to be dangerously willful in the service of the Soviet Union. Hiss wanted both Field and Duggan as part of his network, and would not easily take no for an answer. It is, finally, a startling tale of the faith three highly intelligent, superbly educated young Americans placed in a country they had never even visited, and on whose behalf they willingly betrayed their own.

Moscow was not pleased with these zealous recruits. "The outcome," replied Hede's Soviet control, code-named "Nord," on April 26, 1936, "is that 17 [Field] and Hiss [and once again Hiss is identified by his actual name] have in effect been completely deprived of their cover before 19 [Duggan]. Evidently [Duggan] also clearly understands the identity of 'Redhead' [Hede]. And more than a couple of months ago Redhead and Hiss [his real name again] also got exposed to each other. Helen Boyd, 19's [Duggan's] wife [strange mix of the covert and overt here] having been present at almost all of these meetings and discussions, is undoubtedly clued in as well, and now knows as much as [Duggan] himself. I think in light of this incident, we should not accelerate the cultivation of [Duggan] and his wife. It seems that *the persistent Hiss* will continue his initiative in that direction."

"We fail to see," wrote Moscow Center to Nord on May 3, 1936, "for what reason Redhead met with [Hiss]." The home office reprimanded this unprofessional trio of spies. "As we understand it, this took place after our directive stipulating that [Hiss] is the 'neighbors' man' [GRU vs. NKVD/KGB] and that *it is necessary to stay away from him.* Experiments of this sort could have undesirable consequences."

"Don't mention [Hiss] ever!" Boris Bazarov, her control officer, finally commanded Hede. "Don't speak about him to Noel or to Herta or to Paul. Never see him again." Alger Hiss was high value and had to be protected.

"Now for the question how to get out of this mess," Bazarov continued. "[Noel] (en route to Europe) is isolated. [Hiss] will gradually forget about him. . . . [Duggan] could be of interest considering his position in the 'Surrogate' [the State Department], his wife as well, considering her connections," Bazarov concludes. "Therefore, it is essential that we skillfully smooth over the emerging situation and steer both of them away from [Hiss]."

Further proof that—despite Hiss's denial under oath—the story of Hede's conversation with Hiss at the Fields' apartment took place comes from this cable from Moscow Center on May 18, 1936. "Redhead met [Hiss] only on one occasion. She went to this meeting at the behest of Comrade Nord. After you informed us that [Hiss] has ties with the Neighbors, we did not meet with him. *After meeting Redhead and speaking with her in our [Field's] apartment, [Hiss] no doubt informed his superiors about that meeting.*"

*

The actual damage to US interests by Field and Hiss's spying often gets lost amid the rhetorical heat of the cultural and political wars surrounding the Hiss-Chambers case. A high-ranking State Department official and close FDR friend, Sumner Welles, when shown the documents Hiss gave his courier, Whittaker Chambers, summed up the real harm. It was not so much the cables' *content*, Welles testified, but the clues they provided Soviet cryptanalysts that would have provided code breakers with texts that could be matched against intercepted telegrams. Finally, whether a man or woman betrays his country is not determined by the quality of documents stolen, but by the act itself. Noel Field may not have been a skilled agent, but his willingness to betray the United States on behalf of the Soviet Union is beyond doubt. The full story of Alger Hiss's betrayal belongs elsewhere.

*

Even as he spied on his government, Noel agonized. "Was he doing the right thing? He kept asking us," Paul Massing recalled. "I won't spy on my own government, he kept saying," even as he stashed State Department documents in his briefcase for the Massings to copy.

Relief from Noel's residual doubt about the rightness of his betrayal arrived in the spring of 1936. Field jumped at a job offer from the League of Nations' Disarmament Section. The Geneva-based League was then still a place infused with hope. Though its greatest champion, President Woodrow Wilson, had failed to persuade his own country to join the body, he considered the League his proudest legacy and the only barrier against the next world war. In the war's aftermath, however, the US turned sharply inward—again reverting to George Washington's counsel to avoid Europe's entangling alliances. Now, Noel was offered a chance to actually work toward his boyhood dream of world peace. Moreover, the Geneva offer was a way out of his dilemma. At the League he would not be betraying his own country—not specifically, anyway—but merely working *for* the Soviets. In Field's convoluted thinking, spying on Stalin's behalf in the League wasn't really spying at all. "In Geneva," Paul Massing recalled, "there was an international situation where loyalties could be distributed as you wanted."

"We told him to go to Geneva," Paul remembered, "because there he could be of great use and extremely important to the anti-Nazi movement. He was being groomed as a liaison for a Soviet apparatus. Noel was not told which apparatus, however."

Once in Geneva, Hede assured Noel that he would be contacted by Ignaz Reiss, the Soviet spy who had trained her. Reiss was the real thing: a Jew from Galicia who had joined the Polish Communist Party in 1919, and by the twenties was a highly decorated Soviet agent. In the company of Reiss and his fellow spy, General Walter Krivitsky, the Massings and others of their generation of Communist idealists forged a tight bond of shared struggle, a life of constant danger and dislocation. Jews and Communists in an anti-Semitic age, they were battle-hardened in the treacherous precincts of Vienna, Lvov, and Berlin, skilled at evading marauding fascist gangs, familiar with life in the underground. Lenin's revolution was a success—but so far only in Russia. Reiss, Krivitsky, and the Massings struggled to ignite it in Germany and the rest of Europe, a continent increasingly enraptured by the hypnotic Austrian orator.

Lenin, however, died in 1924. Bolsheviks plotting world revolution in their clandestine cells from Berlin to Washington, DC, would soon learn that his successor, Josef Stalin, did not share their dreams for international Communism. Stalin, gathering all power for himself, regarded the likes of the Massings, Reiss, Krivitsky, Chambers, and their Old Bolshevik cohorts as dangerous dreamers. Henceforth, the Soviet Union would be the revolution's focus, its purpose and crowning achievement. Energy expended on pursuits that did not strictly serve the Kremlin's interest was energy wasted. The ruthless tyrant in the Kremlin had begun a new era in the history of Communism, a fact the men and women in the underground were slow to realize.

★

Compared to the subterranean world of hardened conspirators he fervently hoped to join, Noel Field's world—from Zurich to the State Department via Harvard—had been sheltered and privileged. Ten years in Washington, however, had transformed him from an anxious outsider to a committed Communist. Henceforth, all other loyalties—family and country—would be sublimated to the one true purpose: serving the revolution. "Personal affections," Field wrote, "cannot be determinant."

The Massings had trained him as well as they could in the spy's invisible trade. It was Field's innate need for a guiding faith to imbue his life with meaning, however, that made him a devoted Communist. "The more irrational, nonsensical the Soviets behaved," Paul Massing noted, "the more devoted he was. For Noel, the leaders of the Revolution can do no wrong."

## CHAPTER 6

# SPIES IN FLIGHT

*I can take no more. I am returning to freedom . . . back to Lenin, to his teaching and cause.*

—Ignaz Reiss

CRISP WHITE SAILBOATS sliced the choppy waters of Lac Leman as the long, low wail of a foghorn signaled the arrival of the ferry carrying passengers from the French to the Swiss side of Geneva's lake. The sober birthplace of Calvinism, Geneva strikes the visitor as cleaner and more orderly than any other European city. When Noel and Herta Field arrived in 1936, they might have been jarred by such a placid place in the sea of European turbulence. But Geneva aspired to be more than a picturesque town in the Alpine foothills. The flags of all the feuding nations snapped in front of the Palace of Nations, the hope-filled fortress against the next calamity. Tragically missing from this colorful display at the League of Nations headquarters were the Stars and Stripes.

Noel and Herta inhaled the bracing air, a nostalgic reminder of their Swiss childhoods. It was sweet relief to be far away from Washington, with all its moral and political confusion. The Fields soon settled in Vandoeuvres, a spotless village perched above Lake Geneva, featuring a simple Calvinist church with a plain wooden steeple and an inn named Restaurant du Cheval-Blanc that served dull Swiss fare and good beer. Skiing weekends in nearby Chamonix reconnected Noel to his childhood love of the Alps. With Herta keeping house, theirs was the very picture of an orderly, petit-bourgeois existence. The reality of their lives could not have been further from that misleading surface.

"Ruddy faced, tall, good clean features," a colleague from those days at the League, Wallace Carroll, recalled Noel, "a man everybody liked." With his gentle, almost whispery voice; his unassuming, flawless manners; and his deceptive, wide-open gaze, Noel was a helpful, hardworking colleague and pleasant neighbor. As at the State Department, Field soon had a reputation as an excellent draftsman and a first-rate bureaucrat in the League's increasingly irrelevant Disarmament Section. "But when we got into League politics," Carroll recalled, "in bull sessions, he seemed so naïve, so trusting. He got teased a lot; 'You big dumb Swiss,' they called him." It was the perfect cover.

★

Paul Massing soon called on the Fields. "Noel wasn't introduced to Ignaz Reiss immediately," Massing said. "That was normal for the Soviet apparatus. Agents were often left to sit around for months, even years, before Moscow gave them an assignment." Though he was thirsting for a chance to do something, to be active, to help, Field didn't complain. Meanwhile, he did what he could for the Soviets. "All Field had to do was to pass on things about the League to me," Massing recalled. "The Russians always wanted concrete facts. The best thing was if you could steal the original document. They liked that much better than photostats. Noel was eager to give me all the gossip."

In the age of Hitler, Mussolini, and Franco—and in the absence of the United States—not much of substance was decided inside the splendid Palace of Nations. Still, Noel continued passing Paul scraps of intelligence, whatever he picked up in the corridors and conference rooms. What mattered was keeping the line to Moscow open.

That summer, the Massings and the Fields, including Noel's mother, Nina, vacationed together, driving through Switzerland and into France. Massing even enlisted Nina Field as a Soviet courier in Germany. It was a dangerous mission for a Jew or a Communist, but Nina, a spry, silver-haired Quaker, was unlikely to arouse suspicion. Though not a Communist, and unaware of her son's real affiliation, Nina, guileless and earnest, was as eager to serve as her son.

*

In late 1936, a portly, carefully dressed man rang the Fields' doorbell in Vandoeuvres. Ignaz Reiss—the agent painted by the Massings in heroic colors—changed countries and identities as others change their shirts. The bon vivant Reiss spoke half a dozen languages with the thick accent of his Galician origins. A man whose obvious pleasure in life belied a diamond-hard commitment to Communism and to Lenin, Reiss's charge was gathering intelligence on the Nazis' war preparations. As he traveled across Europe on false passports and lived illegally in Paris, Reiss never lingered anywhere.

A chasm of cultures and styles yawned between the earnest American and the tough, worldly European Bolshevik. The chemistry between them was toxic. How can America call itself great, Reiss teased the Fields, when it has no cafés? The Fields saw no humor in such flippancy. Later, Noel dubbed Reiss "der Dicke," the Fat One, and called him a "Philistine." Reiss found Noel "neurotic" and "untrustworthy." Thus unimpressed, Reiss did not raise the prospect of the longed-for "important assignment."

Noel, however, was too valuable to be dropped by Moscow on the basis of one master spy's poor impression. The Massings' next choice to connect Noel to the Soviets was another Old Bolshevik. Walter

Krivitsky, a Soviet citizen, had fought in the Russian Civil War and held the rank of general. Since 1935, Krivitsky had been operating as chief of Soviet military intelligence in Western Europe. Running offices and agents in many capitals, the wiry general chose The Hague as his headquarters. There, under an Austrian passport, Krivitsky made his living as a dealer in rare books.

Though neither Field nor Krivitsky ever described their first meeting in much detail, subsequent events imply that it went better than the disastrous Reiss/Field rendezvous. Krivitsky and Field could at least tolerate each other sufficiently to collaborate. They had no choice: Noel was needed to help put out a fire in the closely watched ranks of Stalin's European agents.

The man whom Noel had dubbed the Fat One had "turned traitor." Ignaz Reiss was appalled at the news seeping out of Moscow. Between 1936 and 1938, show trials were Stalin's instrument to wipe out potential rivals and all those who disagreed with him. Reiss was revolted by the image of Lenin's most trusted generals and closest comrades reduced to cringing supplication, begging for mercy. He couldn't silently abide Stalin's break with Lenin's legacy by introducing the death penalty for Communist Party cadres. He recalled Lenin invoking the fatal example of the Jacobins in the French Revolution when he barred the execution of Bolsheviks. Expel heretics from the party, imprison or exile them—but no Communist should be put to death for political offenses! Now, pronounced "fascist, mad dogs, and wreckers," Stalin's victims were led to firing squads or the gallows, including the two chiefs of the Comintern, the organization to which Reiss, the Massings, Krivitsky, Willy Münzenberg, and Noel Field all reported. Stalin's chief rival, Leon Trotsky, in flight in Mexico, was beyond his reach—for now. Reiss observed all this with a slow-rising burn. Stalin was destroying the revolution for which he had sacrificed everything.

In an almost unimaginably bold move, Reiss wrote a letter of protest to Stalin himself. "I have gone with you up to now," Reiss wrote, "not a step further. Our paths part! Whoever keeps silent now becomes an accomplice of Stalin and a traitor to the cause of the working class and socialism." In a postscript, Reiss added that he was returning the Order of the Red Banner he received in 1928, since Stalin was now giving such awards to murderers.

The letter, from a legendary agent, was a thunderbolt in the Soviet underground. It also sealed Reiss's fate. Reiss could not be allowed to escape. If he started talking, all his agents would be exposed. "If [Field] is compromised in connection with [Reiss's] disclosures," Itzhak Akhmerov, the NKVD's New York station chief, wrote Moscow on August 15, 1937, "apparently [Duggan] will be frightened and will want to break contact with us."

Now, finally, Noel received his assignment. He was enlisted in the plot to assassinate the "traitor." Late one evening, in August 1937, Krivitsky called Field and summoned him to an urgent meeting. Noel meekly protested. The Fields were hosting a party at their home. Krivitsky insisted. We must leave immediately for Paris, he told Noel, who agreed and made his excuses to his guests. The general and his agent drove through the night, arriving in Paris in the early hours. "Krivitsky took me to a café," Field recalled, "where he introduced me to a Soviet agent. . . . Later, when I went to Moscow I learned that he was a high NKVD official. He wore the Order of Lenin." In the café, Noel faced Solomon Shpigelglas, who was in charge of the Reiss assassination. Reiss, Shpigelglas told Field, could compromise dozens of agents—including Field himself. "He has to be eliminated." Field was instructed to return to Geneva. "If Reiss contacts you," Shpiegelglas told him, "inform us immediately." The Soviet agent then asked Field if his wife could be trusted with such an operation. "Having received my positive answer," Field recalled, he was told to welcome the renegade warmly, and immediately contact a Soviet agent named "Max." Field agreed to his part in the assassination. Max drove Noel back to Geneva, and, in the days ahead, stayed close.

On the night of September 4, Reiss, fleeing his former comrades, his wife and child hiding in the Swiss countryside, left a quiet inn in the sleepy village of Chamblandes, near Lausanne. An old friend and fellow agent, Gertrud Schildbach, had lured him to the rendezvous. Reiss trusted Schildbach, who feigned disgust with Stalin. As the two walked along the lakefront, shots rang out. Reiss lay dead, twelve bullets in his back. Schildbach melted into the night.

The next day, Swiss papers featured gruesome photographs of a bullet-riddled body dumped by the side of the road—a scene from Al Capone's Chicago, not the Swiss countryside.

"[Reiss] is liquidated," Moscow informed Akhmerov on September 11, adding, ominously, "but not yet his wife. She knows about [Duggan]. . . . We are not aware of what steps she will take in the future. . . . This does not mean that you should work [Duggan] over any less strenuously. . . . Who could influence [Duggan]? First of all [the Massings]. Second of all [Field]."

"For the time being," Moscow Center informed its New York agent on November 9, 1937, "[Field] has not been tarnished in connection with [Reiss] so everything is fine from that end—for now."

Noel had passed his first major test. Though his part in the assassination was more passive than active, he had shown his willingness to do Moscow's bidding—even as an accessory in a comrade's murder. He had demonstrated his absolute loyalty to Stalin. "I helped arrange the assassination of your great friend," he later boasted to the Massings. "He was a traitor," Noel flatly asserted. "He deserved to die." The Quaker youth who had once proudly proclaimed to Allen Dulles that his ambition was to bring peace to the world, and had written to his mother of his goal "to be a light which will brighten the path for others" a decade earlier, had made a very long journey indeed.

★

In Washington, Larry Duggan's torment deepened. As chief of the State Department's Latin America Division, Larry planned a trip to Mexico to visit the artist Diego Rivera, an old friend who sheltered Leon Trotsky. This meeting caused consternation in Moscow. "I warned [Duggan]," Akhmerov wrote Moscow on September 28, 1937, "that they might attempt to brainwash him . . . I did not think it was possible to tell [Duggan] *not* to visit Rivera because he could see it as pressure, as well as lack of trust on our part."

Duggan, Field, and Hiss were never on Moscow's payroll. They betrayed their country out of conviction. However, Moscow occasionally provided small inducements, rewards more subtle than financial ones. On January 26, 1938, for example, Soviet agent "Jung" wrote to his superiors requesting "one or two paintings with revolutionary content [for Duggan], preferably reflecting the lives of workers. . . . Such paintings are hung here in fashionable bourgeois salons. As you know, [Duggan] refuses to accept any gifts from us. My wish is to bring him a birthday gift, rich in content, with the aim of developing our friendship."

Field could rationalize that as a League of Nations official he was no longer spying on his own country. Larry Duggan could not thus deceive himself. He was a tortured soul, alarmed by reports of the Moscow show trials. "He says he just can't wrap his mind around the events in the Soviet Union," Akhmerov cabled Moscow on March 1, 1938. "He believes that something is fundamentally wrong and that there can't be so many [Communists] who have become traitors."

At the State Department, a new, tougher mood prevailed. There was a growing awareness that those "naïve idealists," Field and Duggan, might have been up to something. "[Duggan] was summoned by the Assistant Secretary of State," read Akhmerov's cable to Moscow on March 7, 1938, "who told him that the present situation was exceptionally serious. State Department employees are supposed to be irreproachable and loyal to the US government. Duggan says that this was a direct and serious warning. . . . He feels he is being investigated. He says a couple of days ago, a suspicious man dressed as a heating system repairman came to his house when he wasn't there. . . . He thinks it was one of [J. Edgar] Hoover's agents."

"Duggan is very nervous and frightened," the cable continued, "and asked for the meetings to stop for a few months."

But Moscow would not so easily release such a well-placed and, heretofore, accommodating agent. Three months later, on June 28, 1938, Akhmerov cabled Moscow, "I explained to him the exceptional significance of his help precisely at this time. How fascism and fascist imperialism is brewing world war . . . how by helping Hammer [the Soviet Union] he was helping the world working class and progressive humanity in general. On the basis of all this, I asked him to renew our collaboration and to do everything to benefit our mutual cause." Pressure from both sides was bearing down on Larry Duggan.

★

Duggan could not steel himself to break all ties with Moscow. On February 7, 1937, he met with Agent "Granite" and bared his troubled soul. "[Duggan] can't make sense of the events taking place in the USSR," the Washington-to-Moscow cable reported. "He is very troubled by the charges against Trotskyite-Fascist spies in every industrial branch and government institution. People he learned to respect have turned out to be traitors to their homeland and the socialist cause. . . . How could such prominent people fall into such an abyss? What would happen to him if there turned out to be a 'fascist spy' in the State Department who would unmask him? . . . It troubles him and keeps him awake at night," Granite added. "He wants to cut ties with us and try to get involved with the [legal] American Communist Party."

But, as Ignaz Reiss learned the same year, leaving Stalin's secret service was a hazardous operation. "I spoke with [Duggan] for six hours straight," wrote Granite, "and explained to him the USSR's global position and the . . . capitalist encirclement that sends thousands of spies into the Soviet Union. . . . The extermination of these traitors only strengthens the nation and its army immeasurably. . . . The country is united as never before around the Party and the government."

Granite was a skilled agent—and much tougher than his quarry. "Gradually," Granite wrote his bosses in Moscow, "[Duggan] agreed with my arguments." The Soviet agent had one argument more powerful than any other. "I told [Duggan] that he would have to decide once and for all whether he will stand for socialism and progress, or cross over into the fascist and reactionary camp. He agreed that of course he will remain in the first category and agreed that his proposal had been poorly thought out."

"Let's forget my temporary weakness," Duggan conceded at the end of six hours of relentless argument, "and continue our work together. But," he added, "if there is another purge in the highest circles of the government, I simply won't be able to continue our work."

"And so," Granite concluded, "we were back at the beginning . . . but the whole time, I could feel an ambivalence."

Despite his ambivalence—and his mounting fears that he was within an inch of getting caught—Duggan continued to spy. "I meet [Duggan] in the evenings at a decent, quiet, bar," his new control, Jung, reported to Moscow on April 8, 1938, "or he picks me up in his car. We drive to a dark neighborhood, and talk in the car. He gives me telegrams from the [department] during the day, on his lunch break. I photograph them and give them back to him within an hour and a half . . . as he has to return them to the Department the same day."

On February 10, 1939, Duggan suffered another shock. Jung reported that Larry "arrived at the meeting without his car, looking very sullen and broken hearted. He said he had left his home through the back door, taken a taxi, and gone to the cinema before coming to see me. . . . Undersecretary Sumner Well[e]s called him into his office and told him that the Department had intelligence confirming Duggan collaborated with Hammer [the Soviet Union] passing classified documents to a Kremlin agent." Find another job, Welles advised his friend. "[Duggan] said he is completely isolated." If the Soviet cable is accurate, Welles's reaction to Duggan's "collaboration" seems astonishingly tepid. Welles seemed more interested in protecting Duggan than in rooting out Soviet espionage in the State Department.

Moscow, however, would not release Duggan. "[Duggan] repeatedly and earnestly asked to sever all ties with me," Jung wrote in the same cable. "I tried my best to convince him to meet with me if only two or three months from now. . . . He practically begged me not to do this, telling me not to put him in the unpleasant position of forcing him to say he can no longer meet with us."

Astonishingly, despite a mountain of evidence piling up against him in the newly security-conscious State Department, Larry Duggan's friends in high places—including the secretary of state—still supported him. "According to the *New York Times*," Akhmerov, now in Moscow, wrote, "[Duggan] has been appointed personal advisor to [Secretary of State Cordell] Hull. . . . He has access to absolutely all of the State Department's information." The cable closed with this ominous two-word command: "Activate immediately."

The despairing agent was duly "reactivated," spying for Moscow from 1940 until 1944, the crucial war years. Duggan's torment, however, never abated. In early 1941, "he asked me not to call him anymore," Agent "Glan" reported. "He said that despite the fact that the FBI were still '*like children lost in the woods,*' in matters of counterintelligence, nevertheless he knows for a fact that all the phones in Washington are tapped." Duggan continued to meet his Soviet minders, sometimes in a place not famous for privacy: the exclusive Cosmos Club on Massachusetts Avenue.

★

Noel's new contact, General Krivitsky, could not accommodate himself to Moscow's growing brutality against its own. For him, it was personal. Ignaz Reiss had been Krivitsky's oldest comrade-in-arms. They had started together as young partisans during the Bolshevik revolution. Now Ignaz was dead, and his wife and child were in hiding. Krivitsky had not been as willing an accomplice as Noel was prepared to be in that murder. He, too, would now be suspect. Krivitsky began to plan his own defection from the party—and with far greater caution than Reiss, whose provocation of Stalin was deliberate and public. The general quietly asked for and received the protection of French security services. Then he applied for political asylum in the United States.

Like Whittaker Chambers at around the same time, Walter Krivitsky used publicity as his shield against Stalin's vengeance. Chambers, having joined *Time* magazine as a high-profile editor, went public with his confession of treason. Later he wrote a well-regarded autobiography and was embraced by such anti-Communist politicians and luminaries as Richard M. Nixon and William F. Buckley Jr.

Krivitsky followed a similar escape plan, becoming the first of Stalin's defectors to reach out to the American media. With the help of a ghostwriter, Krivitsky exposed Stalin's rule as just another form of totalitarianism. "Why Did They Confess?" was the title of one of Krivitsky's *Saturday Evening Post* articles. "Stalin," wrote his former agent on June 17, 1939, "has for years been reducing his potential rivals to a condition of desperation through super espionage."

"Soviet show trials," the latest "turncoat" wrote, "were not trials at all, and were nothing but weapons of political warfare. . . . The Old Guard leaders were so crushed they seemed shadows of their former selves." The general had thrown down the gauntlet to Stalin, but he was in New York, and under police protection. He thought he had a chance.

Krivitsky's defection posed a direct threat to his erstwhile agent, Noel Field. In 1939, Noel returned to the United States, partly to see

his ailing mother, partly because of Stalin's latest "traitor." "I made a
one- to two-day detour," he recalled, "first of all to meet Hiss. I knew
from the newspapers that Gen. Krivitsky was hanging around Washington, and I had to count on the fact that he could betray me. . . . Since
Hiss knew all about me, I had to tell him that I was in danger, because
of a traitor. We agreed that if he heard anything, he would send me a
warning under a cover name."

Field's reference to Krivitsky as "traitor" strikes an ironic note from
a man actively betraying his own country. By 1940 Noel had quit his
increasingly futile post in the Disarmament Section of the Palace of
Nations. Suddenly unemployed, "I received a telegram from Alger,"
Noel recalled. "Hiss, then in a high post at the State Department, had
recommended me as an assistant to the newly appointed governor of
the Philippines [Francis Sayre]. . . . A secret battle was going on all
around me. Duggan, Hiss and others supported me."

Despite Hiss and Duggan's energetic efforts on Noel's behalf, the
1938 HUAC testimony of J. B. Matthews, claiming that Field had
been a Communist as early as 1928, continued to impede Field's job
prospects. He was turned down for the Philippines post.

                                 *

Field's troubles were nothing like Larry Duggan's high-wire act as a
Soviet agent in Washington. On February 2, 1942, Duggan told Agent
"Mer," "A month ago [Adolf] Berle [charged with State Department
security], after drinking a good deal of wine, reminded [Duggan]
about his affinity for left elements. [Duggan] says that as long as Berle
is with State, [Duggan] will not be able to get ahead. At present he is
working on Mexico and oil related questions and he promised to tell
us everything he knows. We agreed to meet once a month."

On November 26, 1942, Moscow cabled this stern message to Agent
Glan: "You need to take a firmer stand with respect to [Duggan]. Make
him understand that he is in fact our agent, that this is not his first

year working for us, that he gave us valuable documentary materials in the past and *that we now have a right to demand from him, at the very least, some valuable oral information about important issues.*" Our bond, Moscow reminded the now wary Duggan, is unbreakable.

Two years later, Duggan thought he found a way to escape the tightening vise. On March 1, 1944, *Time* magazine, under the heading "Foreign Affairs," in an article entitled "Going...Going..." reported, "Painters got ready to scratch another name off a State Department door. The latest resignation: genial Laurence Duggan, 38, director of the Office of American Republic Affairs, for 14 years a career diplomat, longtime friend of the recently resigned Undersecretary Sumner Welles."

Even leaving State to work for the United Nations Relief and Rehabilitation Administration, and then succeeding his father, Stephen Duggan, as director of the Institute of International Education, he could not escape. A new Moscow agent, code-named "Saushkin," called on Duggan in 1948. After their meeting, Saushkin cabled Moscow: "Duggan, having led me to the elevator, let me know unequivocally that it was time for me to go. He had no wish to talk about anything other than the Institute and tried the whole time to keep an official tone. I got the impression that he was constantly on his guard.... We agreed to have dinner at the beginning of September."

That fall, in their testimonies before the House Un-American Activities Committee, Whittaker Chambers and Elizabeth Bentley named Larry Duggan, Alger Hiss, and Noel Field as Soviet spies.

Noel Field, desperately seeking a job and a country where he would be safe from Washington's growing interest in his record of betrayal, wrote Larry a typically disingenuous letter—meant for eyes other than Duggan's—on November 9, 1948. "The mail brought a number of *Times* clippings [reporting the allegations about Duggan, Hiss, and Field].... The advice I have been getting from friends and relatives ranges from bringing suit for half a million, to simply ignoring the whole thing. At the moment," Field wrote, "my inclination is to follow the latter course and not to dignify the absurd concoction by any public denial, although I shall bear in mind your suggestion of sending a communication for the record.

"An equally scurrilous attack on me was made back in 1938," Noel adds, in reference to J. B. Matthews's HUAC testimony.

# CHAPTER 7

# DESPERATE COMRADES

*The torch of faith is extinct; let us fall back on the candles of truth.*

—Arthur Koestler

I
N A BOOK-CRAMMED apartment on New York's Upper East Side belonging to writer Isaac Don Levine, during the fateful year 1939, two disenchanted former Soviet agents, Whittaker Chambers and Walter Krivitsky, had an extraordinary meeting. By way of a greeting, Krivitsky asked Chambers if he thought the Soviet government was fascist. After pausing to consider this startling opening, Chambers nodded. "Krivitsky and I began to talk quickly as if we were racing time," Chambers remembered. "We talked about Krivitsky's break with Communism, and his flight with his wife and small son from Amsterdam to Paris. We talked about attempts to trap or kill him in Europe, and the fact that he had not been in the U.S. a week before the Russian secret police set a watch on his apartment. We talked about the murder of Ignaz Reiss . . . whose break from the Party . . . had precipitated Krivitsky's. . . . It was then that I learned that for more than a year Stalin had been desperately seeking to negotiate an alliance with

Hitler. . . . By means of the [Hitler-Stalin] pact, Communism could pit one sector of the West against the other, and use both to destroy the non-Communist world. As Communist strategy, the pact was thoroughly justified, and the Party was right in denouncing all those who opposed it as Communist enemies." Mixing German and English, in the shorthand of the underground, they talked through the night. At dawn, they still had more to say to each other. The pudgy, ill-kempt former American Communist and the short, wiry Central European Bolshevik—men electric with intelligence and rage—bonded in bitterness.

"In our time," Krivitsky concluded the long night, "*informing* [on the Soviets] is a duty." This blunt assertion—almost a command from a respected Bolshevik—prompted Chambers to break his own silence and "inform" on his own life in the Communist underground. Chambers's resolution, reached after that cathartic night between two disenchanted Soviet agents, would have seismic impact.

As they parted, Krivitsky ruefully concluded, "One does not leave Stalin lightly."

A year and a half later, the chambermaid at the Bellevue Hotel, a few blocks from Washington's Union Station, was making her morning rounds. Unlocking room 532 with her passkey, she saw a man's feet and legs on the bed, lying the wrong way around. The maid asked when she should come back, and when he did not answer, she noticed blood pooled by his head. Hotel guests rushed from their rooms at the sound of her shriek. The dead man with a bullet hole the size of a fist in his skull was later identified as General Walter Krivitsky.

The next day, front-page articles raised the obvious question: why was a man so clearly in danger after his very public break with Stalin without security? Krivitsky had been making plans to change his name and to file for American citizenship. He had told State Department officials of his strong suspicions regarding the existence of the Cambridge spy ring burrowed in the British secret services: Kim Philby, Donald Maclean, Guy Burgess, and Anthony Blunt. In 1939, Krivitsky was summoned to London to be interviewed by Dick White, head of British intelligence (MI5 and, later, MI6) and Guy Liddell, of MI5. Krivitsky did not know the names of the British spies, but the descriptions he provided White and Liddell matched Philby and Maclean. White and Liddell, however, failed to follow up on Krivitsky's leads. The general had warned his wife that if he were found dead, never under any circumstance believe that it was suicide. He had reported to the police sighting a man known as "Hans"—one of the KGB's most brutal killers. Yet Krivitsky did not have security.

In a revealing (and shocking) FBI internal memorandum addressed to Director J. Edgar Hoover, Agent C. H. Carson wrote on February 10, 1941, "Agent ___ (redacted) advised that he and Agent ___ (redacted) talked to Krivitsky in the latter's lawyer's office and Krivitsky told his story about how he had been accosted by some people who were Soviet Agents. Mr. ___ (redacted) stated that he and Agent ___ (redacted) were not very impressed after the interview with Krivitsky, and they were both of the opinion that though he did not seem like a Jew, he was alleged to have been Jewish." Though it's inconceivable that anti-Semitism was the primary reason the FBI did not provide Krivitsky with security, the memo is a reminder of the institution's casual racism during that period.

*

Two of Noel Field's three control officers, Ignaz Reiss and Walter Krivitky, had paid with their lives for trying to break with Moscow. The third and most important of Noel's liaisons to Moscow—his recruiters, Paul and Hede Massing—were now also suspect.

In the spring of 1938, in keeping with the Stalinist ritual of recalling to Moscow agents under suspicion, Paul and Hede obeyed their summons. What was the point of defiance? Stalin's reach knew no borders.

Once in Moscow, the Massings were virtual prisoners of the fabled Hotel Metropol, minutes from the Kremlin. Their passports in official custody, months passed and their interrogation did not let up. They grew daily more anxious that they would not leave the Soviet Union alive, when, "One morning," Hede recalled, "while I was picking up a batch of mail, I came across a letter addressed to 'Noel H. Field.' As casually as possible, I said to the girl at the desk, 'Oh, is Mr. Field in town?' " Indeed, the Fields were on their long-awaited first visit to the workers' paradise. (Noel, who received his Soviet visa in Paris, did not tell his colleagues at the League of Nations where he was spending his month-long vacation.) Hede immediately understood that if their old friends had not been in touch with them, she and Paul must be officially persona non grata. But at the same time, she saw a way out of a very dangerous situation. She rang the Fields in their room. Feigning a calm she did not feel, she suggested lunch. The Fields were trapped. The chance encounter saved the Massings' lives.

"When we met in Moscow," Paul Massing recalled, "the roles were completely reversed. We were in trouble, Noel was completely *persona grata*. He followed the official line, not calling us. It was the purest chance we learned he was there."

Noel and Herta filled the awkward reunion with a breathless account of all the wonders they had seen on their tour: Leningrad, Stalingrad, Saratov, Rostov, Baku, Tiflis, Sochi, Yalta, and Kiev. Accompanied by their NKVD "hosts," they had visited factories and collective farms. The Fields were enchanted by everything they saw. Noel related a "touching" incident with their Intourist minder, who, when told by the Fields they wouldn't need her one evening, later found her sitting patiently in front of their hotel room, waiting. It somehow did not occur to them that the minder was afraid to leave her post.

Having cornered the Fields into a meeting, Hede took full advantage of the situation. She picked up the hotel telephone as Noel and Herta stood helplessly by and called Bazarov, her control officer, who held the Massings' passports—and their fate—in his hands. "Hede embarrassed Noel very much," Paul Massing recalled, "with her phone call in front of him demanding our passports. But I think it helped us." Their passports were delivered almost immediately. "I think another reason we were allowed to go," Paul recalled, "was that by then the purge had gone very far. There is a natural tendency to reach a point where you say there has to be a stop—or we will all go under." So the Massings survived—with the Fields' inadvertent help.

Agent Bazarov, however, would not fare as well. A two-word memo in the KGB files reveals the dispatch of another agent who had loyally served Stalin, now perceived as the enemy. "Bazarov shot."

★

Noel still pined for a tighter bond—a cleaner connection—with the Communist Party. It was all too ambiguous and ill-defined for a man who had sacrificed family, profession, and country. Later Noel explained, "My trip to Moscow had several purposes. The most important was to get to know the Soviet Union. . . . The other reason was that after Reiss and Krivitsky's betrayals I was left without any connection to the Party and I had hoped that I would be able to establish such connections for further work."

While in Moscow, Noel and Herta applied to join the CPUSA as secret members. This posed an ironic complication. Since Noel was a spy, the American party would not be informed of their membership. "We asked to be registered in the American Party section of the Comintern," Field recalled. "But we were told that our admission was going to be treated confidentially. They would not forward it to the American Party, because of our confidential work."

To placate Noel, the apparatus gave him a name ("Brook") and told him to expect a contact in Geneva. Noel seemed oblivious to the tangled politics of his situation. As a result of his association with the "traitors" Reiss, Krivitsky, and now the Massings, he, too, was under a shadow.

## CHAPTER 8

# SPAIN

*When the fighting broke out . . . every anti-Fascist in Europe felt a thrill of hope. For here at last . . . was democracy standing up to Fascism.*

—George Orwell

*I lived in a city called Barcelona, which I loved more than any other place—and which is no more.*

—Noel Field

E VERY GENERATION DATES its coming of age from one pivotal, permanently searing event. For Noel Field's generation, the Spanish Civil War was that event. The evil lurking just offstage during the thirties erupted full-blown in Spain, in 1936. The Spanish Civil War—though perhaps not the first total war—wiped out the centuries-old distinction between soldiers and civilians. Everybody was a target for German and Italian carpet bombers who rained their inferno on entire towns and villages. Spain was the first war based on ideology: fascism versus democracy. After Spain, almost nobody could have illusions about what was coming.

★

The war for Spain finally presented the West with a chance to stop talking about fascism and start fighting it. But America and much of Europe still only watched the massacre from the sidelines, hiding behind a policy of nonintervention, the latest excuse for inaction. The heroes were the plain people of Spain who shamed leaders in London, Paris, and Washington who said it was no use—let evil spend itself. The so-called Loyalists—supporters of the democratically elected leftist government— mobilized to resist Generalissimo Francisco Franco's right-wing power grab. Hitler and Mussolini rushed to arm Franco—and test their new weapons of mass destruction before the coming bigger war.

Stalin emerged the winner. By letting Franco and his allies conquer Spain, the West handed him a huge moral victory at precisely the moment the Kremlin most needed it. The Spanish Civil War coincided with Stalin's bloodiest wave of terror. For Communists like Koestler and scores of others with growing misgiving about Stalin, Hitler and Mussolini's bleeding of Spain was reason to jump back in the anti-fascist fight.

It seemed as if every writer, journalist, photographer, or activist sooner or later made his or her way to Barcelona, Madrid, Toledo, and Teruel. Ernest Hemingway, John Dos Passos, George Orwell, Robert Capa, André Malraux, and Martha Gellhorn—and thousands of others—all played their part. "Spain," wrote journalist Murray Kempton, "was the passion of that small segment of my generation which felt a personal commitment to the Revolution."

It was also the war that produced the most iconic and horrifying painting of the last century. Pablo Picasso's *Guernica* depicts the total destruction of a small Basque market town. A billboard-size canvas in black and white, *Guernica* does not depict the destruction from the sky of an undefended town. Rather, it is a shocking evocation of the death of everything: men, women, children, and animals, a light going out over the world. *Guernica* is the Apocalypse rendered visible, and it roused people of conscience more powerfully than words.

By the time the Fields returned to Geneva from their Moscow trip, the Spanish Civil War had been raging for two years. The League of Nations hadn't done much to stop the bloodletting. In the war's hopeless last days, however, the League assigned Noel and a team of "commissioners" to arrange the "orderly repatriation" of thousands of members of the International Brigades. Up to 35,000 volunteers from nearly every country—including almost three thousand Americans— volunteered with the Loyalists. Noel's dismal duty was to extract these fighters from the battlefield and repatriate them to their own countries. Hitler had already occupied Austria, the Rhineland, and Czechoslovakia. It was hard to avoid the obvious fact that a Europe-wide war was imminent. What to do about thousands of defeated, demoralized militia fleeing Franco's onslaught was Field's hazardous assignment.

*

Spain was to be the hinge event in Noel Field's life. In Spain, in 1938, Field, the hardened Communist, discovered his barely tapped humanitarianism, and the sense of fulfillment he experienced in easing others' misery. There was abundant human misery in Spain. "Four stirring months in Republican Spain," Noel wrote, "thought and action then found heartwarming, soul satisfying unity in the absorbing task of giving aid to hundreds of anti-Fascist victims." In Spain, too, Noel befriended and helped rescue hundreds of Communist fighters—members of the International Brigades. "Steadfast, clear eyed," he said of them much later, "they were my guides and mentors. I revere them still." In time, they would bitterly regret they ever heard the name Noel Field.

"I think the happiest time in Noel's life was in Spain," Paul Massing recalled. "There he could actually help people concretely. But," Massing ruefully noted, "he did not seem to have learned any more about practical Communist politics in Spain than in Moscow."

Field was oblivious—willfully so, perhaps—of the fact that Stalin transported his brutal purge to the Spanish battlefield. To his horror, George Orwell soon discovered that this was also a war Stalinists waged against all other socialists. "Aren't we all Socialists?" Orwell asked. "I thought it idiotic that people fighting for their lives should have separate parties. My attitude was always 'Why can't we drop all this political nonsense and get on with the war?' " For Stalin, Spain was just another skirmish in his own war for absolute power.

Even as Franco's forces approached Barcelona, the Kremlin's agents turned on socialists, leftists, and anarchists not directly aligned with Moscow. Stalin's relentless hunt for Trotsky—frustratingly elusive in Mexico—was transferred to the streets of Barcelona. Socialists who volunteered to fight the fascists were suddenly smeared as fascists and "Trotskyites." "This charge," Orwell wrote, "was repeated over and over in the Communist Press—part of the world wide drive of the official Communist Party against 'Trotskyism.' " The charge of "Trotskyite" against the likes of Orwell was as irrational as leveling it against the heroes of the Russian Revolution facing firing squads back in Moscow.

★

On January 29, 1939, across the Spanish border from the dusty, inhospitable French town of Perpignan, in the foothills of the Pyrenees, Noel wrote his family his most heartfelt and moving letter. Revealing qualities new to the man, it is also a vivid document of that savage war.

"I know you will forgive my long silence," he begins,

> We have lived in a horrible daze, both of us, and God knows when we'll be able to snap out of it, if ever. When horror is piled on horror, one ceases even to be able to cry. . . . The calendar has simply stopped for all of us. Yes, if I try to figure it out, it must be that I fled with the remaining members of the [League of Nations] Commission Sunday night, a week ago. And before that I lived in a city called Barcelona—which I loved more than any

other place I have ever been—and which is no more. Barcelona ceased to exist at noon last Wednesday.

I sit in the *Prefecture* here alone for the first time in many days. Herta is somewhere in the border regions helping run a cantine. Thank God for our car. It has saved her. She goes off early in the morning, takes others with her. And reporters come back telling me they saw her among the refugees, handing out food. Refugees. You don't know what that is. You cannot imagine it. Goya's engravings. There's been nothing like it in generations. Hardboiled officers who went through the World War in Flanders and saw the Belgian disaster are speechless with horror—the World War was nothing.

And nothing we can do. Except try to tell about it and get it to the heartless, careless, happy world outside. So I talk to reporters, feed them all I can, tell them of that tunnel between Cerbere and Portbou, in which thousands have been jammed for days, thousands more pushing in, unable to get through because on the other end is happy, peaceful, gallant France. Babies born in the eternal darkness on the railroad tracks, old men dying, famine, human excrement, festering wounds, sleeplessness, terror of every sound that reminds of alarms or bombs. For days on foot, barefoot, in nightgowns, bitter north wind, rain, hour for hour, day and night, planes low flying over the roads, bombing. Machine gunning. Trucks loaded with humans of all ages, standing for hours, moving a few blocks in one day, humans heaped up in the ditch and on the roadside, dead and dying on top of each other, as truck after truck blows sky high.

In the fields all through what remains of Catalonia, thousands and thousands exhausted, starved, calmly lying down to die, chewing bark and grass. The horrors of China in the midst of Europe.

As town after town, village after village is wiped out by bombs and machine guns, they stumble on to the next place, hoping by moving to escape from the inferno.

In a military telephone booth, I was trying to phone our office. Dark, stinking. I hear a moan. As my eyes adjust to the dark, an old woman huddled in a corner, starved, barely able to speak. Beside her, a bundle stirs and groans: her husband, at the point of death. Too late to eat: my chocolate lies in their bony hands, they can't manage it anymore.

Two weeks later, Noel continued his unfinished letter:

During one spectacular battle, we counted 76 planes over Barcelona. . . . As Acting Secretary General (of the Commission) I had to take numerous decisions and deal with high officials in important matters. Thank heavens I didn't pull any serious boners though my hair still stands on end when I think of some of the problems I had to deal with. . . .

Mother, I trust my silence hasn't caused too much worry. The press boys assured me they mentioned me in their stories, so I assume you had an inkling of my doings. . . .

Well, hasta luego and love

Noel

Saturated as Noel's letter is with despair, he writes with the quiet self-assurance of a man who has been to hell and back, who has finally had his testing, and is—perhaps for the first time—proud of himself. As Franco's troops advanced, Noel scurried from makeshift hospitals to refugee camps along the Franco-Spanish border. His official role as member of the League Commission was to count the heads of members of the International Brigades staggering across the border into dismal, jerry-rigged French refugee camps. Fifteen thousand fighters—nine thousand of them German—and others from all over Europe and the United States now needed help repatriating to their homelands, and a high percentage of them were Communists. Surrounded by "comrades" at last, Noel was in his element. In action, he forgot about his anxieties, and collapsed from sheer exhaustion each night.

Shockingly, on the French side of the Spanish border, the heroes of Spain were greeted as criminals. Noel spent days at Le Vernet, a former army barracks hastily converted to warehouse the human flood. From a distance, the fifty acres of parched land surrounded by barbed wire might have been mistaken for a concentration camp. The regime inside Le Vernet was punishing. Four times a day, there were roll calls lasting up to an hour each. Any infraction was reprimanded by the guard's leather crop. Those who could were put to work building roads. Almost everybody was starving. In fact, except for its stated purpose, Le Vernet was no better than a Nazi concentration camp, save that its purpose was not the killing of inmates.

Undoubtedly, Noel's Soviet control had provided him with lists of Communist refugees to contact and try somehow to rescue. At this stage, Field could do little more than offer encouragement and a promise that he would return with more tangible aid later.

In the midst of so much human misery, Noel struck up a friendship that would prove tragic for those it touched.

★

The Glaser family were refugees from Schlawe, Pomerania—a region now divided between Germany and Poland, on the southern shore of the Baltic Sea. The Glasers' journey perfectly distills the tumultuous last century. Wilhelm and Marie Therese Glaser—an idealistic doctor and his cultured wife—had high hopes for their precocious daughter, Erica. Everything changed one morning in 1934, when twelve-year-old Erica, walking home from school with a friend, saw "the scene that will forever stay in my mind," as she recalled. "A group of half naked people beaten through the streets across the market place with sticks, whips, fists by surrounding hordes of uniformed gangsters, followed by a screaming mob. . . . I realized to my horror that the victims were people I knew, ordinary, decent citizens of [Pomerania], middle-aged men and women, little shopkeepers, a dentist and his wife. And here they ran weeping and crying, the men stripped to the waist, the women wearing a few rags, covered with blood and dirt, and tears, around their necks the cardboard stigma of their infamy: 'I am a Jewish swine.' " It was the end of the old Germany, and of Erica's childhood.

Soon Erica was the only one in her high school who refused to join the Hitler Youth. She learned to brawl and defend herself against the schoolyard bullies whose favorite target she became. But far worse was coming.

Erica Glaser's indomitable spirit and reckless courage are rarely found outside the pages of fiction. After Herta, she was to be the most important person in Noel Field's life.

Dr. Wilhelm Glaser was one of those rare Germans who read *Mein Kampf* and took Hitler at his word. He moved his family to Spain, then an island of democracy in darkening Europe. In 1936, civil war tore Spain, and the now fourteen-year-old Erica was again witness to and victim of history. "At first there were only small bombs," Erica recalled, "and the people of Madrid ran out to see what was falling from the sky . . . [only to be] mowed down by machine guns. Soon the big German bombers came in large formations, every two hours on the dot, even at night. When there was no moon and we had hopes for a peaceful night, they began with incendiary bombs, and the city, brightly lit, presented a better target than ever. German precision had one advantage: we all regulated our clocks, our next meals, our lives accordingly."

Schools closed, so Erica was forced to choose a more practical education: nursing. The teenager was soon cleaning and bandaging the wounds of Loyalist soldiers and civilians.

Her parents were preoccupied—her father working in a field hospital; her mother running a boardinghouse, their primary income. Each morning Erica walked to the "front," at the edge of town, and back home at night. "My long blond braids drew special attention in a country where 'rubias' were rare and desirable," she recalled. "Sailors lined the Paseo, and pursued me relentlessly. . . . One of them remarked that I might be a German Fascist. I turned in anger to protest. . . . Luckily, they soon realized that I was only a child, and a foreigner at that."

As Madrid fell to Franco's forces in 1938, Erica—still tending the injured—contracted typhoid fever. Now, again, the Glasers were stateless—and in flight. Erica was too ill to travel. Such were the times that families often faced choices this cruel: whom to save, whom to leave behind. To save themselves, the Glasers left Erica behind in a makeshift clinic.

At an International Brigades hospital near Barcelona, a chance meeting brought the Fields and the Glasers together. The two German-speaking couples quickly found common ground. When the Glasers shared their distress at Erica's condition, and their inability to look after her, the Fields sprung to action. "We have no children," Herta told Marie Therese. "We can take her with us to Switzerland, and look after her." With no better options, the Glasers agreed to this informal adoption.

Shortly thereafter, the hospital where Erica was being treated was bombed. All foreign patients were evacuated north, to "sanctuary" in France. "I found myself in an ambulance," Erica recalled, "squeezed between two severely wounded soldiers. The two men next to me moaned steadily with pain, the one opposite had a head injury, which had affected his mind. Periodically he would roll his eyes and fall on top of me. In the middle of the night we ran out of gas and sat there waiting to be captured [by Franco's forces]. . . . I could not yet walk after four months of typhoid fever and had to crawl on all fours. In the evening of the next day we were finally rescued by a truck and taken to the last assembly place for the foreigners in Spain. It was a sight I have never forgotten."

The legendary war photographer Robert Capa might have captured the human misery that greeted Erica in Perpignan: a surreal tableau of cots and stretchers in ragged disorder around the main square, bearing the abandoned flotsam of war—with no doctors or aid workers to tend them. The locals, hearts hardened by too many such scenes, were not helpful. Erica tottered around the town center searching for her parents. A former militiaman spotted the distraught blond teenager and told Erica he had a letter for her. "It's from someone called Field," he said. He no longer had the letter but he said he had read it. "Field says to contact him in the Grand Hotel, here in town. He and his wife want to adopt you and take you to Switzerland." And so, exhausted, dirty, and hungry, Erica made her painful way to the Grand Hotel.

For the young girl who barely survived the Madrid evacuation, still reeling from the aftereffects of typhoid, the sight of Perpignan's Grand Hotel was a shock. "The big hall was brightly lit," she recalled, "and reeling with elegant, well-fed people, in evening dress. All eyes . . . were on me: tall and thin, with a narrow, pale face, dirty hair with straw in it, a man's leather coat, a worn-out skirt practically down to my ankles."

At the sight of this unsmiling adolescent who had clearly seen enough and lived enough to be a child only in years, the Fields saw a chance for a family. The object of their enchantment, however, was sullen and monosyllabic. Fiercely proud, Erica did not easily accept kindness from strangers. "The Fields," she said, "whom I hated sight unseen, had to be extremely patient and kind to stand my horrible behavior in the beginning of our acquaintance. It took me a long time to be able to admit that they were 'nice.' "

"That child has no heart!" Erica's father—heartbroken at having to part from his daughter—exclaimed when they were briefly reunited in Perpignan, only to part again. (As stateless refugees, the Glasers faced internment in France, and ultimately settled in Great Britain.) Erica took the news of the "adoption" calmly. She had a heart but, more than anything, she was determined to survive. She would not see her parents for seven years.

Before long, Erica, living with the Fields in Geneva, was back on her feet and enrolled in school. Self-confident beyond her years, combative and uncompromising, Erica matured into a tall, athletic young woman, physically and intellectually fearless. Noel and Herta doted on their "dream daughter." (Certain accounts of the Fields allege that their affection for their foster daughter might have crossed a line into behavior inappropriate for "parents," but surviving family members deny this rumor.) Herta and Noel's adoration of Erica shines through their correspondence. "I repeat in writing what I have already told you," Noel wrote her on February 18, 1942. "I admire you and respect you for what you have made of yourself. My confidence and belief in you—which were always there—even in troubled times—have been justified." Erica was as open and blunt as Noel was devious and opaque. He loved her—and saw a great future for her as a Communist.

# CHAPTER 9

# WAR

*It's farewell to the drawing room's mannerly cry,*
*The professor's logical whereto and why,*
*The frock-coated diplomat's polished aplomb,*
*Now matters are settled with gas and with bomb.*

—W. H. Auden

P EACE!" EXULTED THE London *Daily Express.* "No conqueror returning from a victory on the battlefield has come adorned with
nobler laurels," intoned the more staid London *Times.* It was Friday,
September 30, 1938, and British prime minister Neville Chamberlain—
returning from his fateful Munich meeting with Adolf Hitler—was
mobbed by thousands of his grateful countrymen. "The settlement
of the Czechoslovak problem," Chamberlain assured them, "is only a
prelude to a larger settlement in which Europe may find peace." Amid
general European jubilation, five hundred thousand Frenchmen who
had been called up for military service were told to go home.

Three months later, on December 17, at 9:00 a.m., the Wehrmacht's
panzer division clattered over Prague's cobblestones. Later the same

day, Hitler's private train rolled into the Czech capital. Standing in his open-topped car in driving snow, his arm outstretched, the Führer entered the gates of Prague Castle, former symbol of Czech independence. No conqueror in recent memory had so completely savored his moment—and the humiliation of yet another nation. Inside the medieval fortress, Hitler signed a document that proclaimed that Czechoslovakia had "ceased to exist." Hitler thus solved another European "problem" by incorporating it into the Reich.

A near-suffocating gloom hung over much of the Continent that winter of 1938–39. Europe was suspended in anxiety. Everywhere, people rushed to buy gas masks and stockpiled canned food, and cities practiced blackout drills. Listening to staticky radio broadcasts, the French, Czechs, Dutch, and Belgians tried to make sense of the deal Chamberlain and Hitler had hatched. As Hitler filled concentration camps with dissidents, Jews, and Gypsies, an ocean away, Americans by the thousands thronged the World's Fair in Flushing Meadows, New York. Against a swelling tide of panicked refugees, the United States tightened its borders and slashed immigration quotas.

For many Europeans, suicide became a rational option. Koestler—now a stateless refugee—recalled a conversation with his Parisian neighbor, the writer-philosopher Walter Benjamin. " 'If anything goes wrong,' " Benjamin asked Koestler, " 'have you got anything to take?' For in those days we all carried some 'stuff' in our pockets. . . . I had none, and he shared what he had with me, sixty-two tablets of a sedative, procured in Berlin during the week, which followed the burning of the Reichstag. He did it reluctantly for he did not know whether the thirty-one tablets left him would be enough. It was enough. A week after my departure he made his way over the Pyrenees to Spain, a man of fifty-five with heart disease. At Port Bou, Franco's Guardia Civil arrested him. He was told that next morning they would send him back to France. When they came to fetch him for the train, he was dead."

★

What went through Noel Field's mind on August 24, 1939, when he read in the newspapers that the Great Anti-Fascist himself had signed a treaty of nonaggression with Hitler? No doubt Noel found a way to rationalize this latest evidence of Stalin's treachery. "He always said Stalin knows what he is doing," recalled Dr. Zina Minor, a young doctor who later worked for Field in Marseille. "Noel gave the breaking-eggs-to-make-an-omelet argument."

The Communist Party had an explanation ready. The morning after Stalin signed the treaty, the French Communist organ published its rationale. The new treaty, *l'Humanité* explained, was a "supreme effort of Stalin to prevent the threatening imperialist war." While most American Communists were shocked by Stalin's deal with Hitler, their official organ, the *Daily Worker*, continued to end its editorials with "Defend the Soviet Union!" Noel Field certainly did.

Western delusions and disengagement from Hitler and Stalin's lethal race for power finally reaped their reward on September 1, 1939, when German tanks from all directions rolled into Poland. Forty-eight hours later, World War II was under way. The first of the Field family to be swept up in the war was Noel's younger brother, Hermann. A twenty-eight-year-old Harvard graduate and practicing architect, Hermann, too, possessed the family's nonconformist streak. But the younger Field was a more balanced man, sociable and self-confident. Where Noel professed to love humanity, and agonized about how to serve it, Hermann enjoyed its company. In London, he'd met and fallen in love with a bright and outgoing English girl named Kate Thornycroft. Kate shared Hermann's distinctly leftist politics—in the age of Hitler, almost a given for the young. Hermann's girlfriend and soon-to-be wife, a humanitarian activist, persuaded him to go to Kraków, Poland, to do what he could for refugees streaming across the Czech-Polish frontier. In common with much of Europe's refugee population in the thirties, these Czechs were mostly Jewish, socialists, or Communists.

Arriving at Kraków in April 1939, Hermann proved coolheaded and brave in the eye of a powerful storm. Without any prior experience in rescue, working for the newly formed British Committee for Refugees from Czechoslovakia, Hermann saved hundreds of newly stateless Czechs by facilitating their transit to Britain.

On May 13, 1939, he wrote his mother, "I've got 800 human beings to look after . . . and *everything is running out*: the money to feed 800 mouths, the accommodation, the British visas, the patience of the Polish police and the government. Meanwhile the situation along our frontier looks worse and worse," he wrote as German troops massed on the border. And then, in a phrase hard to imagine coming from his elder brother, Noel, Hermann wrote, "I never in my life felt so fond of human beings as I have here. They and life with it are something much richer and more real than ever before."

He describes the cruel triage involved in rescue. "All day long," Hermann wrote home on June 24, "people are breaking down and pleading, going off their heads because of what I tell them, people taken away under my nose because if I save them today, they will only have to go tomorrow. They don't even dare ask me anymore when their turn to go to England comes. Their request is ever so small—just for me to give them 2 weeks protection, or ten days, or a week or two days. . . . It is almost impossible to explain to their faces, but I try, and very often they get quiet, and simply go away and disappear. . . . I often wish they would get mad at me, as they do with the others," wrote the young American, suddenly responsible for life-and-death decisions. "Choosing is very hard and depressing and then what is to happen to those that are left? Poland won't have them. Germany won't let them back. They can't leave, and yet won't be tolerated here," he wrote, providing a thumbnail sketch of the twentieth century—and foreshadowing the twenty-first.

A casual reference to his brother's Communist recruiters, Paul and Hede Massing, underscores the Fields' closeness to the two Soviet agents. Hermann wrote his mother, "Tell P[aul] and H[ede] they would discover lots of familiar faces here. *I did my best for them, you can be sure,*" he wrote pointedly, "The losses have been awful though. If the [Massings] come across any Crakow alumni during the next months, they should give them my love. I feel as if wherever I go in the world, I will always find friends. For, by the time my 400–500 departures [i.e., refugees he rescued] have been scattered to the four winds, there will be hardly a country without them. *Some 200 went East.*" A decade later, those two hundred who "went East" would bitterly regret their association with one of the Field brothers.

On August 31, "at 5:30 in the morning we were awakened by sirens," Hermann wrote his mother, "and went to the window and felt relieved that at last we were getting the air raid drill that had been promised for some days. . . . Then, someone came rushing in, 'Didn't we know that German troops had already crossed the frontier?' "

As the Wehrmacht poured across the Polish border, the Luftwaffe rained fiery terror from the skies and panic spread like lava around Hermann. "All I can remember is the noise of breaking glass all around me, of doors caving in and clouds of plaster dust all around us. Then, after a brief moment of silence, the women (and men) beginning to scream and sob and rush around aimlessly, trying still to hide themselves although the planes had long since departed. Then came the wounded and shapeless pieces of people being rushed past on stretchers." World War II had begun.

*

On September 2, 1939—the day after the outbreak of war—Whittaker Chambers named Noel Field, Larry Duggan, and Alger Hiss among those State Department officials spying for the Soviets. Chambers named Field and Duggan as actual Communist Party members, and J. Peters as "responsible for the Washington sector." He handed his memo to Assistant Secretary of State Adolf Berle, charged with security at the department. In the tumultuous days following Hitler's invasion of Poland, Chambers's memo did not get much attention. President Roosevelt dismissed it with a brusque "I don't want to hear another thing about it!" FDR was gearing up the nation for war against Hitler, not Stalin. More surprisingly, J. Edgar Hoover, the powerful director of the FBI, didn't much care about "reds" in the highest reaches of government either. Germany, not the Soviet Union—considered weak and backward—was the immediate threat to world peace. Deemed least credible was Chambers's charge against Alger Hiss. When asked if Hiss, his former protégé, could possibly be a Soviet agent, Justice Felix Frankfurter snorted in disbelief.

★

In the predawn darkness of September 3, Hermann Field fled Kraków, "without my headlights, my car packed to the ceiling, with the American flag stuck big on all sides, my lights pasted over with blue typewriter paper, my staff all gone . . . moving out of town at snail's pace. Kraków—full of beauty and summer—now it was like a dead thing of stone."

Hermann survived and was eventually reunited with Kate. They married during the London Blitz and sailed for New York during the spring of 1940. Hermann's real nightmare, however, was still almost a decade away.

# CHAPTER 10

# MARSEILLE

*We can delay and effectively stop . . . the number of immigrants into the United States . . . by simply advising our consuls to put every obstacle in the way . . . and to resort to various administrative devices which would postpone and postpone and postpone the granting of visas.*

—Breckinridge Long, State Department official

W ITH FRIGHTENING SPEED, France fell to the German onslaught in June 1940. An enormous Nazi flag soon fluttered from the Arc de Triomphe as the German Eighteenth Army marched through the streets of Paris. In the south, the still unoccupied port city of Marseille teemed with thousands of French Jews fleeing the Gestapo, as well as refugees from Spain, Germany, and the Nazi-occupied territories of Eastern Europe. A handful of American relief workers arrived to attempt to fill the gap left by Washington's shameful policy of non-rescue. Among the brave humanitarians was Donald Lowrie of the YMCA. Lowrie had heard of Noel Field's relief work in Spain, and recommended him to the newly formed Unitarian Service Committee (USC), which was looking for someone to head up its office in Marseille.

The Fields' earnest manner and Quaker simplicity suited the Reverend Charles Joy, the balding, amiable head of the Boston-based USC. The fact that both Noel and Herta were trilingual qualified them to work with a multinational refugee population. Besides, not many Americans were eager to take on a mission this dangerous, rescuing Jews and others trapped on the knife's edge in Vichy France. After interviewing them in their home outside Geneva, Dr. Joy hired them both on the spot. There were no guidelines for their jobs. "Just do what you can for these people," Joy told the Fields. In no time, Noel and Herta packed up their Vandoeuvres house and boarded the train to Marseille, one of the final places of hope in Europe in 1940. Erica, enrolled at the University of Geneva, stayed behind.

★

Among those in flight during the summer of France's defeat was Willi Münzenberg, Lenin's public relations genius who had spun Communist propaganda gold from Sacco and Vanzetti's executions. Now, like Trotsky, Reiss, Krivitsky, and thousands of other Old Guard Bolsheviks, Münzenberg was out of favor with Stalin—and feared for his life. Repeatedly summoned back to the Kremlin, he defied calls whose meaning he well understood. Fleeing south, he was the target of at least two dictators, Hitler—for his years as an anti-fascist propagandist—and Stalin, who did not trust international Communists of Münzenberg's ilk. On October 22, 1940, in the village of Montagne, outside Grenoble, hunters found Münzenberg's decomposing body in the woods under a pile of leaves, a knotted cord around his neck. Suicide or assassination? Impossible to determine with certainty, but another of the twentieth century's little-known but transformational figures had died a violent death.

★

The shimmering Mediterranean in the distance never fails to lift the spirits of new arrivals to the port city. High above the great harbor of

Marseille, the silhouette of Notre-Dame de la Garde has been a symbol of sanctuary for generations of refugees. With its teeming port; narrow, winding alleys; peeling, pastel-colored houses; and active black market, Marseille was a place where one could disappear. Though the Gestapo had not yet arrived, Vichy France's omnipresent, black-caped gendarmes already struck fear in many hearts. An unaccustomed quiet hung over the formerly bustling port. In the fascist mold, Vichy's leader, Marshal Philippe Pétain, replaced *Liberté, Égalité, Fraternité* with *Travail, Famille, Patrie*—work, family, homeland—as France's national motto. Pétain also banned public playing of music and dancing, which only added to Marseille's gloom. Not that French Jews, nor Czech, Hungarian, Spanish, or German refugees who crowded the cafés along the Vieux Port and La Canebière Avenue, were in the mood for dancing. Their chief occupation was waiting.

Until the Fields' arrival, Varian Fry, the head of the New York–based Emergency Rescue Committee, was the refugees' best hope. The tall, ascetic Fry burned with anger at Washington's policy to "postpone and postpone and postpone the granting of visas." Fry's specific charge was the rescue of Germany's great—and now threatened—cultural figures. Arranging swift passage to America for them was his challenge. By breaking rules, bribing and deceiving both American and Vichy officials, Fry eventually saved two thousand writers and artists—among them Marc Chagall, Thomas Mann, Franz Werfel, Jacques Lipchitz, and Max Ernst. But pressure from Vichy was mounting—Fry's work was becoming increasingly more dangerous. Nearly as cold-blooded as Vichy's behavior was that of the American consulate.

The lines of visa seekers formed early each morning in front of the American consulate. Even in sweltering summer, they were neatly dressed, in coats, hats, and gloves—as a reminder to those inside that *We are people here, desperate now, but human beings, like yourselves.* Nevertheless, the heavy, carved wooden door of the consulate stayed firmly shut for most of them. Inside, smug and sometimes cruel officials proved no friendlier than Pétain. America's shunning of refugees came from the top. The State Department's anti-Semitic Breckinridge Long controlled the quota on refugees, and he firmly believed that the fewer Jews admitted to the United States, the better.

While turning a cold shoulder to Hitler's victims, Washington placated Vichy and slammed Fry. "This government," Secretary of State Cordell Hull cabled, "*can not* repeat *not* . . . countenance the activities of . . . Mr. Fry . . . however well-meaning he may be, in carrying on activities that evade the laws of countries with which the United States maintains friendly relations, signed, Cordell Hull, Secretary of State. September 26, 1940."

Fry fired back in the American press. "One vice-consul," he wrote, "receives applicants with his feet on his desk, pipe in mouth. He never gets up from his chair, even for women. Applicants stand for hours in the waiting room, stand again while the vice-consuls question them. One woman swore she paid an American consular employee $12 to get a seat after five hours of standing. . . . A German rabbi," Fry continued, "obtained an immigration visa in Berlin—valid for three months. It took this man many weeks to get out of Germany. He arrived in Lisbon late in July and got a reservation on the SS *Excambion*, leaving for New York on August 8—exactly three months from the day his visa was issued. But the vice-consul wouldn't let him get on the boat. He insisted that the visa had expired at midnight on the seventh, and nothing would move him to give the man the benefit of the doubt or to renew his visa."

Within a year, under State Department pressure, the Emergency Rescue Committee recalled Fry to New York. His absence had devastating consequences. "When I arrived in New York," Fry wrote, "I learned that the State Department had devised a new and cruelly difficult form of visa application, which made it almost impossible for refugees to enter this country."

Fry never let up on his private campaign to rouse Americans from their apathy. Unlike Noel Field, Fry was convinced that eventually his country would do the right thing. Varian Fry and Noel Field—two lanky Harvard graduates of roughly the same age and social background, pedigreed nonconformists—should have been natural allies. Ironically, Fry, an open antiestablishment renegade, was willing to break laws and provoke Washington. Field, a clandestine Communist, was not. Fry—a sharp-eyed observer—saw through Field's facade sooner than most.

Through Fry, Noel befriended French journalist Michel Gordey, who helped the Fields find a room in a boardinghouse on the rue Rouvière. "Noel had a collection of Spanish Republican and Russian records," Gordey recalled, "which he used to play for us. It was very brave to play such things then in Vichy France." Noel's seemingly direct manner impressed Gordey, as it did so many others: "He looked you directly in the eyes, with an open, friendly gaze," Gordey said. "A typical American, kind, big hearted, starry eyed. I had no inkling that he had Communist sympathies. But it was clear that he was very moved by the misfortunes of the anti-fascists. He had a wonderful heart, very generous. He didn't have much money, because he was always giving it away to refugees he thought needed something more than he did. There were often terrible scenes with Herta because he gave money and food away. After the first two or three weeks of each month, the Fields had nothing left to live on, and no more pay until the start of the following month."

It did not then seem noteworthy to Gordey that Noel had a special interest in Communist internees. Those Fry turned down for help as being hard-core Stalinists, Field took a special interest in helping. "He used to speak very indignantly about the West's betrayal of the Spanish Republicans," Gordey said.

Field's assignment as head of the USC in France was to ease the suffering of all thirty thousand refugees from Spain, Germany, and forty-two other countries—languishing in internment camps just outside Marseille—through medical and human intervention. At Field's direction, the USC opened camp hospitals and worked to ease the camps' squalor—insofar as that was possible. Field also had his own plan, however, which he did not share with either the USC or Fry: to help repatriate as many interned Communists as possible to their own countries, to seed the ground for an eventual postwar Communist takeover. Ironically, the same American consular officials who harassed Fry left Field alone. Field was trying to send "his" refugees East, not to America. In fact, one of the more callous consular officials in Marseille, Hugh Fullerton, in a cable to Washington, tore into Fry as a "troublemaker" but expressed concern lest Noel Field damage his own health by working too hard.

★

With USC funding, Noel Field soon opened a clinic at Marseille's 25 rue de l'Italie. Almost immediately, lines of the sick and hungry—and those who had no place to go—snaked outside the building. To help look after them, Noel hired a Russian-born doctor, Zina Minor, herself a refugee. The attraction between the tall, blond young doctor and her new boss was immediate and strong. "Noel was very attractive," Dr. Minor recalled. "He had a long, thin face, a terribly earnest air, gray hair already then, and a boyish manner."

In the intensity of their lifesaving work, Noel dropped some of his usual armor and confided to Zina things he had not shared with his own family. "He never hid from me that he was a Communist," Dr. Minor said. "Even a Stalinist. We used to argue. I would say, 'I can't understand that to make the world perfect for everyone, you have to hurt so many people.' But," Zina said, "he was an idealist Communist. He must have been living a double life, but I didn't realize it at all. I would never have believed he was an agent."

In the chaotic frenzy of the USC clinic, and in the bleak internment camp barracks outside Marseille, Noel was surrounded by people who were not only hungry and ill, but traumatized from all they had witnessed. Here, amid so much visible agony, Noel found a state of well-being. He was serving humanity—as he had dreamed as a youth. His new self-confidence and pride shines in a June 14, 1941, telegram to USC's Boston headquarters. "Supplement clinic highly welcome . . . have rented large apartment for Unitarian medical and dental dispensary . . . other half use with social work. Our staff includes chief doctor, assistant physician, surgeon, dentist, pediatrician, social workers. Signed, Field."

Anyone who has spent time in refugee camps knows that the sight of children—idle and quiet—amid such misery is a particular heartbreak. One of Noel and Herta's first initiatives was to organize a kindergarten at Rivesaltes Camp, housing entire families of Spanish Civil War veterans. Like Le Vernet, it was a heartless place on a barren patch of land surrounded by barbed wire, without heat, and with open sewers. Into this bleak, malodorous camp marched the once squeamish Noel, who pitched himself into setting up a school for the unhappy children. "At Rivesaltes thousands of children are being educated and occupied," Field proudly informed the USC board of directors. Back at their Boston headquarters, Noel's stock was rising.

But even as he gave of his last measure to feed the hungry and care for the sick, Noel's focus never wavered. "I lived and worked more and more completely as a Communist," he later wrote of this period, "without inner doubts. And the harder the work, the happier I was. I was conscious that I was making a valuable contribution to the antifascist struggle. . . . My goal," he said, "was to set up a Red Aid—to save our *cadres*." Red Aid on the Unitarians' dime was not what the church elders had in mind. For quite a while, however, the fog and chaos of war, infrequent communications, and Noel's talent for duplicity kept the USC in the dark.

★

For the first time in his career, his colleagues were not bureaucrats or diplomats, but humanitarians. Saving lives or, at a minimum, easing the pain of those written off by others, was their shared mission. Dr. Joseph Weil, the head of the Jewish Children's Aid Society in Marseille, was also impressed by Noel and Herta's dedication. "They radiated goodness," Weil said. Like Zina Minor, Dr. Weil gained Field's confidence and recalled his astonishment at Noel's "burning sympathy" for Stalin. "When I tried to timidly insert a little realism, Noel looked at me with a sort of rapture, which he always had when he spoke of his political vision." Noel spoke of the imminent birth of a classless society, and the end of corrupt, American capitalism. Weil recalled that all the Communists in the camps seemed to know Field, and thought of him as romantic and generous, but a political innocent.

There was at least one American official who shared Varian Fry's humanitarian values and pierced through Field's facade. Among the refugees' staunchest allies in France was US vice-consul Hiram Bingham IV. Bingham, a son of US senator Hiram Bingham III, sheltered refugees—including novelist Lion Feuchtwanger—in his own home. He also freely issued Nansen passports, the lifesaving, internationally recognized travel documents sanctioned by the League of Nations for stateless refugees. None of this pleased the State Department, and soon Bingham, like Fry, was recalled to Washington. Transferred first to Lisbon, then to Argentina, Bingham was passed up for promotions. "Excessive activism" blotted his copybook. Hiram Bingham finally resigned from the Foreign Service in 1945, driven out by those willing to implement a cruel policy. Bingham—like Fry—tried to warn others about Field. "Bingham was the first to tell me to beware of Noel," Gordey recalled. "It was in August 1941. The consul came to Marc Chagall's house in Gordes, to see the painter," Gordey said. "Referring to Noel, Bingham alerted me that 'things were not as simple as they looked.' I was very surprised, and had no idea what he meant."

In March 1945, Fry wrote his friend and colleague Daniel Bénédite, recently freed from a Gestapo prison. "You remember Noel," Fry wrote. "If you or any of your friends still have any relations with him at all, I advise you to *break them immediately and completely*. . . . I can only add that I am in possession of evidence against him which I am sure you would accept as adequate ground for an immediate rupture, if I were able to send it to you."

Bénédite already had his own suspicions. After Varian Fry's recall to New York, Bénédite asked Noel if the USC could take care of Fry's refugees. "What sort of people are they?" Field asked. "All sorts," Bénédite answered, "except Nazis and Communists." Noel declined to help, revealing to Bénédite a hard core usually masked by his earnest dedication.

Herta shared her husband's single-minded preference for saving Communists above all others. A Hungarian refugee named Eugene Gonda and his pregnant wife had been receiving a monthly allowance from the USC while waiting for passage to Martinique. Gonda's USC stipend was suddenly cut off—without explanation. When Gonda asked why, Herta answered, "You are too noisy an anti-Communist." To what extent this was mere accommodation to Noel's Stalinism is speculative at this remove. If it is possible for two human beings to fuse into a single one, however, Noel and Herta Field achieved such a melding to a remarkable degree.

A sad coda to the story of two principled and fearless public servants, Varian Fry and Hiram Bingham IV, is that only in death were they recognized for their courage. Neither man's career ever recovered from the lifesaving and State Department–defying rescue of Jews. Today, however, the square in front of the American consulate in Marseille, where once the hopeless waited in vain for the door to open, is named

Place Varian Fry. Few passersby appreciate that bit of historic irony. In 2006, the US Postal Service issued a stamp honoring Hiram Bingham IV, diplomat and humanitarian.

★

Sometime in 1941, Dr. Zina Minor introduced Noel to Jo Tempi. "Dark, thin, harsh, a terror of a woman," Gordey remembered the German Communist. "Tempi was full of enormous vitality and will power. Noel developed a wild passion for her. Jo," said Gordey, "was a fanatical communist." The Berlin-born Tempi (who, like so many in the Communist underground, had a string of aliases) was a Comintern agent, in and out of German prisons. Like Arthur Koestler, Tempi, too, had worked for Willi Münzenberg as a Comintern propagandist.

Noel loved and needed women and felt his affairs were unrelated to his marriage—his source of comfort and stability. The Fields' relationship may have been extraordinarily close, but it was devoid of passion, almost platonic. However practiced a deceiver Field may have been in matters of espionage and national loyalties, he could not hide his love affairs from the woman who had shared his life since childhood. "Noel and Jo's affair lasted from 1941 to 1946," Gordey said. Tempi's presence shattered Herta. "She was terribly jealous," Zina Minor said, "but also terribly afraid of losing him, and Noel was dependent on her. He was fond of Herta, but Noel's eye roved. Herta adored him completely." Noel was now frequently absent on "field trips" with Tempi, leaving Herta disconsolate. Unlike his dalliance with the sweet-tempered Zina Minor, the affair with this "terror of a woman" would exact a high price.

Noel soon hired Tempi to run USC's clinic in Toulouse and, when Paris was liberated, to run their new office in the French capital. "I once asked Noel who were the people in his Unitarian outfit," Paul Massing said. " 'Oh, well, they are Unitarians,' he answered. 'But in my office, I have only Communists. My right hand, Jo Tempi, is a Communist, and a good one.' " Some of his colleagues found it hard to tell if Jo worked for Noel or the other way around.

As the war ground on, Noel spent more and more time delivering messages between Communist exiles interned in France and .those hiding in Switzerland—where the Communist Party was illegal. Together, Noel and his comrades dreamed and planned for a bright Communist future in their own countries, once the Nazis were defeated. Meanwhile, Noel did his best to keep them healthy, well fed, well funded, and connected to each other.

Until 1945, the Boston Unitarians were oblivious to Noel's misuse of their philanthropy. Field's reports reassured the USC that "With every day that passes," as he wrote Dr. Joy on May 1, 1942, "we can point with increasing pride to the fact that we are an American organization and that the help we are giving has its source in America."

In November 1942, as Allied forces landed in North Africa, German troops marched into Vichy France, making all of France part of the Third Reich. The roundup of Jews started immediately. Thousands of Jewish refugees were dragged from French internment camps, and deported and gassed by the Nazis in Auschwitz. Americans in Marseille were now enemy aliens—marched off to the same camps where the Fields had been helping others.

Minutes ahead of the Gestapo's arrival, on November 10, Noel and Herta boarded the train from Marseille to Geneva. At Annemasse, the final French station before the Swiss border, Vichy police stopped the train. The Germans had instructed French gendarmes to detain all Americans. In a show of anti-Nazi defiance, however, the local French police chief offered the Fields his own car for a getaway. With its official Vichy tags and a French gendarme behind the wheel, the Fields tore past German roadblocks into Switzerland—and safety.

Mont Blanc's icy peak peering through the clouds over Lake Geneva was a welcome sight after the Fields' heart-stopping escape. Once safe in too-calm Switzerland, however, the couple felt strangely deflated— overcome with a realization that their most intense and productive period had just ended. Field had proved a resourceful, energetic, and inspiring leader where lives were at stake. At the same time, he felt immensely proud of his role in preparing for a postwar Communist Europe.

# CHAPTER 11

# THE SPY IN WARTIME

*Spies know things one step ahead of the rest of us.*

—Tom Stoppard

NOEL AND HERTA—exhausted and shaken by their close encounter with the Gestapo—were reunited with Erica, still studying at the University of Geneva. "It's not quite the thing," Noel wrote his mother describing the women's dormitory in which they made their temporary home, "me, lone male among a batch of females, from sweet 17 on up. But then, my hair is gray, my wife is with me, and Erica is our daughter, even if only foster . . . and so, at long last and most unexpectedly, we're again reunited with our beloved child."

Noel now increasingly blurred the lines between his two lives: humanitarian and Stalinist. Though still with the USC, he was no longer saving lives. Mostly, he was acting as a courier, carrying messages between Communists in France and Switzerland. He missed, however, the soaring feeling that easing human suffering gave him. "I think of the past with a growing nostalgia," he wrote his mother. "For, though it was hard and often depressing, never in our lives before had we been

so intensely alive." To Dr. Joseph Weil he confided that he "would like
to go to the East, to serve the people who were achieving their liberty."

★

Surrounded by Axis troops in France, Germany, Italy, and Austria,
neutral Switzerland was, once again, as during World War I, the ideal
listening post, this time for the newly formed and blandly named Office of Strategic Services. Precursor to the CIA, the OSS was the brain-
child of the swashbuckling William Donovan. Determined to build
a small and efficient organization, "Wild Bill" didn't much care who
brought him the intelligence. "I'd put Stalin on the OSS payroll," he
once said, "if I thought it would help us defeat Hitler." Later, Donovan
became fanatically anti-Communist, but in the forties he claimed that
leftists were often the bravest spies and saboteurs. "You can have an
organization that is so secure it does nothing," he noted, "or you have
to take chances." He took chances. "Every man or woman who can
hurt the Hun," Donovan said, "is okay with me."

All that remained was to find the right man to run covert operations—
under diplomatic cover. "We have finally worked out with the State
Department," Donovan wrote FDR, "the appointment of a representa-
tive of [the OSS] to proceed to Berne as 'Financial Attaché.' . . . A man
of a different type; a person who can mingle freely with intellectual and
business circles in Switzerland to tap the constant and enormous flow
of information that comes from Germany and Italy. . . . As soon as we
find the man we need . . . I shall advise you."

With his thinning gray hair and bemused twinkle behind round,
professorial glasses, there was nothing of the dashing secret agent about
the new spymaster. Allen Welsh Dulles looked every inch a high school
physics teacher. Dulles, whose brother, John Foster Dulles, would be
secretary of state under President Dwight D. Eisenhower, had sterling
establishment credentials. He shared his boss's view that agents and
informants must be recruited from unlikely places. He still regretted

passing up a chance to meet Lenin, who showed up unannounced in his office in 1917. Dulles, who had a rendezvous with his mistress, gave the Soviet leader the brush-off. "The first chance," he recalled, "to start talking to the Communist leader was lost." Never again would Dulles pass up a potential source—however suspect.

Dulles soon settled into a fourteenth-century row house with idyllic views of the Bernese Oberland, and a hidden back door. In his cozy sitting room, an Alpine vista to one side, a roaring fire on the other, the avuncular Dulles puffed on his pipe and coaxed information out of a growing net of informants. Based on their reports, the OSS conducted airdrops and sabotage behind Nazi lines.

In 1941, Robert Dexter, another public-service-minded Boston Unitarian, took charge of USC's European operations. Dexter burned to do more than humanitarian work to fight the Nazis. Moonlighting for the OSS, he thought, might deliver a stronger punch against the loathed enemy. Dexter assumed that the USC's man in Geneva shared his values and patriotism. "Come along to Berne next time," Dexter urged Field. "Talk to Dulles."

Allen Dulles remembered when he first met Noel, in Zurich in 1918, when the youth proclaimed his dream of bringing peace to the world. He also recalled that Noel's father had been a useful "asset" during the past war. Many of Field's Harvard classmates and fellow Ivy Leaguers—Richard Helms, William Colby, Arthur Schlesinger Jr., and Stewart Alsop, as well as such unlikely figures as Julia Child—had signed up with the still largely clandestine OSS. Noel now enthusiastically joined their ranks.

Field never cleared this new role as OSS informer (agent number 394) with Moscow. Wartime communications made such an exchange virtually impossible. Besides, Field's comrades in the exiled Communist underground in Switzerland and France saw collaborating with the OSS as a great opportunity to infiltrate Nazi-occupied Central and Eastern Europe.

For the next three years—with Noel as go-between—these Communists benefited from OSS financial and logistical support. In exchange, they provided Dulles with intelligence from the largely Communist French and German resistance. United in fighting the "Hun," this arrangement seemed in everybody's interest.

In a secret internal cable to the OSS Paris office, Dulles wrote, "Noel Field, our #394, prior to liberation of France maintained close contact with an anti-Nazi German group composed of German political refugees, deserters, etc. Since November 1942, this group has been actively engaged in clandestine propaganda and sabotage, with headquarters largely in Marseille, later Paris. *Thru Field we furnished part of the funds for financing this group's activities. From Field I understand group is now continuing active work in France under the name, 'Nationalkommittee Freier Deutschland fur den Western.'* While the group is now working largely with the Free French, Field understands they have some representatives working with our troops. It's possible that the group contains valuable personnel for German penetration and consider it urgent that Field discuss this problem with you, and put you in touch with certain of their leaders who are now in Paris and whom he knows personally."

Following Dulles's instructions, OSS Paris agent and the future historian Arthur S. Schlesinger Jr. received Field—and raised an alarm. "Soft spoken but intense in manner," Schlesinger wrote of Field, "his notion . . . was that OSS subsidize a group of German 'anti-fascist' refugees in France so that they could set up a Comitee de l'Allemagne Libre Pour l'Ouest (CALPO), to conduct 'political reeducation' in Prisoner of War camps, and recruit agents to be dropped in Germany, for espionage and sabotage."

"Field's [plan]," Schlesinger continued, "was obviously the extension to western Europe of the Soviet controlled Free Germany Committee set up in Moscow in 1943 behind a facade of captured German officers. Field's list of potential recruits had a strong Communist flavor. Giving them priority seemed a poor idea," Schlesinger concluded.

"My impression in the course of several conversations was that Field's passion for the project and his studied evasiveness about its details and political implications *exceeded the reasonable bounds of innocence or enthusiasm.*" Schlesinger blocked Field's plan.

Dulles nevertheless continued to use Noel's contacts within the exiled Communist Parties, and to fund their return to their Nazi-occupied homelands. Neither Noel nor any of the Communists supported by the OSS had Moscow's approval for these missions. German, Hungarian, and Czech émigrés assumed that Stalin—as Roosevelt and Churchill's ally—would be in favor of such collaboration. They falsely assumed defeating the Nazis and setting up postwar Communist states in Central and Eastern Europe to be Moscow's paramount goal.

In 1944, Field played a minor role in an OSS mission—essentially writing a brief letter of introduction on behalf of a group of Hungarian Communists—to Dulles, with fatal consequences to one of its participants. Tibor Szönyi, the group leader, and Ferenc Vai, György Demeter, Gyula Kuti, and Andras Kalman had spent the war in precarious clandestine exile, in and out of Swiss and French internment camps and prisons. All were committed Communists, impatient to start building a people's republic in their devastated homeland. Through OSS funding, and with Dr. Joseph Weil's help in getting them Yugoslav Army uniforms and fake Yugoslav identification papers, they set off on their mission to Nazi-occupied Hungary. A US aircraft flew them from Naples to Bari, and then to Belgrade, finally reaching Budapest in late March 1944. In 1949, Stalin would use each detail of this heroic mission to destroy its participants.

★

After years of silence, Moscow had finally reached out to Field in 1943—and presented him with a dilemma. "Brook," the contact he was promised during his Moscow trip in 1938, called. "He asked me whether my earlier political views had remained the same," Field recalled. "And if I was willing to work for the Soviet Union again. I gave a positive answer. . . . He instructed me to break all my Party contacts, and live like an apolitical man. He also asked me to build good relationships with people at the American Consulate and other Americans."

Moscow thus asked him to choose between work he loved on behalf of his comrades and the uncertain rewards of a shadow life as a secret agent. To befriend his former American colleagues and break ties with Communists like Jo Tempi and others was too high a price for Field. But, as usual, he equivocated. "I told this person," Field said, "that at that moment I was not ready to give an answer. I must discuss this question with my political advisers." The Soviet agent did not appreciate such indecision. "He sharply replied that I was probably going to discuss the matter with the Americans." The Kremlin's agent left, and never reached out to Noel again. Field's next contact with the Soviet secret police would be in prison.

In his vacillating way Noel had made a choice: he was with the expatriate Communists. He did not understand that by Stalin's lights one could not be loyal to Moscow as well as to the international Communist movement. In fact, Stalin, deeply suspicious of all Western Communists, had virtually ended the international movement. Noel Field was oblivious to these shifting Kremlin policies. He was an inactive agent freelancing in isolation in wartime Switzerland. Nor did he understand that he had just added to the Kremlin's list of reasons to be wary of him. Krivitsky, Reiss, the Massings—all traitors—were all connected to an agent who just said no to Moscow.

## CHAPTER 12

# CHILD OF THE CENTURY

*You might as well live.*

—Dorothy Parker

ERICA GLASER WALLACH'S life, a parable of the violent past century, is yet another tangled thread in Noel Field's journey. Accustomed to making her own decisions, trusting only her own judgment, Erica's tough shell enabled her to survive two seismic dislocations. "I was against *everything*," she said. Though the Fields' dogged devotion softened her resentment of them, nothing could soften her rage at the Nazis. Twice they had made refugees of her family: forced them to flee their homeland, Germany; and then destroyed her second home, Spain. The Nazis had turned Erica into a stateless migrant. They had to be defeated—by any means.

In 1942, Erica, a headstrong twenty-one-year-old, fell in with a group of Communist students at the University of Geneva. Unlike Noel, who embraced Communism as a faith that imbued his life with meaning, for Erica the appeal of Communism was not ideological;

it was a way to fight the Nazis. "I was perfectly willing to help the Communist Party," Erica said. "They were the only ones actively fighting the Nazis. We were all naïve," she said.

Through Noel she met Leo Bauer, a German Communist in Swiss exile. Bauer pulled Erica into serving as a courier between Field and underground party members. With Noel, she smuggled Communists across the French border into Switzerland. Some of those Communists were also part of Allen Dulles's network. Erica, however, was unaware that Field was himself a Communist. "He knew Communists from Spain," she said, "where he went from hospital to hospital making lists of every foreigner on the Republican side . . . and naturally he met practically every Communist there." This much she knew. She also recalled Noel studying Marxist tomes on doctrine and ideology. "Noel was completely without intuition," Erica said. "He arrived at everything with pure, tortuous thought. He plodded through volumes on ideology." But she considered herself more radical than her foster parent, whom she regarded as a woolly intellectual. Noel Field as Moscow's agent? Impossible.

As the Red Army approached Berlin, and the Allies continued to roll back the Wehrmacht in Western Europe, Erica was eager to get back to Germany, "to set up a new democratic government," she said. "Without me, it couldn't be done!" she recalled with a self-deprecating laugh. Through Noel, she found a job as secretary to Dulles's deputy, Gerhard van Arkel. Her friend Leo Bauer instructed her to tell him if she heard "anything interesting." "Why not?" she thought.

But by April 1945 Hitler had committed suicide in his bunker and the glue that temporarily held the Moscow-Washington alliance dissolved. In Yalta, a gaunt and frail Roosevelt faced a resolute Stalin. His armies occupied Central and Eastern Europe, and they had no intention of budging. Quite the contrary; they were about to unroll Moscow's blueprint for postwar Europe. Those Communists who had spent the war in Moscow, not Switzerland, were streaming back to take control of Communist Parties in Prague, Budapest, East Berlin, Warsaw, and elsewhere.

The early shoots of the coming Cold War were sprouting—nowhere more than in Berlin, where Moscow and the Western powers were joint occupiers. Collaboration between the OSS and the German Communist Party was no longer possible. Erica was instructed by the Central Committee of the German Communist Party to quit her job as OSS secretary. In her typical, blunt style, she pronounced such advice "stupid." Nevertheless, by 1946, bowing to party pressure, she did resign her OSS position, and formally joined the German Communist Party.

For the next year, while studying law at the University of Frankfurt, she edited a German Communist magazine. "I often did not like the way things were written," she said, "and thought it was just silly . . . too much the Moscow or the Berlin Party line. So I would rewrite it. I had a lot of fights, and the more time went on, the less I agreed with the policy, which had come from Berlin. Well, the stronger this policy of anti-Americanism grew and a 100 percent defense of everything Moscow did or said—the worse it got for me, and the less I could actually work under those conditions."

Soon, her personal life became as tangled as her politics. In 1946, Erica met and fell in love with US Army captain Robert Wallach, a boyishly handsome Virginian posted to Germany. "Of course," Erica said, "as far as the Party went—that was pure treason. I thought that it was my private life, and it's nobody's business. I was going to see Americans as long as I wanted to." As she and Wallach became more seriously involved, her role as editor of the Communist publication became less and less tenable. "I was thinking of getting married," she said, "and thinking of having children, and I was thinking of just withdrawing from all this [political engagement], and having a peaceful and quiet life."

Unlike the Fields, Erica was never blinded by her faith. "The Communist Party policy of attacking everything American and saying everything that comes from Moscow is just gospel," she said, "I considered ridiculous. Surely there can be things with which you disagree and have different opinions." But there was no room for a scintilla of disagreement in the newly empowered German Communist Party. By 1947, "all these things came together," Erica said, "and made me decide that I was in the wrong boat. My decision was to leave that boat."

The boat, however, was not ready to leave Erica.

# CHAPTER 13

# COLD PEACE

*Other civilizations rolled and crumbled down, the European
civilization was . . . blown up.*

—H. G. Wells

WHEREVER YOU LOOKED in the spring of 1945, it seemed as if
European civilization had vanished. The ancient cities of
Eastern and Central Europe had been blasted into rubble—the great
cathedrals, palaces, and monuments—skeletons in mountains of de-
bris. Pitiful lines of orphaned children and shaven-headed deportees,
skin and bones, streamed homeward, only to find that there was no
such thing as home anymore. Everyone nursed a grievance; nearly
everyone had suffered. Thirty-six and a half million Europeans were
killed between 1939 and 1945, nineteen million of them civilians. Two
out of every three men born after 1918 in Hitler's Germany did not
survive his war. No civilian population was spared six years of total
war. With so many hearts hardened by too much suffering, pity was as
scarce as food.

One hour before his death, in his final note, Roosevelt sent Churchill a terse message: "We must be firm." Though the nation was tired of war, this time around, few Americans saw retreating from the world as a serious option, not with Great Britain on the brink of economic collapse and the rest of Europe on life support. The nation's new and untried president—Harry S. Truman—had no choice but to confront Josef Stalin.

For Eastern Europe, it was too late. Stalin's handpicked, Kremlin-trained puppets—ready to implement their scheme for a gradual Soviet takeover—arrived with the Red Army to East Berlin, Warsaw, Prague, Bucharest, and Budapest. Noel Field was eager to help rebuild the ruined East in the image of his cherished utopia. The American dreamer and the hard man in the Kremlin did not share a common vision of the future.

"I saw Noel in 1945," Joseph Weil said, "looking older and more furtive. He'd become more guarded . . . agitatedly traveling between Berlin, Paris, and Budapest. In parting, he told me he considered it his duty to head East, to work for the People, to help them achieve their freedom."

Desperate to join his comrades in the East, Noel had no interest in returning to his own country. Nor did he want to break ties to America, or to lose his job with the Unitarians. As usual, he thought he could have it all ways: an American who no longer shared his country's values, who in fact was working for its soon-to-be enemy, and yet still thought of himself as an American.

Increasingly, Noel's double life broke through the smooth surface of his deception. In a letter protesting USC's plan to work with Ukrainian refugees, Field pointed out that Ukraine was part of the Soviet Union, and thus America's ally, which made Ukrainian refugees anti-Soviet and, according to Field, "only a little less reactionary than Nazis."

Later in 1945, Noel warned his Boston employers of the danger of being anti-Soviet, a position which, he claimed, will lead to renewed

war. Anti-Communism, he told them, in practice inevitably spells
"fascist." Brandishing the threat of World War III, Field was repeating
the Kremlin's warning to the West.

Summoned home to Boston by the USC, Noel, the dedicated humanitarian, dazzled even his critics. "He was the hero of the piece just
then," the Reverend Ray Bragg, soon to be the executive director of
the USC, said. "A knight in shining armor. Everybody was captivated.
They called him a Lincolnesque figure, a quiet, persuasive sort of fellow, very simple in expression, but moving. I came away thinking, *Isn't
this a wonderful guy*. He explained that the new Europe is not going to
be a historical succession of the old. It would have a new orientation."

But Noel felt a stranger in his own country. America was turning inward, losing interest in Europe. "It is so utterly different from
Europe," he wrote Erica from Boston on December 6, 1945. "I have
gone from group to group with hat in hand. . . . I've tried to rouse
interest right and left. . . . There has been some interest but mostly
failures. . . . That is just one among the many disturbing aspects, as a
result of which we shall go back to Europe very much sobered."

From Boston, the Fields traveled to Mexico, where some of Noel's
Communist friends from Spain had sought asylum. "We have met
some old acquaintances from Marseille days," Herta wrote Erica on
December 17, 1945. "They are most eager to return to their respective
countries . . . we are also seeing some of the people we met years ago
in Barcelona, faces out of the dim past."

These letters also reveal how attached both Fields were to their
"daughter." Weil remembered a bronze bust of Erica on Noel's desk.
"We really did not know how much you had become part of us," Herta
wrote her on March 27, 1946, "till one day in the States we sort of
wondered why laughter seemed to have departed from our life. It then
dawned on us that you, little wretch, had taken it with you when you
left. We have become terribly serious people. I can't get Noel to produce his famous silly grin. . . ." Herta, who left behind so small an

imprint beyond being Noel's devoted partner in all things, reveals her human warmth in her letters to Erica. No doubt, too, their devotion to their foster daughter was yet another bond shared by Noel and Herta. It was also partial compensation for their decision not to have children for the sake of their great cause.

*

By 1946, questions about Noel's loyalties could not be ignored by even the most credulous Unitarian elders. Field—so recently greeted as a "knight in shining armor"—was now under fire. A tense confrontation played out between Dr. William Emerson, chairman of the USC board (and grandnephew of Ralph Waldo Emerson) and Francis Henson, director of Varian Fry's former organization, now renamed the International Rescue and Relief Committee.

"Individuals have come to me," Henson began, "and said they had been refused aid by the USC because they were not Communists."

"If your statements are true," USC board member Dr. John Lothrop said, "we are done for."

Jo Tempi, who accompanied Noel, heatedly denied the charge. "We don't ask people who come to us for aid what political party they belong to," she protested. "But we have limited funds and can't help all."

"At the IRRC," Henson replied, "we don't help totalitarians, either of the right or the left. . . . I fight Communism as one of the greatest dangers in the world today."

Field—with everything on the line—seized the offensive. "You are ready to accuse me of being . . . a member of the American Communist Party and the NKVD," he protested. "I am neither . . . [but] the Communist Party is legal. . . . In accusing me of belonging to the NKVD, however, you are accusing me of treason."

That word brought a powerful current into the polite gathering—as Noel intended. Henson backed off. The meeting soon ended, inconclusively. For Noel's supporters, the question of how anyone could accuse this self-sacrificing "Lincolnesque" relief worker of treason silenced any other consideration—for now.

"I would prefer to combat [the treason charge] in court," Field wrote Dr. Emerson. Henson did not raise it again.

Field survived this round. "Emerson was a very kind, gentle man," Elizabeth Dexter, wife of the USC's Robert Dexter, said. "He just couldn't believe ill of people . . . would not recognize a Communist under his nose." Larry Duggan also came to his defense, writing Emerson, "It is distressing to find these old charges about Noel Field still being repeated. . . . They related to a time when Noel was like a brother to me, so that I feel in a position to speak with knowledge. With all the conviction in my power I affirm that *to the best of my knowledge* neither of the two charges is correct." Duggan's line was to become the standard line of scores facing the House Un-American Activities Committee. "To the best of my knowledge" was that corrosive era's pathetic refrain. Technically, Duggan was not lying. Noel was neither a member of the American Communist Party nor—at that time—an NKVD agent. Duggan, like Field, evaded the substance of the charge: that Field, under cover of relief work, was almost uniquely serving Communists. The Unitarians continued to support their man for a while longer.

*

Noel's blazing love affair with Jo Tempi having burned out, she now set her sights on Dr. Charles Joy, the head of USC European operations. "Dr. Joy was not very good looking and had an unattractive wife," Mrs. Dexter bluntly said. "Jo made a pass at him, and he was swept off his feet. This was something quite new to him. All over Europe, there was already comment about their traveling together, having adjoining rooms, how he couldn't keep his hands off her in public." In an essay for the *Christian Register*, Joy published this embarrassing paean to Jo: "She perceives quickly the true inwardness [*sic*] of any problem, and elucidates it with equal ease in French, German or English. . . . She is sometimes severe with her subordinates, but they worship her in spite of it. They work as late as she does, and weep sometimes when she compels them to go home. . . . She is essentially and charmingly feminine, and sometimes craves a security that she has never since her earliest childhood known. She is the strong oak on which the weak lean, she could be the vine that clings lovingly to it."

The enraptured reverend grew careless. The couple was sighted sharing an overnight Pullman from Boston to New York. The affair exploded in public and Dr. Joy was fired from USC. Noel continued to defend Jo, and threated to quit if she, too, were fired.

As suspicion about Noel's Communist ties mounted, Ray Bragg— Joy's successor—invited Noel to his home in Minneapolis. "We sat up half the night talking," Bragg recalled. "I remember asking him—in the early morning hours—'Noel, can a Communist—with his commit- ment to a class cause—be a conscientious relief worker?' And he did not answer—didn't argue, didn't make any response at all. And I felt uneasy. Next morning, at breakfast, before going to the airport, Noel said, 'That was an interesting question you asked last night. The min- ister of the State of Württemberg [in West Germany], who is a Com- munist, enjoys a very fine reputation in his relief program.' I thought, this is no answer! Obviously Noel thought it was, but I did not. I felt his own mind was very subtle. He was trying to hoodwink me. And it annoyed me, hurt my pride."

Noel, however, felt confident he had again outsmarted his enemies. He was excited about the prospect of heading postwar USC relief efforts in Eastern Europe. Caught between the Nazi onslaught and the Soviet "liberation," no region was harder hit than the region between Berlin and Moscow. First, the Nazis deliberately tried to destroy a civilization they considered inferior. Then followed the equally brutal Soviet westward advance. In his memoirs, George Kennan, the noted American diplomat and historian, described the devastation. "The disaster that befell this area with the entry of the Soviet forces has no parallel in modern European experience," Kennan wrote. "There were . . . sections where . . . scarcely a man, woman or child was left alive after the initial passage of Soviet forces. . . . The Russians . . . swept the native population clean in a manner that had no parallel since the days of the Asiatic hordes."

For Field, in the destruction of the old civilization, there was opportunity. "People's democracies" could rise from the rubble. That is what he had been working toward since he joined the USC: rescuing and returning Communists to their homelands, to start the revolution of his dreams. In addition to the Paris office, Noel planned operations in East Berlin, Warsaw, Prague, and Budapest. On June 10, 1946, he wrote Erica from Berlin, "This is my first long separation from Herta in years, and I'm gradually going nuts for lack of her and for lack of feminine company generally." Erica and Herta were the twin pillars of his emotional life. "Kid," he wrote later that year, "I needn't tell you how much I miss you; I guess you know it without my saying it."

*

On the other side of the ocean, vague rumors about Field were hardening into facts. A State Department official, Woodbridge Wallner, who had served in Vichy France, notified Bragg that Field was a "Stalinist." "State," Bragg said, "was eager for me to go to Europe [to investigate Field]. I asked for a visa Friday afternoon. Monday morning I had it."

In contrast to the gutted coastal towns of Caen, Le Havre, and Rouen, Paris miraculously survived the war more or less unscarred—on the surface. But two years after the end of fighting, when the Fields picked up Ray Bragg at Orly Airport, Paris was dark and poor, and Parisians hungry. Noel, however, was in a cheerful mood. "He was at home in Paris," Bragg said, "knew the city well. We watched the May Day procession from the Place de la Concorde. Noel translated the speeches, and then we drove up to Montmartre and ate some good cakes—hard to get in those days. We had dinner overlooking the Seine."

Only then did Bragg reveal what brought him to Europe: to learn the truth about the USC's European chief. "I told Noel I wanted to speak with people of the Spanish Government in exile," Bragg recalled. "Noel said, 'OK. I'll go with you and interpret.' 'No, Noel,' I told him. 'I'll get an interpreter from the American Embassy.' Noel's presence would have undermined what I learned. So the Embassy gave me an interpreter and I went with her." Ray Bragg got an earful. "These Spaniards—[anti-Franco] Social Democrats—were violent in their denunciations of Noel Field and of the USC. They said that Communists got all the relief. They didn't get any."

"I told him, 'Noel, you are one heck of an embarrassment to me,' " Bragg said, "because from every quarter, suspicion, accusations, doubts are rolling in. I can't defend you." Bragg said. "Noel expressed sympathy for my position. . . . His position was that Americans don't understand that Europe in 1945 is totally different than it was in 1939, and that Europe will never be the same again. I don't think he ever denied anything I ever confronted him with. Rather, he argued that people don't understand that this [new Europe] is not a bad thing."

"Noel," Bragg said, "was essentially a decent guy. One night, I went out and bought a bottle of Hennessy cognac, and we sat up until four or five in the morning. He loved wine, and I was purposely trying to get him loosened up as we sat up drinking brandy. But," Bragg said, "he did not." Cognac was a feeble weapon against Noel's decades-old Communist discipleship. "I don't recall he said anything he wouldn't have said otherwise."

Bragg never forgot Noel's chilling nondenial of the most disturbing charge leveled against him: complicity in the murder of Ignaz Reiss. "There are suspicions being circulated about you in the U.S.," Bragg said, as he and the Fields drove through picturesque Vichy, France. "One of them is that you were implicated in the murder of Ignaz Reiss." There was a long pause, Bragg recalled. "Herta didn't say anything. Neither did Noel. I didn't press it. After considerable delay, Noel just laughed. But he said nothing at all."

The Unitarian's most urgent problem, however, was how to contain the explosive Jo Tempi. "I had breakfast with Tempi in Toulouse, in April 1947," Bragg continued. "I pointed out to her that she had become an embarrassment [to USC] and there was nothing she could do to correct it, so I would be very happy to receive her resignation right then and there. She said, 'I won't resign, and what's more I will sue you to maintain my rights.' I said, 'All right. You are fired as of the last day of May.' I'll never forgive myself," Bragg said. "If I had fired her as of that moment, according to French law, she would have lost all authority. But I gave her forty days."

Forty days was long enough for Tempi to wreak havoc. "She went back to the USC office in Paris, gathered her staff and told them, 'I've been fired as of the last day in May.' " Seventeen of her staff of nineteen offered to resign in protest. "No," Tempi told them, "let me fire you, so USC will be forced to pay your three months' salary." Bragg shook his head. "Jo was a very shrewd gal. I thought she was a bitch."

Reviewing USC's records, Bragg found massive relief—food, clothing, and medicine—going to Communist organizations. "I never wanted to *bar* Communists from receiving aid," Bragg noted, "but I found it *all* went to Communists. When I visited some of our installations, I was welcomed as a *comrade*. The meaning was political, not humanitarian." Noel Field had fulfilled his dream of creating a Red Aid organization. But now the game was up.

"After I fired Tempi," Bragg continued. "Noel became quite helpless . . . which led me to conclude that while Noel was USC's European director, he was Tempi's subordinate in the Communist hierarchy."

What to do with Noel Field was a difficult problem for Bragg. "Lacking legal proof [against Noel]," he said, "I decided to bring Noel home. I offered him a job. But he said that he wouldn't come home, because Larry Duggan had been so abused. So, in September 1947, I told Noel we'd pay his salary until October 31. Then he was through."

"I should have made a much more intensive study of Noel Field's record," said Robert Dexter, who had urged Dulles to recruit him into the OSS. "The USC paid a very high price because I was so impressed by the Fields."

"Dear Kid," Noel wrote Erica on August 13, 1947, on Unitarian Service Committee letterhead. "Just a line to tell you that my service with the above organization will come to an end on September 30. What I shall do thereafter is still too early even to guess, except that both of us intend to take thorough vacations."

Instead of a "thorough vacation," Noel collapsed, mentally and physically. "He is being treated for stomach ulcer," Herta wrote Erica on January 1, 1948, "gastritis and colitis, both severe. . . . Noel has not been in a very cheerful frame of mind since we left the USC."

★

For a decade, the slippery J. Peters, gray eminence of the Washington cell, outfoxed an FBI manhunt. Melting into the ethnic brew of Kew Gardens, Queens, he assumed yet another identity as Alexander Stevens, small-time businessman. After years of false leads, the FBI finally tracked him down in 1949. The firebrand had morphed into a courtly Hungarian émigré in a community where almost everyone spoke with an accent. Subpoenaed to testify before the House Un-American Activities Committee, Peters invoked his constitutional right to remain silent to all questions regarding the Ware group, his relationship to Alger Hiss, and the spy ring he ran on Moscow's behalf. Deported to his native Hungary in 1949, he kept his pledge of public silence regarding his successful run as spymaster in the heyday of the Washington Communist underground. He and Noel Field would meet again, however.

# CHAPTER 14

# MAN WITHOUT A COUNTRY—1948

*I spoke with Lenin of the cruelty of revolutionary tactics. . . .*
*"What do you expect?" he asked in wonder and anger.*

—Maxim Gorky

THERE WOULD BE no peace—just another sort of war, this one cold. Even as Europe dug itself out from the rubble, it was clear that the battered continent would be divided. The Soviet empire would stretch, in Churchill's words, "From Stettin in the Baltic to Trieste in the Adriatic." Moreover, people trapped east of the divide would be prohibited from accepting lifesaving American aid in the form of the Marshall Plan, and would thus be condemned to years of misery. Far worse, under Stalin's total control, their ancient lands and cultures would be recast in the Soviet image.

By 1948, not one country had freely elected a Communist regime. A string of rigged elections forced Communist rule on Poland, Hungary, Czechoslovakia, and East Germany. Instilling fear in their population was the only way for these unpopular regimes to hold power. Terror was their chief weapon. Vigilance against the invisible enemy was the order of the day. Every poster, rally, and trade union conference hammered a single message into a cowed people: the danger of foreign subversion is ever present; sometimes the enemy wears Communist clothes. A state of constant anxiety was the way to make the population submit. Who would be next to vanish in the night, me or my neighbor? "We slept," one survivor recalled, "with one ear cocked for the sound of the elevator coming up at three in the morning, holding our breaths until it went past our floor."

By 1948, one million Hungarians, nearly one-tenth of the total population, had been arrested or prosecuted for some crime "against the state." Starting in May 1948, the Soviets blockaded West Berlin to starve it into submitting to Soviet control. The US response was swift, showy, and effective. Each day, the Berlin Airlift flew eight thousand tons of food, coal, and other necessities to the blockaded city. Berliners grew accustomed to the steady drone of planes over their still war-dark city, one every thirty seconds, dropping not bombs this time, but nourishment. In what has been called the first battle of the Cold War, the West was the clear winner.

These hardening lines between former allies presented a personal crisis for Noel Field. How could he continue as his country's low-key deceiver when straddling the East-West divide was no longer an option? Typically, Field tried to delude himself into thinking he could. "In the long run of course I'll want to go *home*," Noel wrote Erica, "but I feel as though I still have something to contribute from over here." Field still thought of America as "home," believed he could continue to be American and work for America's destruction, call himself an American relief worker while saving Red cadres. Somehow he would get away with it all as he had for so long. Searching for a new role, and income, Field explored a career as a writer who would explain to Americans why this was a grand and historic moment. "The peoples of Eastern Europe," Noel wrote in an April 14, 1948, book proposal, "are reconstructing and remodeling their countries along paths so new and untrodden, under such difficult circumstances. . . . It is my purpose to spend several months in each of the countries of Eastern Europe and to devote myself to getting as complete a picture as possible."

He knew many of the players in the new Soviet bloc, and some owed their survival to Noel. With OSS support, he had speeded their passage back to build their people's democracies. It was their turn to throw him a lifeline. In theory, Noel's plan made sense. In reality it was a dangerously delusional dream.

The Communists Noel Field had supported were suspect in Stalin's eyes. "Contaminated" by too much time in the West, they had mingled with too many non-Soviet Communists. Moreover, many had fought in the Spanish Civil War, which was perceived by the man in the Kremlin as an international affair. Noel's comrades wanted to rebuild their own countries—along Stalinist lines, of course—but still, they were essentially patriotic Poles, Germans, Hungarians, and Czechs. Stalin did not trust them.

Noel understood nothing of this.

*

Noel scrambled to find a role for himself in the newly "liberated" lands east of the Rhine, crisscrossing among Warsaw, East Berlin, and Prague. Where others were shocked by scenes of misery and mass starvation, Noel saw a steady march to the Promised Land. He wrote Erica, whom he hoped to lure East, from Warsaw. "Food is plentiful everywhere, in fact there is almost a superabundance, and the eyes of people who come here from England almost pop out of their heads when they see the thousands of overflowing shops (not merely food but clothing and virtually everything else). We have eaten so many strawberries in cream that we are almost sick of them."

On a Moscow-bound train at roughly the same time, French foreign minister Georges Bidault observed a different landscape. "Going

West to East, the train went slower with each country . . . and peoples' faces got progressively sadder and more expressionless as we journeyed toward the East. . . . East Germany was perceptibly sadder than West Germany. Poland was sadder than East Germany. And Russia was saddest of all."

Noel Field was without a job, without prospects, soon to be without a country. Meanwhile, his friend Alger Hiss, in another of his soft landings, was now president of the Carnegie Endowment for International Peace. Noel wrote him asking for help in finding a publisher. On May 7, 1948, Hiss wrote back, suggesting Noel reach out to American magazines. "This would make you known as a reporter on Eastern Europe. . . . Last night," Hiss wrote, "I spoke to Miss Freda Kirchwey of the *Nation* about you, and Larry [Duggan] tells me he will be speaking to the people in charge of *Harper's Magazine* and will let you know."

Noel was desperate to keep Erica in the party's fold, living a "healthy life"—even, he wrote, if it meant working "in construction in a People's Democracy." For her, he painted the East in the brightest colors. "We've been here two weeks," Noel wrote Erica from Warsaw, on June 23, 1948, "and planning on remaining for several more . . . we attended two meetings and they insisted on putting me right up on the platform . . . in full view of the public, and cameras, and surrounded by many dignitaries from different countries! I felt decidedly odd!"

He should have felt more than odd. At a time when Americans were at the very least an oddity, when smoking an American cigarette was considered suspicious behavior, and most people behind the Iron Curtain kept their heads down, awaiting Stalin's next move, this conspicuous *American* was posing with Communist dignitaries—old comrades from Spain and France, all living on borrowed time.

★

It was not in war-ravaged Europe, however, but in New York City, where a grand jury was empaneled to hear evidence regarding a Com-

munist conspiracy to overthrow the US government, where everything changed forever for Noel Field. The country Noel had betrayed
with impunity for a decade and a half was itself turning.

The national mood was different a decade after Adolf Berle
showed FDR and J. Edgar Hoover Whittaker Chambers's list of
Communists in the highest reaches of the government—only to have
the president dismiss it as a distraction from the war effort. The war
was over and Americans were shocked by their erstwhile ally Stalin's
brazen power grab in Central Europe. Other events converged to
raise anti-Soviet fears in Washington. Canadians unmasked a Soviet
spy ring operating in Ottawa. Most significantly, Republicans won
control of Congress for the first time since Herbert Hoover, giving
the largely marginalized House Un-American Activities Committee
a new shot of life.

On August 18, 1948, federal agents delivered Chambers a subpoena to appear before a New York grand jury. Chambers named
Alger Hiss as part of the Ware group—provoking Hiss's categorical
denial and an aggressive counterattack against Chambers. Back and
forth, the two former comrades lobbed charges and countercharges
at each other, as each struggled to salvage his own reputation by destroying the other's.

They were almost comically a study in contrasts. While Hiss remained pitchfork straight and icily composed through the proceedings
before the House Un-American Activities Committee on August 27,
1948, the slouching Whittaker Chambers's jowly features seemed to
melt under the blaze of klieg lights. Hiss, a gifted public performer,
coolly requested permission to examine Chambers's teeth to identify—
and degrade—his old comrade. But he overplayed his hand. Hiss's
denial of ever having known his accuser provoked Chambers into revealing much more than he originally intended. His back against the
wall, Chambers now unmasked the Soviet spying operation for which
he had been a courier and Hiss a spy. Chambers produced microfilmed

copies of classified State Department documents he had hidden in a hollowed-out pumpkin on his Maryland farm—the famed "Pumpkin Papers"—traced to Hiss.

Still confident he could bluff his way out of any trap, Hiss sued Chambers for libel. Ultimately, Hiss was convicted of perjury, the statute of limitations on spying having expired. It amounted to much the same thing. Alger Hiss had perjured himself by denying he was a Soviet spy.

"Hiss," his former control officer, J. Peters, said, "made a great mistake in suing Chambers." That "mistake" destroyed Noel Field's cover. It was Hiss's libel suit against his old comrade for calling him a Communist that provoked Chambers into revealing not only Hiss's role in the underground, but that of Field.

★

Remarkably, Hiss continued to enjoy the unflinching support of the American establishment. Dean Acheson, John Foster Dulles, and Felix Frankfurter all leaped to the defense of the man partly responsible for drawing up the UN Charter. (California congressman Richard M. Nixon doggedly pursued Hiss and kept the investigation alive.) Noel Field, absent from Washington for more than a decade, did not have the protection of Alger's many friends in high places.

At precisely this most dangerous moment for Field, his US passport was about to expire. More than ever, he yearned to be a certified, card-holding member of the Communist Party. In an attempt to find a line to Moscow and clear up his confused party status, he wrote Jakub Berman, the head of the Polish secret police. Noel knew Berman's secretary, Anna Duracz, from the USC. Now he pleaded with her to deliver his letter personally to Berman. It is an astonishing and painful missive, and for once candid about his deep need for the party's full embrace—a need that goes to the core of a man possessed.

"Dear Comrade Berman," Field wrote on September 9, 1948,

Anna Duracz, who is my good friend, told me she had discussed my case with you, and as you have been very busy, could not see me during my stay in Poland. So, I have sent you the certificate of my recent Party activity and wish to inform you of my current situation. I apologize for writing in such detail . . . [but] my story is very complicated. . . . I ask you to believe me that I would not [bother you] if I were not in a very difficult situation. I tried repeatedly to solve the problem but without result. Resolving *this situation is a matter of life or death* for my wife and me. After what I have been through—without the Party's support and unable to participate in the Party's life—*our existence is meaningless.* . . . My wife and I have been Party members for twelve years. We have always been vigilant to the Party's needs, loyal to the Party's ideology and—except for one mistake—[when he broke the code of silence and told Hiss he was working for Hede Massing's apparatus] have never been criticized by the Party. But because of the reasons detailed in the attachment, we have been unable to certify our Party membership or establish contact with anyone who could certify it for us.

We joined the Party during our Moscow stay [in 1938] and submitted our applications to the American section of the Comintern. But as we lived and worked in Europe, and due to the dissolution of the Comintern [in 1943] the American Party has not received information regarding our affairs. . . . I would humbly ask you where to turn for clarification regarding my Party status.

Not having a Party certificate has caused me difficulties during our stay in Poland. It is painful for me as I feel an extraordinary love for the People's Republic of Poland, and admire its great successes. . . . I think this is an intolerable situation for a Communist.

Comradely greetings,

Noel H. Field

Neither Comrade Berman nor any other high party official anywhere in the Eastern Bloc answered Noel's plea. His persistence,
however, was increasingly noted in the only capital that really mattered: Moscow. Foreigners in Warsaw, Prague, and East Berlin were
now routinely followed, their mail opened and their phones tapped by
the local offshoots of the NKVD, soon to be the KGB. Why was this
former State Department official so desperate to come East? Moscow
had a file on him dating at least from the mid-1930s. The Field dos-
sier revealed a troublesome record. Most potentially explosive was his
wartime freelancing with Allen Dulles, soon to be the first director of
Central Intelligence.

# CHAPTER 15

# THE END OF THE LINE

*How did a snake get in the tower?*
*Delayed in the democracies*
*By departmental vanities*
*The rival sergeants run about*
*But more to squabble than find out.*

—W. H. Auden

O N OCTOBER 15, 1948, Field's world was shattered. In Prague, looking for work, he picked up the *New York Herald Tribune* and was stunned by the headline: "Ex State Department Aide Called Red by Chambers—Noel Field Named in House Inquiry." "Hitherto secret testimony by Whittaker Chambers, self-confessed former Communist, that an important official in the Western European division of the State Department in the 1930s was a Communist—was made public today. . . . Mr. Chambers identified the State Department official as Noel Field. He charged that Alger Hiss, then also a State Department official, attempted to draw Mr. Field into the Communist cell in which Mr. Chambers contends Mr. Hiss was a leading figure. However, Mr.

Hiss failed, the witness testified, because he learned that Mr. Field was working in another (Communist) apparatus."

Herta asked her husband if he had given Paul Massing [now in the United States] as many documents as Hiss gave Chambers. "Yes," Noel said, "I gave him a great deal."

This front-page outing ended Field's double life. In his own country, Noel Field had benefited from the same bias that had shielded Larry Duggan and Alger Hiss. How could such an earnest, courteous, well-educated Quaker humanitarian be a traitor? "His colleagues still could not believe it," Paul Massing remembered. "Even Wallace Carroll—the respected editor of the *Winston-Salem Journal and Sentinel*—wrote that it was ridiculous, unbelievable, quite out of character." "He fooled us all," said Elizabeth Dexter. The mild, open-faced, always-helpful Noel had turned out to be someone quite different— capable of deceiving his family and closest friends for the only cause that mattered to him.

Now, without a country or a job, Field was a desperate man. Out of the question, after Chambers's revelation, was his plan to try his hand at journalism reporting from the East for "progressive" American publications. What he most feared, however, was an FBI subpoena to testify in a New York court. "I was afraid I might harm others [if forced to testify]," he said, "primarily my friend Alger Hiss. . . . Alger defended himself with great intelligence; he had been trained as a lawyer and knew all the phrases and tricks. I, on the other hand, had no experience. . . . I did not trust myself enough to stand in front of my accusers and shout 'innocent' in their faces. . . . I also understood the same from a short letter from Hiss, who obviously could not write openly."

Back in Geneva, Noel avoided places where he might run into Americans, giving especially wide berth to the American consulate. Herta now answered the phone and the front door of their apartment on the rue de Contamines.

"You may or may not have heard," Alger Hiss wrote in a typically insincere letter to Noel on October 19, 1948, "of the irresponsible smearing of [your] name before HUAC. . . . I am enclosing [the testimony] for your information. The man seems to be *unbalanced and to be given to hallucinations.* There have been no further press accounts and the chances are that you will hear no more of this foolishness."

★

In New York, Larry Duggan could not so easily elude the FBI. Pressed to name his recruiters and his comrades in the Washington Communist underground, Duggan withheld Hiss's and Field's names. In late November, two FBI agents called on Duggan at the Scarsdale home he shared with his wife and four young children.

On December 20, 1948, Duggan's broken body was found on the Fifth Avenue sidewalk below his sixteenth-floor office window.

On Capitol Hill, Congressman Karl E. Mundt of South Dakota, chairman of HUAC, did not allow this tragic event to pass unexploited. At a hastily summoned midnight news conference, Mundt revealed that Duggan had been mentioned in recent closed-door hearings, one of six State Department officials named by Whittaker Chambers. Asked by reporters when Mundt would release the names of the five others, the Republican congressman replied, "We will give them out, as they jump out of windows."

In his eulogy, Sumner Welles, Duggan's former State Department boss, praised the forty-three-year-old diplomat for his "high patriotism," adding, "he typified the finest kind of public servant that the United States has produced." Welles concluded by sternly rebuking "a handful of fanatical or unscrupulous slanderers that Laurence Duggan was sympathetic to the doctrines of the Communist Party," concluding, "If there was ever an American who in his daily life practiced democracy as Franklin Roosevelt defined it—it was Laurence Duggan."

Welles did not live to see his fellow American Brahmin, Exeter and Harvard graduate, and Soviet spy, Larry Duggan, exposed.

For the rest of his life, Noel Field blamed the FBI's harassment of Duggan for his suicide. As usual, he missed the point. The Soviets never released Duggan. KGB files reveal that just three weeks before his suicide, Agent "Shaushkin" called Duggan's office and left his name with his secretary. "Tell him Shaushkin called."

The KGB, at least, acknowledged its possible role in Duggan's suicide. "I do not exclude [the possibility] that . . . [Shauskin's persistence] promoted his decision to commit suicide. . . . We can cause great damage to our country by striving to get information from old agents who are exposed, and information acquired from them . . . has no value."

For Duggan, the acknowledgment was too late.

*

Increasingly, the Fields were only furtive visitors everywhere, even in Switzerland, where they had just lost their resident status. Michel Gordey spotted Noel at the Communist front "Partisans for Peace" conference in Paris's Salle Pleyel. "I saw Noel, hanging around," Gordey remembered, "trying to get in. He looked very bad; thin, sick, poor, badly dressed. His shirt was frayed. He had no delegate's pass, couldn't get in, but he wanted badly to hear the speech that was scheduled. I think it was [Soviet author] Ilya Ehrenburg. I got him in as a newspaperman.

"I didn't have much money either," Gordey said, "but I took the Fields out to lunch. They ate and ate, like really hungry people who haven't had a meal for some time. Herta had turned gray, become an old woman since I last saw her. They were obviously broke and both were extremely depressed. Noel said he wasn't making any money, was in a bad way but that he had an offer to teach American civilization at Prague University. I told him it was a very bad time to take a job in Prague—just after the Communist coup. He said, 'But I have no other job, I'm starving and sick. They've offered the job with a guarantee of complete freedom in teaching. I just have to take it.' He said I could get in touch with him at the Prague Press Club."

In another blow, his beloved Erica followed her heart in a different direction than Noel had hoped. Though she had briefly joined the German Communist Party in 1946, two years later, in March 1948, in Epsom, Surrey, Erica married her GI sweetheart. Noel was crushed. "One of my greatest disappointments," Noel later wrote, "was that she never returned [to the East]."

"As to ourselves," he wrote Erica, in March 1949, "the sky certainly hasn't brightened. I'm getting pretty sick and tired. Our friends," Noel concluded this doleful note, "all seem to have forgotten us."

What depth of despair prompted the once proud and ambitious man to write his foster daughter, "Do you suppose that it would be possible for Bob [her husband, Robert Wallach] to lend me some dough— maybe twenty or thirty thousand francs . . . paying him back when we come to Paris?"

"My own mood at the moment is particularly black," he wrote Erica for the last time on April 10, 1949. "I woke up feeling just about ready to jump out the window."

# CHAPTER 16

# BLOODLUST AGAIN

*A better Socialism! Different from Stalin's! The pipsqueak! Socialism without Stalin was no different from fascism!*

—Aleksandr Solzhenitsyn

A N EPIC FALLING-OUT between two giants of the Communist firmament, Stalin and Tito, ultimately sealed Noel Field's fate. The Soviet-occupied lands of the East were run from Moscow and nominally headed by little Stalins—puppets whose every move Moscow monitored and controlled. All but one. Yugoslav leader Josip Broz Tito was his own man. A hero of the anti-Nazi resistance, Tito had built both the Yugoslav army and its secret police. He did not need Soviet troops to keep himself in power; he was that unique Communist leader whose own people largely supported him. A handsome, charismatic, ruthless dictator, he was loyal to Stalin but put Yugoslavia's interests a shade ahead of Moscow's. By 1948, Stalin demanded absolute fealty and could not abide Tito's independence, nor his talk of a Balkan federation of Communist states.

Aleksandr Solzhenitsyn brilliantly captured Stalin's agony as he pondered the young Yugoslav "upstart" in an imaginary internal mono-

logue. "On the ottoman lay a man," Solzhenitsyn described Stalin in
*In the First Circle,*

> whose likeness has been more often sculpted, painted in oils,
> watercolors, gouache, and sepia; limned in charcoal, chalk, and
> powdered brick; pieced together in a mosaic of road maker's
> gravel . . . etched on ivory; grown in grass; woven into carpets;
> spelled out by planes flying in formation . . . than any other face
> ever has been in the three billion years since the earth's crust was
> formed. . . .
>
> He had run rings around them on the Danube and in the
> Balkans. . . . All Soviet prisoners returning home after living in
> Europe were sent to the camps. All prisoners who had served only
> one ten year sentence were sent back to serve another.
>
> In a word, things seemed to be coming right at last. But when
> the Siberian taiga no longer rustled with hints of alternative so-
> cialism, the black dragon Tito crept into the open and blocked all
> roads ahead. . . . How could he have let himself be misled? Failed
> to discern the scorpion soul of the man! In 1936 they had Tito
> by the throat! And they let him get away! Ay . . . ay . . . ay . . .
> ay . . . ay!
>
> A better Socialism! Different from Stalin's! The pipsqueak!
> Socialism without Stalin was no different from fascism!
>
> Stalin groaned, swung his legs off the couch and clutched his
> balding head. Vain regrets rankled in his bosom. He had toppled
> mountains and he had tripped over a dunghill. . . . Not that Tito
> would get anywhere. Nothing would come of his efforts. As an
> old horse doctor who has slit open any number of bellies, chopped
> off innumerable extremities in smoky peasant huts, looks at a lady
> medic in the making, come to do her practical work in spotless
> white, that was how Stalin looked at Tito. . . .
>
> But Tito made play with long forgotten slogans from the early

days of the Revolution: "workers control," "land for the peas-
ants" . . . soap bubbles to fascinate idiots . . .

He took a deep breath. Stroked his face and his mustache.
Took another deep breath. He must not let it all get him down.

Ah yes, he had to see Abakumov. . . .


Viktor Semyonovich Abakumov—as head of the Soviet Ministry of
State Security, the second most feared man in the Soviet empire—was
instructed to put in motion the liquidation of the bothersome Yugoslav.
In June 1948, the members of the Communist International "voted"
to expel Yugoslavia from their ranks. Henceforth, the "hero of the Yugoslav resistance" was "the chained dog of the imperialists." The news
that Stalin had expelled Tito and Yugoslavia from the Comintern—the
first fracture in the postwar, Kremlin-controlled, Communist border
states—broke like a thunderclap over Europe and the United States.

Tito, though distressed by his excommunication, was safe in his
Belgrade stronghold, and unbending. Confident of Yugoslav support,
he would weather the Kremlin's ban.

Stalin upped the ante. He had to make an object lesson out of
this renegade Communist. He would demonstrate the high cost of
veering one inch from the Kremlin's leadership, and instill terror in
both the occupied populations and their leaders. Those Communist
leaders who were within his reach—however faithful they might
be to Stalin—would be liquidated. They would be tried in people's
courts and revealed to be "Titoists"—the highest crime since the sin
of being Trotskyite in the thirties. To be a Titoist meant working for
the Americans.

Now, all who had spent time in the West, who had not spent the
war years in Moscow under Stalin's watchful gaze, who had been part
of the International Brigades, all those who did not owe the little father
their positions in their own countries, found themselves in Stalin's
crosshairs.

All that was missing from the scenario hatched by Stalin, Aba-kumov, and Lavrenti Beria, head of the NKVD, was a key witness, someone who could tie Tito and all the other now undesirable and dangerous international Communists to the New Enemy: the United States. That detail would nail all of them as spies and traitors. All of Eastern Europe could then finally be cleansed of "foreign" elements. Stalin's dream of absolute power would be fulfilled, his rage at Tito calmed.

There was one man who could fill that role. Noel Field could con-nect Eastern Bloc leaders—Tito among them—to the camp of the imperialists. Through his "Red Aid," compliments of the Unitarian Service Committee, Field had provided exiled Communists funds and logistical support in getting back to Germany, Czechoslovakia, Poland, Hungary, and Yugoslavia. Best of all: Noel could link them to Allen W. Dulles. It mattered not that the American was a true-believing Stalin-ist, a traitor to his own country, desperate to come East and serve. Field had recently been outed as a Communist in his own country, thus, Washington might not make a big fuss if anything were to happen to him. Therein, too, lay opportunity.

Show trials, like today's terrorist videos of beheadings, were meant to spread terror and fear. Unrelated to justice for the accused, debased and brutalized before their executions—these "trials" were intended as graphic lessons to the living. A similar script had enjoyed a huge success in a prior run in Moscow between 1936 and 1938, when Sta-lin liquidated his "enemies" in sham trials. A stunned world had wit-nessed the heroes of the Bolshevik revolution confess to treason and beg for the gallows as their just punishment. Instead of Trotskyites, the 1949 suspects would be Titoists, but the methods for extracting confessions, and the judicial travesty that followed, would be a precise replay. Again, as in the thirties, hard-core Communists would be in the dock, performing their final "service" for the party—after torture, of course. Only the cast, led by an American, was new.

Stalin chose Budapest as the venue for the world premiere. In Hungary's little Stalin, Mátyás Rákosi, the Kremlin had its most eager and subservient partner. By offering his unflinching support, Rákosi was assuring his own political future. Moreover, under the guise of liquidating Hungarian Titoists, the much-loathed Rákosi could eliminate his own most dangerous rival in the Hungarian Communist Party: László Rajk, a genuine Communist war hero. Unlike Rákosi, who spent the war in Moscow, Rajk, after bravely fighting in the Spanish Civil War, joined the French Resistance before returning to fight fascists in Hungary. Tall, handsome, and charismatic, Rajk loomed too large next to the short, bald, neckless Rákosi.

Happily for Stalin and Rákosi, there was a tiny shard of "evidence" against Rajk that could be magnified into "treason." As foreign minister, Rajk had warmly greeted Tito on the Yugoslav's state visit to Hungary, before he became public enemy number one of the people's democracies. Minor technicalities—the fact that Rajk had never actually met his alleged "coconspirators" Noel Field or Allen Dulles—the scriptwriters could easily fix.

In a matter of months, the judicial screenplay "unmasking" the Dulles-Field-Rajk conspiracy to overthrow Rákosi and Stalin and restore fascism to Hungary was ready.

How to get Field into Rákosi's custody was the stage managers' next challenge. Given Field's desperation for sanctuary in the East, this proved to be remarkably light work.

Oblivious to the conspiracies swirling around him, Field was an easy mark. Having failed to get hearings in East Berlin and Warsaw, his last hope was Prague. With growing agitation, Noel wrote the Czech minister of information, Oskar Kosta. "I need hardly tell you how much we are looking forward to coming back to Prague again," he wrote. "In one form or another, we shall put our shoulders to the wheel of progress and once more absorb something of the new spirit and life which we so sorely miss here."

This was astonishing zeal to enter a country slowly morphing into a prison state. In 1948, Prague was wrapped in sullen gloom. Stalin forced Czechoslovakia to refuse the Marshall Plan economic assistance—a political and economic catastrophe for its war-ravaged economy. Czechoslovakia's once thriving free-enterprise economy was forced to duplicate the one-size-fits-all Soviet model. Czechs with the means were packing up and fleeing west. Stalin had recently summoned their popular foreign minister, Jan Masaryk. "I went to Moscow as foreign minister of an independent sovereign state," Masaryk said. "I returned as a lackey of the Soviet government." On March 1, 1948, Masaryk was found dead in the courtyard of Prague's Czernin Palace: another plunge from another window dressed up as suicide.

General Fyodor Bielkin, the regional Soviet proconsul, now ordered Czech president Klement Gottwald to immediately issue Field a visa. Mobilize the Czech security services, the Russian instructed the Czech president. Prepare to kidnap the American.

In early March 1949, Noel received a letter from a Czech Ministry of the Interior official, inviting him to Prague to discuss a teaching position at his earliest convenience. For the frantic Noel this was the long-awaited break: a job, a country, a chance for a new life safely out of the reach of the House Un-American Activities Committee. "Noel told us he was going to Prague," his assistant Hélène Matthey said, "to study at Charles University. I asked, 'Study what?' 'Just study,' he said."

On May 9, Noel wrote Herta from Prague, "Today I'm sticking close to my room, waiting for a call from the Foreign Ministry. . . . It's lunch time, and still no call for me yet, so shall go over to the Press Club [underlined by the secret police] to mail this letter . . . and then come back to my room, Thine, Noel."

# CHAPTER 17

# KIDNAPPED

*The deliberate increase in the chances of death,*
*The unconscious acceptance of guilt in the necessary murder.*

—W. H. Auden

N OEL FIELD'S CAPTORS slapped a chloroform-soaked rag on his face and shoved him in the back of an unmarked car. He was unconscious during the drive to Bratislava, near the Czech-Hungarian border. There, dazed and unsteady, Field was handed over to a new set of agents who spoke a language the multilingual Noel did not understand. Field and his captors rode in silence until they reached the Danube bend, and Budapest's lights flickered in the distance. Noel, however, could see none of this through his blindfold, briefly removed during a stop for the bureaucratic matter of registering the new prisoner at the Andrássy Út headquarters of the Hungarian secret police (today a popular tourist attraction known as the "House of Terror"). Field was then shoved back into the car, which soon accelerated as the driver shifted to a lower gear to grip the hairpin turns to the top of Szabadság Hegy—the ironically named Freedom Hill, one of Buda's highest peaks. Across the river sprawled the city's iconic Parliament, a new red star atop its cupola lighting up the black night. As the car slowed down, the crunching sound of gravel under tires signaled to the blindfolded prisoner that he had arrived somewhere. Tightly gripped by his guards, Field felt the soft spring night air. No sound of traffic or human voices broke an eerie stillness. Still blindfolded, the guards led him inside.

The Villa, as it is called, is still a place that chills the blood. Surrounded by gnarled trees, coiled with vines, its overgrown garden is littered with the rusting hulks of abandoned cars. Though it is no longer a crime scene, even today it is as if no one wants to get too close to this place. A man could scream his lungs out and no one would hear. No. 41 Eötvös Utca was one of the secret interrogation houses of the AVO—the Hungarian secret police.

When his guards removed his blindfold, Noel finally saw his jailers: expressionless, grim-faced men, the hammer-and-sickle insignia on their shoulder boards indicating they were "his" people. No doubt that for a moment Field was paralyzed by horror. What was happening? Why? As they led him up the stairs to a hexagon-shaped room with windows covered by thick blackout curtains, his guards did not treat Field as a comrade. Helpless in their grip, he was positioned at the end of a T-shaped table to face his accusers. In heavily accented German, a Hungarian barked at him. "Tell us about your spying activities for Allen Dulles!" A small man, a former tailor named Gábor Péter, was now the chief of the Hungarian secret police and in charge of Field's interrogation. It was the first time Noel Field heard himself called a spy—not by his own country, but his spiritual homeland. A Russian officer sat in the back, silent, but in charge.

Stunned at finding himself the captive of the people he served for decades, Noel stammered astonished denials. Then the blows began. Most records of his initial interrogation were destroyed by the AVO during the 1956 uprising. There are, however, only so many ways to break a human body and crush the human spirit. From the existing records it is clear that the AVO used all the time-tested methods— sleep deprivation, verbal abuse, and relentless beatings. Field's "co-conspirators" in the same "Titoist plot" have recounted precise details of their interrogation in the same villa. Forced to stand for hours on end, Noel was repeatedly told that his role as an American spy had already been confirmed by many of the people he had helped in his humanitarian work. His torturers turned a two-line note Field sent to Dulles in April 1945—urging Dulles to support the repatriation of the Hungarian Communist exile leader Tibor Szönyi, to mount anti-Nazi resistance in Hungary, passing en route through Yugoslavia—into proof of both Field and Szönyi's treachery. Obviously, both Field and the Hungarian Communist were Dulles's agents.

Exhaustion and a sense that he was abandoned by the outside world were the two necessary conditions for a prisoner's interrogation. A relay of well-rested interrogators, each eager to succeed where the agent before him failed, worked on Noel Field. "The sessions always took place at night," said Gyula Décsi, one of Field's interrogators. The blows stopped only when the prisoner agreed to confess to the crimes. "We didn't have time to find out what precisely Field was guilty of," Décsi added. The torturers were merely told that Field and his cohorts were "bourgeois careerists, without a conscience, who wanted to harm the working class," his interrogator said. "I accepted this explanation as satisfactory." Field, according to his friend Tonia Lechtman, a Polish "Fieldist," "sometimes had to be carried back to his cell on a stretcher."

One of Field's codefendants, Béla Szász, a Hungarian Communist who returned from exile in Argentina to help build the new people's democracy, described the method used to "persuade" him to confess to being Field's recruit. "I stood for nine days and nine nights without food and without water." The AVO, according to Szász, also favored "soling," the beating of the soles of the victims' feet with rubber truncheons.

If the show trials had been less murderous, it might be tempting to find humor in certain moments of this judicial farce. Szász was asked, "When did you meet Noel Field?" "But I don't know him!" the prisoner protested. "This Field is in our hands," his interrogator proudly proclaimed. "I could only shrug my shoulders," Szász said. "I had never heard the name of Field." "How did you come back from [Argentina]?" the interrogator pressed. "I went to France by ship, from there by train." "Through Switzerland, perhaps?" "Yes, through Switzerland," Szász replied. "My interrogator was so pleased with my reply that his face brightened. 'Well, then the whole thing is simple. Field was in Switzerland at that time. When you were passing through Switzerland, Field boarded the train and recruited you as his agent.' It was hair raising," Szász said, "that [his interrogator] should be content with such a transparent fairy tale. When I said that it appeared unimaginable to me that anyone should permit himself to be recruited into a foreign secret service by a complete stranger on a train, the colonel shrugged his shoulder. 'If you don't like it, write something more convincing. . . . Write also about Field,' " he was ordered. This was a challenge for Béla Szász, who had never even heard of the American.

★

His interrogators turned every facet of Noel's work for the Unitarians into a crime. Field was tortured into confessing that his rescue of Communists was a cover for recruiting them for Dulles and the other archtraitor, Tito. He was ordered to list all the Communists he had ever met and helped to return to Poland, East Germany, Czechoslovakia, and Hungary. Field listed 562 names. Once he had "confessed" to being an American spy, all his contacts were considered to have been his "agents."

As Moscow ordered other Soviet satellites to prepare similar show trials of Titoists, Polish, Czech, and German Communists Noel had known during the war (a chance encounter in a restaurant was sufficient) were soon dragged to other houses of torture in other Eastern Bloc capitals. All paid with their lives, their freedom, or—the lucky ones—merely their livelihood, for the crime of being "Fieldists."

In a nightmare season, Field's worst moment was when he was forced to face one of those he "confessed" he had recruited for Dulles. Tibor Szönyi, his face bruised and swollen beyond recognition, was dragged into the room with the T-shaped table. A legend in the underground, Szönyi had until a few weeks before been head of Communist cadres in Hungary. As an Old Guard Bolshevik, a non-Muscovite who had spent the war years in Switzerland, he was automatically suspect. Now, Field was ordered to accuse to his face a man he had seen casually twice before of being his agent. Field did as he was ordered. Szönyi was later sentenced to death and hanged.

On July 7, 1949, a broken and desperate Field resorted to the unthinkable: an SOS to the American embassy in Budapest. "Urgent and Secret," Noel scrawled on a scrap of paper addressed to the American ambassador:

> The undersigned American citizen swears to the veracity of the enclosed: On May 11, at 3:30 in the afternoon, the Hungarian Secret Police abducted me in Prague, and transported me to Budapest and has since kept me confined against my will with the ludicrous charges that I am the arch American spy against the East. I am undergoing third degree treatment—including beating and starvation. My wife was in Geneva but the police claim she is their prisoner too.
>
> I request urgent intervention,
>
> Noel H. Field

"As reference," Field added in a postscript, "I give Allen Dulles and John Carter Vincent, Ambassador to Switzerland."

Noel entrusted this message into the hands of a cellmate placed there to tempt him into just such an act of desperation. His SOS traveled as far as the desk of the colonel in charge of his interrogation. After this, Noel's "third degree" interrogation picked up renewed steam. Field had, in effect, confirmed in writing his close affiliation with Dulles.

By the end of summer, Stalin and Rákosi had their confessions. "Rákosi travelled twice to Moscow to consult Stalin [during the Field case]," Gábor Péter later testified, "and informed him personally about the [Field] case. In August, Rákosi presented Stalin with the text of the indictment which he had written himself. . . . Gen. Byelkin [sic] instructed Rákosi three times a week. . . . Rákosi had to have Stalin's consent to carry out the death sentences."

On September 16, 1949, in Budapest's cavernous Great Hall of the Iron and Metal Workers' Union, the curtain rose on the show trial of "László Rajk and His Accomplices before the Peoples' Court of Budapest." Seated under giant portraits of Marx, Engels, Lenin, Stalin, and Rákosi, seven defendants sat hunched, their beefy police guards squeezing the accused together. After their two-month ordeal, the accused no longer filled out their old suits; their collars hung loosely around their necks. But though they seemed calm—sedated for the occasion—all had the haunted look of those condemned to die. László Rajk, György Pálffy, Tibor Szönyi, András Szalai, Milan Ognjenovich, Béla Korondy, Pál Justus—and, for good measure, Yugoslav diplomat Lazar Brankov, there to connect the proceedings directly to the traitor Tito. All had been, until recently, ranking members of the Communist Party.

The defendants were charged with attempting to overthrow the peoples' democracy on behalf of the American imperialists, and their local "running dog," Tito. In their testimony, the accused embraced the charges and piled on others the court had overlooked. Though he had never met Field, Rajk testified, "In the Le Vernet internment camp an American citizen named Field, who was, as far as I know, the head of the American intelligence agency for Central and Eastern Europe, visited me. . . . He referred to instructions he had received from Washington that he should speak with me and help me to get out of camp and return to Hungary, to dissolve the Party and possibly take leadership into my own hands. But my contact with the Americans ended after my meeting with Field." Rajk then volunteered a jaw dropping plot detail, "Field arrived in the camp after I had already agreed to work for the Gestapo."

Even in this grim setting, humor occasionally made an inadvertent appearance. Judge Peter Janko asked Szönyi to identify two photographs. "Who is that?" the judge demanded. "Noel Field," the accused confidently answered. "And this?" Szönyi shook his head. "This man I don't know," he said, staring vacantly at the image of Allen Dulles. "You don't recognize Allen Dulles!" roared the judge. "Oh, yes!" the accused man hastily corrected himself. "I do recognize him. But at that time he did not wear glasses," a fact which would have been news to the director of the CIA.

In contrast to Alger Hiss's perjury trial at roughly the same time, no battery of aggressive lawyers defended the accused. In fact, no real evidence was presented in court at all. My parents, reporters for the Associated Press and United Press, covered the Rajk trial in Budapest. "Everybody performed a role—the judge, the prosecutor, the so-called defense lawyers, the defendants," my father wrote, "after endless rehearsals. . . . The excessive zeal of some of the defendants was almost unreal. They accused themselves of unheard-of crimes bordering on the ridiculous. At times I thought this was their secret message to the world, saying, in effect, no sane person should believe the nonsense they were confessing to."

Noel Field did not testify in the people's court. To have the ravaged American appear in person and testify in English would have been too risky—and perhaps too provocative for even Stalin's taste. But to those in the dock, invoking Noel Field's name was their death knell.

In his summation, the prosecutor said, "Of Tibor Szönyi it was proved that during the war he became an American spy, that in Switzerland he received instructions from Noel H. Field and Allan Dulles . . . returned to Hungary with the aid of Yugoslav agents of the American spy organizations and . . . placed American and Yugoslav spies into important administrative posts in Hungary."

"Our people demand death for the traitors," the prosecutor concluded. "The head of the snake which wants to bite us must be crushed. . . . The only defense against mad dogs is to beat them to death."

"Long live the Party!" were László Rajk's final words as the hangman tied the noose around his neck on October 15. Four others went with Rajk to the gallows; another fifty followed in their wake.

★

Stalin's bloodlust was not yet slaked. The show-trial producers—including Bielkin—moved to Prague next. There, two years later the same scenario, an all-Soviet production, was reenacted, with certain modifications. The Slánský affair started with the arrest of Czech Communists tainted by the double sin of Swiss exile and Noel Field's friendship. However, for the Czech inquisition, the "crime" of Zionism (thinly camouflaging Stalin's anti-Semitism) supplanted Titoism as the Kremlin's new obsession. Czech prime minister Rudolf Slánský, the target, was, along with ten others accused, Jewish. Noel Field once again conveniently linked the whole sham trial to Washington. "Let us remember," the Czech information minister Václav Kopecký intoned, "how the whole international network of Anglo-American espionage was unmasked in connection with the well-known Noel Field."

In the Prague trials, the "master spy's" brother, Hermann Field, played a supporting role. His 1939 rescue of fleeing Czech Jews in Poland was invoked as American cover for espionage. "Hermann Field," read the indictment, "under the guise of humanitarian aid, recruited from among the refugees in Kraków a number of agents and turned them over, as did his brother Noel Field, to British and American espionage agencies," adding that, "in the selection of refugee agents, the Field brothers followed two criteria. First, they must belong to the political left, and second, they should be Jews."

More than one hundred ranking Communists were executed, and tens of thousands jailed, before the fever broke in Czechoslovakia.

No show trial was staged in Berlin. Though Noel had named three dozen of his closest German Communist contacts, the proximity of West Berlin likely made a spectacular show trial in the Eastern sector too risky, and liable to antagonize West German Communists. Instead, Field's East German comrades from the Spanish Civil War and the Le Vernet internment camp were imprisoned or, at a minimum, expelled from the party. Of Noel's closest friends in the East German Communist Party, one—Paul Berz—committed suicide in custody, and the other, Willi Kreikmeyer, was tortured to death.

★

Having performed his service, Noel Field was moved from the hilltop house of torture to the first of several maximum-security prisons in Budapest. Though he was of no further use to the party, the presence of an American citizen, never officially convicted of anything, languishing in a Hungarian jail had to be kept absolutely secret. Similarly, shooting or hanging an American was more potentially explosive than executing one of their own. Besides, why bother? There was no shortage of space in the Gulag or in the Soviet satellites' vast network of camps and prisons. Field thus spent the next five years in solitary confinement.

When, in 1954, Field learned for the first time that his testimony led to the execution of Tibor Szönyi, he collapsed. His interrogating officer during this time (when Field was still in jail but fighting for a new hearing), Major Arpad Kretschmer, also interrogated my father the following year. Kretschmer told my father that Field suffered a "complete breakdown" and blamed himself for his "weakness" in implicating an innocent man. He excused his own brutalization and imprisonment without charge as the "mistake" of a few zealots. Field, who would revere the Great Leader for the rest of his life, never learned of Stalin's intimate involvement with his case. The files were not opened for more than two decades after Field's death. No doubt, however, that he would have found a rationale for Stalin's brutality.

"My arrest," he wrote, "was the right and duty of the authorities. . . . My accusers essentially have the same convictions that I do."

Field listed all the reasons why his accusers did the right thing in beating a confession out of him.

1. I am an American
2. I worked for the State Department
3. I worked for a Christian philanthropy [USC]
4. I was in touch with Dulles
5. I snooped around the East Bloc after the war
6. I was born bourgeois

Field even apologized for his SOS to his own government from prison. "A Communist," he wrote, "cannot behave like that."

This was the ultimate triumph of totalitarianism: the accused accepted, even embraced, his guilt. The party can never be wrong.

# CHAPTER 18

# TWO MORE FIELDS DISAPPEAR

*Here they hang a man first, and then they try him.*

—Molière

T wo weeks after her husband vanished, Herta had not alerted anyone, least of all any Americans. She blamed Washington for his disappearance. If not the FBI, she reasoned, then perhaps Moscow had reactivated Noel as agent, which of course she must not reveal either. With each day without news, her anxiety mounted, however. It wasn't like Noel to be out of touch for more than a few days. "She was very secretive about it," Hélène Matthey, with whom Herta was staying in Geneva, recalled. "But I told her, that if she was going to be my guest and my friend, I couldn't help her if she wouldn't say what was worrying her." Herta, like Noel, was practiced at keeping things to herself.

On May 22, 1949, Herta wrote to Noel at the Palace Hotel. The letter was intercepted by Czech security services and passed along to Budapest, where I found it in the Hungarian secret police archives. It is a heartbreaking account of a woman at the very edge of despair. It is yet another example of the breathtaking depth of Stalinist cruelty.

"It's a long time since I have had news from thee, dearest," his wife wrote. "These past ten days seem like so many weeks, a small eternity. First I thought I would wait with writing till I had heard from thee. But thee may come back to the hotel, where I imagine my previous letters are waiting for thee and then thee will be upset if thee finds no recent news. . . . It is not like thee to keep me waiting like this," Herta wrote plaintively of the longest separation of their two and a half decades of marriage. "In my imagination I saw thee run over by a car, sick in a hospital, burned to death in a hotel fire. . . . I called the Palace Hotel and [was told] thee had left without leaving an address. So the hotel had not burned down, it did not sound like sickness or accident and I calmed down considerably . . . and decided that I had better just wait patiently til thee is going to communicate with me again. . . . I read a lot and go for very long walks, to smooth my ruffled tranquility and to make the days go a little faster. And my thoughts are with thee all the time, dear, beloved husband. Ever thine, Herta."

"Finally," Matthey recalled, "Herta announced, 'I'm going to Prague. I would rather be in prison with Noel in Prague, than be free here in Switzerland.' "

Herta asked Hermann to go with her. Noel's brother was in Italy, leading a tour of architects around war-devastated sites. He had just accepted the job of dean of the School of Architecture at Western Reserve University in Cleveland, Ohio. He and Kate and their two young sons were soon to leave for America. But Herta pleaded with Hermann to help her search for Noel. Reluctantly, Hermann agreed.

They met in Prague on August 4, 1949. Making the rounds to several ministries, Czech officials promised they would investigate Field's mysterious disappearance, and told the Fields to come back in a week.

To pass the time, Hermann decided to visit his architect friends, Szymon and Helena Syrkus, in Warsaw. Mr. and Mrs. Syrkus were obliged to report to their local party official the American's visit. Another Field, in another Soviet satellite planning its own show trial, was an unexpected gift for Moscow. Warsaw was ordered to gear up for Hermann's visit.

After a week spent looking at war destruction in Warsaw, Hermann was dropped off by his friends at the Warsaw airport for his return flight to Prague. He passed passport control and cleared customs. Then a porter politely ushered Hermann to a special departure room. Field assumed the room was for VIPs. Instead, Hermann was greeted by an unsmiling, heavyset man blinking behind thick horn-rimmed glasses: Josef Swiatlo, deputy head of the notorious Department 10 of the Polish Ministry of Public Security. "Just a few questions, Mr. Field," Swiatlo said. "Please follow me." Annoyed but not unduly concerned, Hermann assumed he would be queried about photographing unauthorized sites. He did not ask to see anyone from the American embassy before he was bundled into the back of a van with blacked-out windows and driven to Warsaw's secret police headquarters, from there to Miedzeszyn, a dungeon in Warsaw's outskirts, and oblivion.

Hermann's Prague-bound plane took off without him. Mr. and Mrs. Syrkus, who had dropped him off at the airport, were arrested within days. The Moscow-ordered purge of Polish "Fieldists" was under way. For the seemingly innocuous act of handing Noel's letter to her boss, Jakub Berman, Anna Duracz—age twenty-five—was arrested on October 15, 1949, as a "Fieldist." She survived an attempted suicide, was eventually freed, and quit the Communist Party shortly thereafter.

*

Herta stood for a long time on the tarmac of the Prague airport, eyes fixed on passengers disembarking from Warsaw, waiting for Hermann. The airline had told her that though his name was on the flight manifest, no one had seen him board the plane.

Seized now by panic, Herta wrote Hermann's wife, telling Kate that her husband, too, had gone missing. On August 26, 1949, three months after Noel vanished, Kate Field called the American embassy in London. It was the first word the US government had of the disappearance behind the Iron Curtain of two American citizens.

The same day, the Czech secret police received Moscow's order to arrest Herta Field, still in Prague. Agents now called on Herta at the Palace Hotel and told her that they had located her husband in a hospital, in Bratislava. The agents offered to drive her there. Unlike her husband, she needed no chloroform for the drive to the Slovak capital. "You're going to your husband," her guards assured her. "We have promised him so." "I had the impression," she later said, "that this reunion would take place in the next few days. The guard even said, 'We let you come to help your husband.' "

In Bratislava, Herta was handed over to Hungarian agents. By day's end, she was prisoner of the villa on Eötvös Utca. Instead of a reunion with Noel, her interrogator told her, "Your husband is a criminal. You are in our hands. . . . You cannot live in America or the West . . . but [if you cooperate] you can live here." She was unaware that she and Noel were under the same roof. She was merely told Noel's life depended on her "good behavior." In her cell, she "imagined" hearing Noel nearby—which, indeed, he was. "I heard my husband groan," she said later. "A heavy, shuddering groan, as if he were in great pain. It seemed to come from the floor above. . . . One night, my husband was placed in the cell next to mine. He woke up, as he often does from dreams, with little moans. I heard him say, 'All gone, all gone.' "

After a few weeks of interrogation at the villa, Herta was moved twice more. Most cruelly, she, like Noel, was kept in solitary confinement—for their capture was too explosive to risk exposure. Around Christmastime in 1953, Herta experienced a moment of searing heartache. "I had asked the prison doctor to give me my glasses back," she recalled. "The commanding officer showed me a pair of glasses and asked me if they were mine. . . . The glasses were my husband's. I recognized them by their peculiar gold frame and their green tinted lenses."

One wonders what went through their guards' minds, as they shuf-
fled from the despairing Noel to the broken Herta driven nearly insane
with worry and longing, three cells away.

★

In the light of all we know about the Stalinist capacity for brutality, the
Fields' pursuit of Noel straight into the monster's maw now seems
incomprehensible. What were Herta and Hermann thinking as, like
lambs to slaughter, they made themselves available for victimhood in
Budapest and Warsaw? The answer is, first, that we benefit from a
hindsight they could not draw on. Second, they were sympathetic to
the stated goals of the Soviet system, and dangerously naïve about its
ruthlessness. Herta, moreover, would have followed Noel anywhere.

Arthur M. Schlesinger Jr. captured Hermann's innocence prior
to his imprisonment. Lecturing in Cleveland in 1948, Schlesinger
had a chance encounter with Hermann. "Henry Wallace had just announced his presidential candidacy," Schlesinger recalled. "I found
myself embroiled in an increasingly angry argument with the Fields
[Kate and Hermann]. Hermann was glowingly and naïvely enthusiastic about the 'people's democracies' of Eastern Europe and bitterly
critical of 'pro-fascists' in the State Department. Identifying communism with city planning and land reform, he was cheerfully oblivious
of any machinery of repression and terror. Hermann Field," he notes,
"was no Communist himself but a hopeful liberal whose Quakerism
would not permit him to see evil in people who, like Communists,
professed good."

There was one other equally strong motive for Hermann to temporarily abandon his wife and two young sons to cross the Iron Curtain
in search of his brother. He admired Noel, six years his senior, and
considered him a role model and father figure. "The moment in 1921,"
he recalled, "when I was eleven, when everything changed, with my
father's premature death, Noel became my mentor, determined that

my father's Quaker humanism should continue to guide us as a family. The image of Noel," he mused, "before we left [Switzerland] in 1922 addressing a student 'No More War' rally in the big hall of our villa overlooking the lake and the Alps. . . . Me, the kid brother, sitting on the fringes, but listening, absorbing, Noel emerging from Harvard as an authority on world disarmament." Thus, Hermann, the loyal and admiring younger sibling, made easy prey.

From the depths of despair in the dungeon outside Warsaw, which would be his home for five years, Hermann reflected on his fate. "Was this to be the end of my life as I had known it?" he wondered. "Were Kate and the boys in Cleveland—and America itself—gradually to become distant memories, part of a wonder that once was called life? . . . How blind of me not to have seen the writing on the wall. . . . Don't worry [he had told those who tried to warn him to be careful]. *What could anyone have against me?*"

It never occurred to Hermann Field that as an American probing around Soviet-occupied Eastern Europe in 1949, he had crossed into enemy territory, and that it was not personal. He was not only the enemy, he could be extremely useful. In party jargon, Hermann was referred to as a "useful idiot." Now, in the inhuman silence of his freezing cell, he had time to "search for a clue." "Images of my brother enveloped me," Hermann recalled. "Noel at the State Department . . . at the League of Nations. Noel in Paris the last time I had seen him, in 1947 . . . depressed." Hermann realized how little he actually knew the brother for whom he had given up his freedom.

# CHAPTER 19

# ERICA FALLS IN THE NET

*Old Joe Stalin certainly knows how to play for keeps.*

—Alger Hiss

HREE AMERICANS HAD vanished without a trace—and no one seemed to be doing anything on their behalf. To Erica, the last free member of Noel's immediate family, this was incomprehensible. Noel and Herta had rescued her in Spain, and then helped to raise her when her parents could not. That was not a debt Erica would leave unpaid.

A year after their disappearance, with only silence from Washington, Moscow, Prague, and Warsaw, Erica—the mother now of an infant and a toddler—decided to take matters into her own hands. She had a powerful contact in the German Communist Party, Leo Bauer, who had first pulled her into clandestine work during the war. She now wrote Bauer, asking for help in finding the Fields. Erica asked to meet Leo in Frankfurt, in the Western sector. Bauer wrote back saying he had interesting news regarding the Fields, but asked her to come to East Berlin. The State Department offered her security for her trip East. Washington, too, was interested in information about three missing American citizens. Erica turned them down. She could handle things better unencumbered by security. She would find out from Leo what happened to the Fields, and be back in France with Bob and her two babies in a couple of days.

Checking into the Hotel am Zoo off Berlin's Kurfürstendamm, Erica was suddenly gripped by anxiety. "I saw my bed in that room," she wrote, "and I had just one desire: to crawl in and pull the blanket over me." But she steeled herself. "Why should anything happen?" she asked. "Nothing ever happened before. . . . You go," she urged herself on, and took the subway to East Berlin, crossing from the Western into the Eastern sector at the Brandenburg Gate.

The once buzzing intersection was now quiet. Erica could barely recognize Berlin's prewar landmarks. The burned-out shell of the Reichstag, and the bare bones of the former great department stores, were still visible. But Cyrillic graffiti was scrawled on the walls of Hitler's foreign ministry, and red flags flew along Unter den Linden. A year after the Berlin Airlift, she read tension on the set features of the uniformed guards she passed. A tall, elegant woman, tanned from her Riviera vacation of a few days before, in a well-cut suit and high heels, was a remarkable sight in East Berlin in August 1950. Soldiers in Soviet-style uniforms along the Wilhelm Strasse appraised her with hard looks. There were no idle strollers on the streets, and the echo of her heels on the deserted pavement amplified Erica's anxiety. But she kept walking. She knew if she hesitated, she would turn back. She was determined and, as she later said, "my arrogant self."

When she reached Communist Party headquarters off Unter den Linden, she passed smoothly through several checkpoints. In the lobby, she was informed that Leo Bauer had already left for the weekend. Striding out to the sidewalk, she released all the tension she had contained since her arrival. She had done her best for the Fields—she could return to her family with a clear conscience. To celebrate, she bought a lemonade from a street vendor. That was when she heard steps behind her. She did not turn around because she knew. A hand on her shoulder signaled that she would not be leaving. "*Kriminal Polizei*," the voice said.

★

Thus began Erica Wallach's own journey through the Gulag Archipelago—for that is where she was eventually dispatched. But Erica was a radically different inmate from the man she had tried and failed to rescue. The same qualities that led her into the Soviets' trap— her cocksure self-confidence, her fierce pride, her disdain for authority, and her contempt for dogma—proved powerful survival weapons.

Station one on her journey was cell 7 in an old Nazi fortress—the notorious Schumannstrasse Prison. "Tell me," Erica taunted her first German interrogator, "are there always Russians present?" She knew this was a sensitive point, since Germany was supposed to be a sovercign statc. But from hcr first session, she noticed "a Russian sitting at the table . . . in civilian clothes, a well fed, well dressed, well groomed intellectual type, with gold-rimmed glasses. . . . He never said a word, carried on his conversations with the Germans in writing, on little scraps of paper, pushed back and forth."

Erica, like Noel, was asked to name all the German Communists she had known in Switzerland. She was flatly informed she had "turned them all into American agents"; she had given them "espionage instructions" when they became high officials in Germany. Her wry retort—"I never knew what a successful seducer I was"—did not amuse her interrogators. But she never lost her sharp wit or her sense of the ridiculous. "I shall soon develop a superiority complex," she mocked an agent she dubbed "Caraway." "Just think of it," she told him. "There were all these old [Communist] war horses, with years of training and experience, who went through hell and persecution. . . . And then one day, they meet a little nineteen-year-old girl, and she just waves her hand and the fighters for a better tomorrow follow her blindly!"

She was still their prisoner, and would be for five years, but Erica declared her freedom from the start. Unlike Noel Field—or the broken Bolsheviks in the Budapest courtroom—she could laugh at their ludicrous fantasies because she was not—and never had been—a believer. To Erica, the party was not holy; it was cruel and ridiculous.

By giving her jailers nicknames, she diminished their power over her. Of a particularly brutal Russian interrogator she dubbed "Ivan the Terrible," she said, "A scent of peaches surrounded him. Russian men love perfume . . . especially fruit perfume. . . . I knew from former experience how accustomed the Russians in East Germany had become to the submissive attitude of the Master Race toward their present rulers . . . but I was not going to give him the pleasure."

Gradually, Erica began to understand why she was their prisoner. "The spy Field," as Noel was called by her jailers, had "bought" her from her parents while he was spying in Spain. "It was not quite clear," she wrote, "whether I had already been a spy in my own right, at the tender age of fourteen, when I started to 'infiltrate' the International Brigades in Spain, or whether Field had schooled me for special services in Switzerland . . . and then made me his top agent. . . . It was up to me to choose."

Erica's deep longing for her children ultimately shattered her defiance. "All I had to say was that I had been a naughty American spy," she reasoned with herself, "and I was sorry, and wouldn't do it again and everyone would be happy. What difference," she concluded, "as long as I could get back to my children or at least hear that they were all right?"

"I was an American spy!" she blurted out at the end of a long night's session. But even this lie was not enough to end her ordeal. It was one thing to implicate herself. She still refused what they most wanted from her: to name her "coconspirators."

"Five days and five nights without one minute of sleep," she re-called, "without once stretching out for even a second, with cold cab-bage soup . . . and icy nights of mental and physical torture. . . . Every morning it was harder for me to walk back to my cell. The fifth morn-ing, I was no longer able to stand up straight, and it took me an endless time to creep down the halls, my back bent . . . edging along the walls."

For two and a half years she resisted. Two days before Christmas in 1952, Erica Glaser Wallach was tried before a military tribunal in Ber-lin's Lichtenberg Prison, in the prison chapel with portraits of Lenin and Stalin as the new icons. She had neither a defense counsel nor any witnesses. Her codefendant was Leo Bauer, the man who had lured her to East Berlin—now accused of the same crimes. In the final words granted the accused, Erica said she would not defend herself against absurd charges. "The Spanish experience," she told the tribunal, "was something so decent and so clean that . . . I would let no one, not even the Soviet Union, drag it into the mud. You have taken everything away from me: decency, fairness, and belief itself. Leave me at least one thing I can hold on to."

The tribunal was unimpressed. Erica and Leo were sentenced to death by shooting.

Only once she was marched back to her cell did the full force of her sentence hit her. "Death," she thought. "That meant not only the end of my life when I had barely begun it, it meant that I would never again see my children, my husband, my mother . . . never again taste all the beautiful things life has to offer. . . . Nothing ever again."

Now, awaiting death, she reviewed her improbable life of thirty-one years and twenty-nine homes, and considered the journey well worth it. "I had known the luxuries and carefree pleasures of semi-feudal life in Pomerania; privations, hardships, and strenuous work in Spain and the rewarding, gratifying feeling of dedication; I had tasted the exciting life of a student in Switzerland, poor and hungry most of the time, spending my little bit of money on art, music, books, philosophy, politics, love, friendship. And I had met the cruelty and the ordeal human beings go through in order to exist."

Erica thus faced death squarely, and did not buckle. Nor did she offer up names to save herself. She waited for her death sentence to be carried out. "I lived a full, almost complete life during this eternal year. Acquaintances were timidly struck up, friendships developed, even love affairs ensued—all through the thick prison wall. To keep my balance, I followed a rigorous schedule for the entire day. I had learned to judge the time almost perfectly, and I kept strictly to my hours, from the ten-minute exercises in the early morning, to writing poetry and books in my head in the evening. I made myself review all the knowledge I had ever acquired, and went back to school, with regular half-hour lessons each of French, English, Latin, history. . . . I composed thirty-six poems in prison, which later I was able to write down without hesitation. . . . I made menus for a week of freedom. . . . I composed songs for my children and I played chess." Behind the high walls of her Berlin prison, Erica declared her freedom. She even managed to connect with other prisoners, despite the walls separating them.

One of Erica's fellow inmates in the cellar where she awaited her death sentence, Curt Pohl, recalled their intense, life-saving interaction. "Can you still remember?" he wrote to her once he was free and living in West Germany. "Narrow corridor in the NKVD cellar, dim light, foul air, mysterious sounds, and a wall too thick to always understand the knocking signs? True, you already understood everything. . . . Nevertheless I managed to remember: 'Inform Robert, Hopefield, Warrenton, Virginia, USA.' I was almost happy being your neighbor, and forgot where I was. Indeed, I firmly believed I would soon be freed, and I wanted to do everything from my home-town for my courageous 'neighbor.' I thought of your two children who were deprived of their mother in such a cruel fashion. Perhaps you remember that I was very worried about my pregnant wife, and you knocked consoling words from your cell. That calmed me down for quite a while. . . . That house of cards was knocked down when I was, sentenced to fifteen years of hard labor. . . . How I missed your consoling knocking . . . but I was already in Vorkuta in the Capital Mine. . . . I secretly feared for your life since you always 'knocked' the notion of 'international case.' "

Meanwhile, Erica's husband waged a desperate search for his wife. A University of Virginia graduate whose taste in women had previously run to blond socialites, Robert Wallach never wavered in his five-year campaign to find and free Erica. "Once you've been married to Erica," Wallach told his sister Hope Porter, "you can never be married to anyone else." On August 29, a distraught Wallach wrote his mother-in-law, Marie Therese Glaser, "I haven't yet decided what to do as far as the children are concerned," he wrote. "They are all you and I have left now." The following month, on September 23, 1950, Wallach again wrote Mrs. Glaser, "If, as U.S. officials believe, Erica is still in Germany, the only thing that can be done is to arrange an escape. This, they say has been done more than once, and though it requires the payment of tremendous sums of money, they assured me that they would make every effort," he wrote Erica's mother, adding ominously, "If, however, they found that she is no longer in Germany, they think that there is little if any hope."

*

Cruelty and paranoia had their mirror image on the other side of the East-West divide. On February 9, 1950, Republican senator from Wisconsin Joseph R. McCarthy, speaking in Wheeling, West Virginia, launched a ghastly era. "While I cannot take the time to name all the men in the State Department," McCarthy told the Ohio County Women's Republican Club, "named as members of the Communist Party and members of a spy ring, I have here in my hand a list of 205 that were known to the Secretary of State as members of the Com-

munist Party, and who nevertheless are still working and shaping the
policy of the State Department."

Erica's distraught husband fell victim to the State Department's hysteria. Later that fall, while Erica was still held in Berlin's Schumannstrasse prison, American authorities gave Bob Wallach forty-eight
hours to leave Germany. "No reason whatsoever was given," Wallach
wrote his mother-in-law. "Nor am I told where this order originates.
My passport has been restricted to France and Switzerland, which im-
plies that it is perhaps the State Department which is behind everything. You can imagine what this means—having to leave Germany."
It meant giving up his quest to rescue his wife.

"What happened to you," Noel's younger sister, Elsie, an Urbana,
Illinois–based physician, wrote Wallach on November 24, "is incredible and abominable. . . . For a year and a half, Kate Field and I have
been trying to convince [the State Department] that none of the
Fields disappeared *voluntarily.* I thought we had finally been listened
to, but apparently not. . . . Every time I go to Washington there are
fewer and fewer of my former friends . . . because of this infernal red
hysteria."

On the first anniversary of Erica's disappearance, her husband, back
in Virginia, wrote her mother, "It is now almost a year since our Erica
vanished—the loss, temporary though it may be, becomes more painful as time goes on. It is only the children that keep me back, even
though I realize that any personal efforts of my own would be futile."

Wallach closes with a powerful reminder of just how high the cost to
the Field family Noel's disastrous life choices had become. "Elsie Field
was here again last week," he wrote. "She has given up her doctor's practice, and travels the country seeing influential people, and trying to do
what she can to persuade the State Department to move vigorously."

A year later Elsie Field—now working full-time on her brothers'
cases—again wrote Wallach. "Kate [Field] and I have been getting absolutely nowhere. After submitting our reports and pleas to [George]

Kennan [a Soviet specialist at the State Department] and getting assurances that Kennan would explore the situation for possible approaches to the Soviet Union, the State Department let us know that Kennan did not consider it in the best interest of this country or our people to open up the subject in Moscow. And now he got himself kicked out [in September 1952, Kennan was declared persona non grata, five months after he arrived as ambassador, for comparing the Soviets to the Nazis.]" Elsie closed on a note of despair; "The Department has told me that it can make no further approaches to any other country unless we come up with some new evidence; and this we are unable to do."

Nonetheless, Bob Wallach continued to pressure the State Department. "I went to the State Department," he wrote Mrs. Glaser on November 20, 1952, "and made another request that they at least ask the Russian authorities for information. I believe that when the Republicans take over the Government, there is at least a chance that they will do this. The Democrats are of course terrified of doing anything for anybody connected to the CP."

But by late 1952, Erica was no longer in Berlin. Shipped to Moscow for execution, she was held in a "death cell" for six months. Then, on March 5, 1953: the miracle. The Little Father of the People breathed his last. Though Stalin's death did not result in the immediate end of the Gulag Archipelago, executions became more rare, and the inmates' lives somewhat less brutal. Instead of being shot by a firing squad, Erica was dispatched to the most punishing of all the stations of the Gulag. Reserved for the toughest criminals, Vorkuta, north of the Arctic Circle, was where Erica Wallach discovered her real strength.

Behind three rows of barbed wire, under the relentless gaze of soldiers from four watchtowers, in the biting frost of the Arctic winter, Erica rarely saw the sun. With her fellow convicts, she laid railroad ties in subzero temperatures. Somehow, she more than merely survived this punishing regimen; she was strengthened and humanized by it. Her relationships with her fellow inmates—and even her guards—

were based on an honesty unimaginable to those outside the barbed wire in the Soviet Union. There is a stunning contrast between the grotesque lies she and Noel and hundreds of thousands of other Soviet prisoners were forced to concoct as "confessions" and Erica's blunt yet human interactions in the frigid Vorkuta bunkhouses.

In a vodka-fueled outburst, one of Erica's guards recklessly confessed how much he hated his job, and said he, not Erica, was the real prisoner. "In a wave of affection," Erica recalled, "I drew off my gloves and took his head in both my hands. . . . 'Misha,' I said in my limited Russian, 'you are a good man. . . . You must not do anything foolish. You are not the only one whose eyes have been opened here. Things are different now. A lot has changed already, and you can speed the process." The irony of the inmate trying to lift the guard's spirits is rich.

Real change arrived at a glacial pace to the labor camp. At the end of 1953, Erica was finally allowed to write her family for the first time. "Dear Bob," she wrote on a postcard addressed from Vorkuta Barracks, "So happy to be able to write for Xmas. I am healthy and well (have gotten fat). Honestly, you need not worry. Only a terrible longing for you all. Please write detailed news about yourself, the children and mother. . . . I want her to know how sorry I am for having caused her such suffering. I do hope I'll soon get home and be able to make good a little bit. I have been thinking continuously about my darling children. Please send pictures of all of you. . . . Can't wait to hear from you. Please hurry and I'll hurry to get home."

For her mother, this first sign that her daughter was alive was a moment of pure joy. "I recognize my child very well in this letter," she wrote Bob on April 23, 1954, "the sweet, affectionate little girl she was before Hitler ruined our home. . . . She never had a teenager's carefree youth," Erica's mother noted, adding bitterly, "In Switzerland, she was under Noel's influence." But, she warned Bob, "Be prepared for a changed woman. The years of being treated as a criminal, mistrusted by people . . . of course she longs for love and understanding. We must not fail her. . . . If only I could take her in my arms. I know what it means to lose everything in life . . . Erica is a broken woman."

Her mother underestimated her daughter. Erica was miraculously unbroken. She was buoyed by her first letter from her family and—best of all—a photograph. "The photograph showed two children standing in front of a fireplace, a little boy of four, and a six-year-old girl," she said. "Both were very blond, both looked happy and healthy. Both were complete strangers to me."

Her release, however, did not come. Her mother continued to send heartbreaking pleas for help to everyone, from the members of the Soviet Politburo to the Archbishop of Canterbury. "I appeal to you to grant the release of my daughter," Therese Glaser wrote in 1954, "the only surviving member of my family. . . . We were formerly refugees from Nazi oppression. . . . I lost my only son, killed in action while serving as a Captain in the last British air battle in April 1945. My husband died three years later. My daughter Erica is all that is left to me." The Archbishop's secretary sent a polite form letter expressing His Lordship's regret.

\*

At last, in September 1955, Erica was shipped to Moscow, to the notorious Lubyanka Prison, to begin her "rehabilitation." The KGB officer charged with her case listed all the spurious charges for which she had been sentenced to death, and asked her to plead guilty or innocent. Erica, ever straightforward, pleaded innocent to all charges except one: "Propaganda and Agitation against the Soviet Union." "I criticized the Soviet Union," Erica bluntly admitted. "Well, then," Agent Gorbunov replied, "tell me what you don't like about our country." "The lack of freedom to say, write, paint, and compose," she answered. "I do not like that." Give examples, he said. "There are so many, I can't remember them all. . . ." Erica cited Shostakovich and Picasso as two great artists vilified by the Soviet Union. How good it felt to speak plainly to power that seemed actually to listen.

Gorbunov had one other piece of business to take up with the inmate: a letter from Noel Field, recently freed in Budapest.

"Dear Kid," Field wrote, "You are always in our thoughts and hearts. Please let us hear from you. Hoping to see you soon. Noel and Herta."

As always, Noel had more than one agenda in mind. "It is more than likely," Field wrote his Hungarian minder, Comrade Toth, "that Erica is being torn by conflicting loyalties and that this will be exploited in the interest of the 'Cold War' advocates. We have no idea what Erica's present outlook is, but if there is any chance of influencing her in a positive direction, we should like to contribute toward this aim, especially since we fear that the other members of her family will drag her in the opposite direction."

The idea that the man who was the cause of her five-year Soviet captivity now wanted to keep her there is almost beyond belief. When told that Noel Field was living in Hungary, and offered her a home there, Erica reacted sharply. "Hungary!" she exclaimed, "What in God's name is he doing there?" "I was not only surprised," she wrote, "I was upset."

"Where do you want to go, then?" Gorbunov asked. "The United States," she answered, "where my family is."

"All that is left for me to do then," the KGB officer said, "is to apologize. In the name of the Soviet Government, I have to ask you to accept our honest apologies. . . . We took five years of your life and there is no way to give them back to you." Erica accepted his apology, but turned down Gorbunov's offer of monetary compensation.

She did ask for one thing. "After I was sentenced, they took all my belongings," she told Gorbunov, "including my wedding ring. I want the ring back." The ring, however, was lost. Erica would not relent. She was not leaving without her wedding ring. "I waited around for three weeks . . . I would ask them every day about it. Finally," she said, "one day, they found it." She began her homeward journey the following day.

Alger Hiss—who, like his friend Noel Field, betrayed his country in search of a Communist utopia—is shown with head bent just behind a haggard and ailing President Franklin Delano Roosevelt at Yalta. Field, like Hiss, began as an idealist and ended up serving a brutal system.

Below, FDR's successor, President Harry S. Truman, clasps Hiss's hand, oblivious that it is the hand of a traitor.

3

Noel Field (far right), with his mother and three siblings, set off
for America from Switzerland in 1921.

Fresh out of Harvard, Field landed his dream job as a Foreign Service officer assigned to the State Department's Western European division in 1926. He was launched on a brilliant career, but within a few years he would be recruited by Moscow's agents.

Already a Soviet spy, Field (seated, back row) attended the 1935 London Disarmament Conference and passed classified documents to the Soviets. His colleagues did not suspect the well-mannered, well-bred Noel Field of serving Moscow.

6

During HUAC hearings in 1948, Hiss calmly denied he was a spy. Icily composed throughout, Hiss was nonetheless convicted of perjury, the statute of limitations for spying having expired.

Field and Hiss stayed in touch throughout their lives, before and after prison. This letter—which calls ex-spy Whittaker Chambers "unbalanced and given to hallucinations"—was found in the Hungarian Secret Police archives in Budapest.

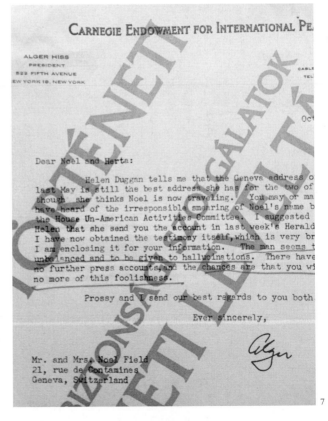

CARNEGIE ENDOWMENT FOR INTERNATIONAL PE.

ALGER HISS
PRESIDENT
522 FIFTH AVENUE
EW YORK 18, NEW YORK

Oct

Dear Noel and Herta:

Helen Duggan tells me that the Geneva address o last May is still the best address she has for the two of though she thinks Noel is now traveling. You may or ma have heard of the irresponsible smearing of Noel's name b the House Un-American Activities Committee. I suggested Helen that she send you the account in last week's Herald I have now obtained the testimony itself, which is very br I am enclosing it for your information. The man seems t unbalanced and to be given to hallucinations. There have no further press accounts, and the chances are that you wi no more of this foolishness.

Prossy and I send our best regards to you both.

Ever sincerely,

Alger

Mr. and Mrs. Noel Field
21, rue de Contamines
Geneva, Switzerland

7

Field left the State Department to work for the League of Nations. Dispatched to civil war–torn Spain in 1938, he was charged with helping refugees, such as those shown here, to flee Franco's savage onslaught. In Spain, Field befriended many future Communist leaders.

9

With desperate refugees fleeing the Fascists by the thousands and the US government tightening its quotas on immigrants, American humanitarians formed the Unitarian Service Committee to rescue those it could. Field and his wife, Herta, shown here at an internment camp at the base of the Pyrenees in Rivesaltes, focused almost entirely on saving Communists and sending them back to Eastern and Central Europe to start planning postwar satellite states.

Field hired Jo Tempi, a Berlin-born Stalinist, as his aide in 1940. Their love affair lasted for five years and wreaked havoc in his marriage and later with the USC— which did not realize Tempi and Field had turned the Boston-based charity into a Communist rescue organization.

10

11

Whittaker Chambers named Hiss and Field as spies, ending Noel Field's career as a Soviet agent and sending him in panicked search for refuge in the Eastern Bloc. Instead of providing sanctuary, Stalin ordered his faithful acolyte arrested, tortured, and imprisoned for five years.

At first, few believed Chambers's accusations against the popular Hiss and the proper Field. One who did was the junior California congressman Richard M. Nixon, shown here examining the now famous "Pumpkin Papers": microfilm of classified documents stolen by Hiss and hidden by Chambers in a pumpkin on his Maryland farm. The future president (pictured here with Robert Striping, HUAC's chief investigator) doggedly pursued Hiss and kept the investigation alive.

12

No one paid a higher price in the search for the illusory utopia promised by Communism than Larry Duggan. "My best, my only friend," Noel Field called Duggan, shown here receiving last rites on a New York City sidewalk on December 21, 1948. Duggan, age forty-three, plunged to his death shortly after he was exposed by HUAC investigators as a member of Hiss, Chambers, and Field's Washington cell.

14

This house of horrors was the first stop on Field's journey as a key witness in a new wave of Stalinist show trials. Abducted from his Prague hotel, he was bound, blindfolded, and driven to this secret interrogation house in Budapest in 1949. Here, Moscow's agents tortured him into confessing that he was actually an American spy, not a Soviet agent. Unbeknownst to Field, his wife was also a prisoner here, and at times could hear her husband's late-night torment.

Having beaten a fake confession from Noel Field, the Kremlin raised the curtain on the show trial of Hungarian foreign minister Laszlo Rajk, accused of being Field's agent in the CIA. Seven defendants—squeezed between their secret police guards—were charged as "Fieldists." Though Field never appeared, his name was frequently invoked as the spy at the center of Washington's anti-Stalin plot. My parents, though not shown, were in the Budapest courtroom covering the trial for American wire services.

15

16

Freed from Stalinist captivity in June 1956 was the widow of the executed "Fieldist" Laszlo Rajk, shown here with her son, Laszlo Jr. Julia Rajk called her former jailers "criminals and murderers who should be punished." Two weeks after this ceremony marking the reburial of her husband, revolution erupted in Hungary. Noel Field, even after torture and prison, remained a true believer. He called it a "counterrevolution."

A notorious Polish secret police agent, Josef Swiatlo brutally interrogated both Field brothers, and then, five years later, when the Fields were given up for dead, defected to Washington. Here, the secret police agent reveals that Noel, Herta, and Hermann are still alive in Soviet prisons. With a new identity, shrouded by the FBI, Swiatlo disappeared forever under the Federal Witness Protection Program.

Though released from jail, Noel Field was never really free. As these documents in the Budapest Secret Police files attest, his every letter was opened and translated from English to Hungarian by scores of agents whose job was to keep him under tight surveillance. He never returned to America.

Budapest, 1955 december 23.

Kedves Erzsi:

Mellékelek két levelet, melyekhez nem szükséges magyarázat, hogy Maga és az elvtársak elolvassák, Herta és én nagyon szokat elküldeni, de nem akarjuk azt az elvtárak engedélye ellenére. Mi ugy érezzük ugyanis, hogy az időtáj annyira vagyuk a kapcsolatot egyik másik elvtárssal azok közül, akik nak idején a legszorosabb kapcsolatban voltunk. Ugy érezzük karácsonyi időszak a legjobb jó alkalom erre, és a legsikali mély Maria Weiterer, minthogy Paul Berz már nincs életben. "Maria" legközelebbi barátunk volt és abban az időben részt folithommasszar" féle. Másrészről mi Professzor Rompe-t vá közvetítőnek, miután ő biztosan tud Maa hollétéről és miután gokból tudjuk, hogy ez NDK-ban nagy hírnévnek örvend.

Részben a következők inditották el határozásunkatt Néhány lött olvastuk a Neues Deutschland-ban Németország Szocialista Pártjának hivatalos lapjában, hogy Otto Niebergall nem régen nevében beszédet tartott a Saar vidéken, nyolc évi távollét után a cikk legfontosabb részét Saarbrückenből: "Itt Burbac munkásnegyedben beszélt vasárnap este Otto Niebergall. Nyolc tották meg a Saar KP alapító tagjának, hogy látná a Saar vid re tegye. 1947-ben a Szeparatisták kiutasították. Mos ezer napestén eljöttek a munkások, hogy megszorítsák Otto Niebergall de biztosítsák öt barátságukról." . cikket igen feltünöen 2. oldalon nagy cimmel: "Otto Niebergall-al Burbach-ban." Sa különtudósítónktól M.Grey-től. Csak emlékeztetnem kell Magít Niebergall a párizsi Szabad Németország szervezet elnöke vol Weitererrel együtt a "Partvezetőség tenja volt Franciaorszá már is megérti a cikk jelentőségét. Niebergall rehabilitálták jelenti, hogy Miát is rehabilitálták.

Hozzá kell tennem, hogy Tonia ujra boldogan dolgozik régi mint nem rég hallottuk; egy közös barátunkon keresztül róla gyerekéről kaptunk képet. A cimet azonban még nem kaptuk meg

Szerettem volna eztek a legészvetárdést közvetlenül Magá al i, azonban tudva, hogy milyen elfoglalt, azt gondoltam, hog aritok meg, ha irok. De nagyon kérem tegye lehetővé, hogy egymást miniēlőbb. Nagyon hiányzik. Nagyon jó lenne, ha s velet ek mindi előbb "tisztáznd", hogy ne sokkal érjenek oda tán. Ugy gondolom, hogy ajánlva adom fel öket légipostán.

Szeretettel üdvözlöm
Noel

.I. Miének szóló levelet ujra lemásolom, minthogy a második életlanül, forditva gépeltem.

Dear Noel and Herta:

Our christmas letter of this year, if
Kate and I felt we could bring ourselves
at least. All we wanted was to cre l away
wounds like injured animals. And so we di
unchanged quiet. And Alan and Hugh, feel
thing, joined us and we had a lovely fiv
and her 2 year old baby -not his-). I su
as things stand now , we would find ourse
a year and a half ago. So much for that -

May

Dear brother:

Just a short note to bring you up to dat

June 17 evening we fly to London. June 9
rael. June 30 I fly from Israel to Athen
mornin  from Athens to Vienna where I me
from London, and we continue at 4.45 to
at 5.30 (must be a change of time since
more than 15 minutes to Budapest)  sorry
It's actually 45 minutes which I guess i
We continue July 11 at 11.30 to Warsaw,
Then on the 15th we fly via Brussels to
take possession of a Volkswagen 1500 3 V

20

Hermann Field, who went looking for his vanished brother and was himself jailed by the Soviets, was suddenly freed five years later, in late 1954, following Swiatlo's astonishing revelations. Here, Hermann is reunited with his wife, Kate, and sons Hugh and Alan at London's Victoria Station.

The fourth member of Noel Field's family to be kidnapped by the Kremlin, his foster daughter, Erica Glaser Wallach, was freed in October 1955. The bouquet she holds is from the CIA, which was not yet prepared to let her rejoin her American husband and children. It took Erica almost two years to win that struggle.

22

Erica found domestic happiness in the Virginia countryside, after the most turbulent twentieth-century life imaginable, with husband Robert Wallach, who had waged a heroic campaign to free her from Soviet custody.

23

24

Together since age nine, Noel and Herta are shown in a flatteringly touched-up photograph taken in the late sixties in Budapest. Though they look like an ordinary elderly couple, their private correspondence and surveillance records reveal the depth of the torment they suffered at the hands of those they loyally served. Used and abused by the Communist Party and by Josef Stalin, the man they most admired, they never recanted their faith.

25

In Budapest in the midsixties, the two brothers were briefly reunited, and
Noel met his niece, Alison, born after Hermann was freed. They never
spoke of their prison experiences. The subject was too fraught for Noel,
who would spend the rest of his life in Budapest.

# CHAPTER 20

# THE PRISONS OPEN

*Both of us sought to forget the existence—the very names—*
*of those we loved.*

—Noel Field, letter to Erica

AROUND THE TIME Erica received the photograph of her children, Noel—still in custody—began a hunger strike. During four years as an inmate in various Budapest maximum-security prisons, he had never been charged with a crime, never faced a judge or jury. Nor did the Soviets ever intend to free him. Field—a ghostly shell of a man, an American—was too grave an indictment of the Soviet Union to expose to the world. Since the Soviets kept denying he was in their custody, Noel was kept in solitary confinement with only his Hungarian guards as his twice-daily sullen—and at times brutal—companions. Having served his purpose, Field was now a useless encumbrance.

On June 20, 1954, the despairing prisoner handed his guard a letter that contains the almost unbearable depth of Field's private agony—as well as his extraordinary love of Herta. "After long personal struggle," he addressed his interrogator, Major Kretschmer, "I have decided to turn to you with a question, I decided years ago not to ask, partly out of fear that I would not be told the truth, partly out of fear of hearing the truth. . . . I am putting this in writing to avoid a mutually uncomfortable situation, and also because I don't want to see the answer on your face. So, for that reason I ask that you also put the answer in writing, which I can read when I am alone. The question: Is my wife alive or not? . . . Just so you understand the significance of this question, I add my autobiography's most significant fact—something I barely touched on in my confession: that since age nine . . . I have loved one and the same woman."

He had also begun a hunger strike. To stop him, his Hungarian captors made a deal with Noel: resume eating and we will review your case. "Write to the Soviet authorities," he was told, "Maybe you'll get a new hearing." So Noel did. During the spring of 1954, Noel wrote a sixty-five-page letter addressed to the Central Committee of the Soviet Communist Party. Without a trace of anger for the terrible wrongs he had suffered, drenched in wretched humility, the letter makes painful reading. Field still grovels before authority, still pleads to be let into the magic circle of the party that degraded and brutalized him.

"Honored Comrades!" he addresses the people who came within a breath of destroying him, his wife, and his family, "I am not asking for my freedom," he assures them. "My future life has no sense or meaning—it is broken—and at age fifty it holds no real appeal for me." Field then tells his "honored Comrades" that his case cannot be honestly aired because "imperialists and warmongers" would only exploit it for their own purposes. Thus, he humbly asks for the party to allow him and his old comrades [for he is unaware of their fate] to return to the good graces of the party, and live as good Communists. Field outlines how loyally he has served the party, and accepts total blame for his punishment. He faults himself for lack of "Communist character" to withstand torture. Everything is his fault. "We are

Communists," he declares, "not traitors." He calls himself a "pathological coward" but one who never betrayed the cause. Everything he ever did, from working in the State Department, to his humanitarian work rescuing refugees, was for a single cause: the party. Perhaps the most bizarre part of the letter is that Field declares himself a loyal American.

Finally, Field requests a new investigation of his case—not for himself, but for the party's own good. This, he tells his Soviet comrades, would "fulfill my final, most sacred duty." No faith could ask for a deeper submission.

Field's reprieve came not from Moscow, but from Washington. On September 28, 1954, the man who supervised the arrest and torture of Noel and Hermann Field appeared in a State Department auditorium and faced the world media. In a CIA-organized news conference, Josef Swiatlo, reviled Polish secret police agent, awkward in his ill-fitting new suit, stunned the press with his announcement. The Field family was alive, Swiatlo said. Unaccustomed to the harsh lights now aimed at him, the former torturer admitted that the charges against the Fields were fake, and that their imprisonment was a travesty of justice. He spoke with authority, Swiatlo assured the astonished reporters, because he had interrogated the Field brothers.

Josef Swiatlo's own escape from the East could have been lifted from the pages of a John le Carré thriller. While on a West Berlin shopping trip the prior December, Swiatlo slipped away from his Polish delegation and turned up at the American embassy in Berlin. He requested, and was granted, political asylum in the United States. An extremely high-value defector, Swiatlo had been confined to a CIA safe house outside Washington for nine months of debriefing prior to his press conference.

Even as Swiatlo related details of the Fields' incarcerations, the State Department filed notes of protest to Budapest, Warsaw, and Moscow, demanding the immediate release of Noel, Herta, Hermann, and Erica.

As reporters rushed to file their stories, Swiatlo, under heavy guard, was quietly whisked out of the State Department. Under a new identity as part of a witness protection program, he disappeared forever.

Swiatlo's announcement, and the Radio Free Europe broadcasts to the Soviet empire that accompanied it, roiled the already choppy waters of post-Stalin Eastern Europe. In Budapest, American ambassador Christian Ravndal delivered a note to the Foreign Ministry, demanding to see Noel and Herta Field. At the Fő Utca maximum-security prison, a redbrick fortress on the Buda side of the Danube, a startled Noel was rushed from his cell, shaved, and showered. "I am led to a large office," Noel recalled. "I am solemnly told that I am free. My mind does not take it in. 'My wife, where is she?' I manage to stammer. 'You shall see her in a few minutes.' Tears now, the first in years. In a little while the door opens and in its frame stands she who has been part of my life since the age of nine."

Two shell-shocked survivors, Herta and Noel, faced mirror images of each other, a gaunt, gray-haired, ghostly pale couple who had been robbed of middle age, relieved now that they were both alive, their devotion to each other and to their faith intact. "Have you remained true?" Noel asked his wife. "Yes," she answered, "never for one moment have I doubted." "Nor I," Noel answered. Then, turning to the guards, he asked, "Is Stalin still alive?" "No," he was told. "He died more than a year ago." The Fields were shaken by sobs.  .

When told of Noel's first words to Herta, "Have you remained true [to our cause]?" Erica was shocked. "This is not the man I knew," she said. "Not a word about the lives ruined? Those killed or forced into suicide? This is just a Party man. The human being has disappeared."

On October 28, 1954, Noel and Herta Field walked out of the Fő Utca Prison. But they were not free.

"They must guarantee their loyalty to the Hungarian Republic," read a memo from the minister of the interior, László Piros, "and that after their release they will make such a declaration in front of journalists and condemn the American government's policy of war and announce their desire to settle in Hungary. They must guarantee that they won't seek any relationship with the American or other capitalist country's embassies."

★

Hermann, also suddenly freed after his five-year ordeal in a Warsaw dungeon, wanted only to be reunited with Kate and the sons he barely knew. Not for a minute did he wish that reunion to take place in the country that had imprisoned him without ever charging him with any crime. "I first got the news [of Noel's release] over the radio," Hermann recalled. "Hungary had released Noel and Herta. Had this event been timed to upset my plans once more? Instead of relief and joy," he said, "I felt a kind of resentment. . . . [But] no—nothing would delay my departure [from Warsaw] at this late point, not even Noel's being freed, not even *his need for me.*"

Prison freed Hermann of his illusions about a system that promised everything and delivered jail, torture, and total control over its population. His older brother's power over him would take longer to shed.

# CHAPTER 21

# STILL NOT FREE

*I met many people in the camp who managed to combine a shrewd sense of what was going on in the country . . . with a religious cult of Stalin.*

—Eugenia Ginzburg

W AS IT A final shot of cruelty on the part of the Hungarian authorities that Noel and Herta's first night of freedom should be spent in the same hilltop villa where they were tortured five years earlier? This time, however, the Fields were provided a comfortable apartment and—without blackout curtains and blindfolds—a spectacular panorama of the Danube below. For the first time, the Fields appraised the city where they had spent the past five and half years. They had seen nothing of this exotic place, with its amalgam of Romanesque, Gothic, and Baroque architectural styles—all blended into a wholly different esthetic called Magyar.

As the secret police records reveal, however, they were far from free. Also clear is that in the minutely calibrated Cold War chess game, with two Western prizes at stake, Moscow had an unbeatable advantage. The Kremlin was privy to the Fields' most "private" thoughts.

The transcripts of their taped conversations capture every sigh and moan as the sleepless couple compare prison experiences.

"You don't want to go home," Herta whispers to her husband on October 29, 1954. (Did they perhaps suspect they were being recorded? The listeners express frustration at the Fields' low voices and their nearly incomprehensible blend of English and German.) "And neither do I." "It would make no sense," Noel replies. "I read Stalin's collected speeches," Herta tells her husband. "Do you think it's possible for a great hero to die?" she asks. They exchange stories of humane jailers and cruel ones. Noel speaks of the great changes since 1949, when a hunger strike would have only earned him extra beatings, instead of a chance at "rehabilitation." On November 12, the recorder picks up Herta's enthusiastic "It always gives me such a thrill," she tells Noel, "when they call me 'Comrade'!" She seems the stronger of the two now, and her role is to prop him up. "I have no future," Noel moans. "My life is over." "How can you say such a thing?" Herta rebukes her husband. "That we have no future? That is not in my vocabulary!"

Late at night, holding each other, the microphone records the Fields' incoherent sobs as they recall their worst moments of captivity. "Those tortures," Noel whispers, "those terrible tortures." "Oh, I know," his wife says, comforting him. "But Noel," she said, "somehow you have to find the will to live." After a lifetime by his side, she knows how to rouse Noel from the depths of despair. "You cannot die here," she declares. "What do you think the Western press would do with that? They are all our enemies." Stay alive for the cause that nearly killed us both, is her bizarre message. Herta, whose adoration and admiration of Noel since early childhood knew no bounds, had always expected great things to come his way. Now she bitterly recalled their pre-jail humiliation, and blamed America for the time when, as penniless fugitives, they lived in fear of an FBI subpoena. After five years in a Communist prison, she had no desire to face American justice. Listening to these late-night conversations, the Hungarian authorities and their Moscow minders hatched their plan.

Soon, the Fields were moved to a villa of their own. Perched on a steep hill, 38 Meredek Utca was the ideal location for a pair of soon-to-be defectors in whom Moscow and Budapest still had little confidence. There was little chance of a random encounter on Meredek Utca. Even today it is eerily quiet, without shops, restaurants, or street life. An owl's hoot and a dog's distant bark are all that break the perfect stillness of midday. The hum of the sprawling metropolis in the distance is muffled. Behind a high iron gate, the Fields' modernistic house is a graceless hulk of poured concrete. A full complement of secret police agents posing as "staff" moved in with the Fields. Even during Noel and Herta's frequent stays in various hospitals, they were taped, their telephone bugged.

A top secret internal memorandum, addressed to Minister of the Interior László Piros and dated November 1, 1954, outlines just how little actual freedom the newly freed Fields enjoyed:

> *We have fulfilled the following tasks:*
>
> *Villa on Szabadsag* [Freedom!] *Hill with a garden, which will ensure the couple can stroll unseen and isolated from the outside world.*
>
> *The following team will supervise them: Rudolf Nagy—whose cover will be that he is there to help with household chores, errands. etc.*
>
> *We will also place hidden guards on the Villa premises. The guards are forbidden from communicating with the couple.*
>
> *Dr. Laszlo Bence* [an AVO officer] *will supervise their health.*
>
> *For now, we advise good cooking, to be provided by the Comrade Janitor's wife, who will also clean.*
>
> *Regarding reading matter: all languages, but only those available in the East Bloc.*
>
> *No permission for radio or press for now.*

*Record player and records are all right.*

*Captain Tibor Metzler, who speaks perfect German, is a good conversationalist, and was head of intelligence in Vienna, should handle the couple's political indoctrination.*

*Comrade Captain Mrs. Molnar, age 32, will be assigned to Mrs. Field.*

*Captain Metzler and Captain Molnar are to spend 3–4 hours a day with the Fields.*

*Their assignment: to assure the couple's loyalty, to assure that they express criticism of the US warmongering to journalists—which is why they wish to live in Hungary.*

*To assure that the couple do not contact any capitalist Embassies, or do anything to harm the interest of the People's Republic* [of Hungary].

*To assure that they will agree to spend at least 1–2 years here.*

*Tell them that their case is "still under review."*

Noel's jailers were able to dictate the precise terms of his "freedom" because he was still the penitent, seeking the high church's blessing and forgiveness. Noel's single-minded goal was Soviet certification of his innocence of the fake charge that he was a CIA agent.

No outpouring of emotion or compassion from fellow victims of Stalinist injustice greeted Noel and Herta in Budapest or elsewhere. The Fields never denounced the brutal regime whose victims they had been, nor condemned the crimes committed in Stalin's name. Nor was their return to "freedom" celebrated by joyous reunions with loving relatives and friends. Only one American came to call on them: Ambassador Christian M. Ravndal. Ravndal, a handsome and sociable diplomat, arrived at Meredek Utca with a thick bundle of back issues of the *New York Times* and a warm welcome to the Fields. Over tea and cookies, the three Americans chatted amiably about common friends in the State Department. Noel expressed dismay at Joe McCarthy's harassment of two colleagues, Owen Lattimore and John Carter Vincent. He was silent regarding his own—and his wife's, his brother's, and his foster daughter's—treatment by the Soviets.

On Christmas Eve in 1954, a curt Hungarian government press release announced that Noel and Herta Field had requested political asylum in the country that had jailed them on false charges. At a time when thousands were desperately trying to escape the giant prison of the Soviet empire, the announcement may well have been unprecedented. In the game of Cold War chess, Moscow achieved checkmate.

Now, Ambassador Ravndal requested a second meeting with the Fields. For this visit, the AVO instructed Noel to be "polite, but cooler" than the last time. Field performed according to instructions, and stated that his asylum request was genuine and made of his own free will. A formal note from Ambassador Ravndal immediately confirmed the exchange and its consequences.

"I am authorized to inform you," Ravndal wrote,

> that in view of your voluntary request for political asylum in Hungary, your repudiation of the United States, your sympathy with and intention to work actively for Communist objectives, including those directed against the United States Government, all responsibility of the United States to assist and protect you has ceased. In these circumstances the United States can take no further responsibility for your well-being or for your safe return to the United States.
>
> I am further authorized to inform you that while your request for asylum in Hungary is not of itself a hostile act, the coupling of this request with your indicated desire to render service to a foreign state and to work against the interests of the United States is wholly inconsistent with American citizenship. You are advised that you may formalize this renunciation of American allegiance by renouncing your American citizenship before an American

diplomatic or consular officer. . . . *I must further inform you that you will be held accountable at such time as you may again come into United States jurisdiction for all treasonable acts which you have committed while you remain American citizens.*

Field, typically, was shocked by the predictable reaction he provoked. "Neither I nor my wife," he wrote Ravndal on February 16, 1955, "willingly renounce our American citizenship. Even if we should be deprived of our formal citizenship . . . we should not recognize such unilateral action, and should continue to regard ourselves as Americans. . . . In our conversation to which you refer, I drew a clear distinction between the United States and the present policy of its government. It is this policy which I repudiate, and not the United States. . . . It is my intention," Field closes, with the clearest expression of just how far removed he was from reality, "to work for international peace, an activity which, if it should clash with the 'interests' of the United States Government is certainly not directed against the interests of the American people."

Field was equally unprepared for the world's reaction to his defection. "To my utter amazement," he wrote on January 17, 1955, "I have found my name on the front page of some newspaper almost every month, and the end is evidently not in sight by a long shot," he wrote. "I had somehow imagined that little Noel and little Herta had long ago been forgotten." This letter was addressed to one of the few people with whom Noel allowed himself a degree of candor: Monica Felton, a British Communist, dispatched by Moscow to Budapest to shepherd Field's transition to "freedom." "You told me I had been mentioned in the Rajk and Slansky trials," he wrote Monica. "I had no idea of the extent to which my name had been bandied about not only in *the enemy* [i.e., Western] *press, but in our own.*"

Field's interaction with Felton offers a rare glimpse into his generally obscured hard core. Together, they plot how to pull Hermann back into the camp from which he was just liberated. Even after paying the highest price for Noel's treachery, his family is still insignificant compared to the party's need for a major propaganda score. "The fact that Hermann is not planning to return to America," Noel wrote Felton, "is in itself a positive fact. . . . I am sure from all I've heard that there can be no question of *separation* [from his wife!]. On the other hand, it would be worse than useless if Kate went to Warsaw [this at a time when the recently reunited Kate, Hermann, and their sons were about to sail for Boston] and then found after sometime that Kate couldn't stick it out [in Warsaw]. . . . The main thing to aim for in Hermann's case: continued silence [about his prison experience] and a *non-return to America*. . . . After all, the political significance of the actions of the two brothers would still be positive and would supplement each other: both refuse to make negative propaganda [about their imprisonment], both *refuse to go home.*"

Noel's letters to his siblings are uniformly cheerful accounts of his new life. "Herta and I love the place we're in now, and, as we overcome the language barrier, this feeling is likely to increase," he wrote to Hermann on March 11, 1955. "We've been going to the opera on the average once a fortnight. Last Friday, for instance, it was a glorious performance of Mozart's *Don Juan*. We've been to more operas this winter than in ten years of our pre '49 life. Not to speak of the movies. There are some swell films being produced here of late, some of which, I hope, will also find their way abroad." The move to Budapest, Noel seems to imply, was based on its rich cultural offerings.

Weeks passed, and though reports of the Fields' release were front-page news worldwide, Noel had yet to face a single journalist—an event both the Hungarians and their prize feared and were determined to avoid. As a substitute for a personal appearance, a committee of the Ministry of the Interior was dispatched to work with Noel on a press release. The Ministry was not pleased with Noel's draft:

1.  *His statement has to be more decisive, more concrete, more to the point.*
2.  *He should condemn the politics of the United States more sharply.*
3.  *The condemnation of Allen Dulles, who carries on with his dangerous politics should be supported by concrete evidence.*
4.  *The Marxist phraseology, however, should be avoided.*

In other words, Field's statement cannot sound like what it is: dictated by Communist officials. Field was of higher propaganda value as a "progressive American" than as a hard-core Stalinist.

Field, wrote Mrs. Ferenc Kuhari, an AVO major serving as his "secretary," "is trying to *avoid his duty* . . . trying to avoid using stronger [anti-American] language, under the pretext that he wishes to avoid harming American comrades."

Back and forth flew the memoranda. Dozens of agents massaged the "personal" statement from the American; it had to sound firm, anti-American, and pro-Soviet, yet believable too. A tall order, to explain how a man who had passed through the nightmare Field just barely survived could still defend such a system, and hail it as the promise of the future, the camp of peace.

"We are not among those," Field finally declared in his public statement, "who blame an entire people, a system or a government for the *misdeeds of a handful of the overzealous and the misguided.*" Thus did Field exonerate one of history's most cruel human experiments, blaming the jailing and slaughter of hundreds of thousands of innocents on a few excessively fervent bad apples. In closing, Field said he and Herta owed their jailers and torturers "a debt of gratitude" for acknowledging their innocence.

The Hungarians now had another problem: how to keep their Cold War trophies happy. "We have to make plans for some sort of a social life for them," writes an AVO general in another top secret memo, underscoring that it is essential to prevent the Fields from succumbing to homesickness. "They don't know anyone in Hungary," the memo states. "They might fall in with the wrong sort of company, or they might think about leaving. . . . Please find out through their 'secretary' how they imagine their lives in Hungary, what sort of work they would like to do."

★

As usual, Noel's siblings had misjudged their brother. His decision to seek asylum in the East was a blow to his family. After four months of silence, Hermann finally wrote Noel. It was his toughest message, and a departure from his habit of accommodation. "If you had simply made a statement," Hermann wrote, "that you wished to stay on for the time being . . . without implying that you *were seeking Hungarian protection from your own government*, you might have avoided any sharp clash. Instead, after [the United States] made numerous diplomatic efforts on your behalf over many years, you rewarded them by a propaganda coup for Hungary. . . . You have to face the fact that you have put yourself under the protection of a government which is hostile to your own in the Cold War." Hermann reminds his brother of the obvious: "I can only retire into private life if you are out of the news. . . . If you are publicly involved in attacks on U.S. policy, you might well force me to dissociate myself [from you] and take a public position myself to avoid any ambiguity." (The Hungarian authorities may have allowed Field to receive such less than positive letters from his family, but the archives reveal that all the while they monitored, translated, and analyzed his correspondence. Field's surveillance continued into the 1960s, by which time Moscow no longer feared the loss of this Western prize.)

In spite of fresh embarrassment and continued pain caused by Noel, his brother and sister still tried to spare his feelings. "I just can't bring myself to write [to Noel] about the nightmare of the past five years," Elsie wrote Hermann on April 24, 1955. "With all that we did and the

State Department did. I know that [Noel and Herta] have suffered far more than I did. . . . I have no aptitude for conveying the way we tackled the tragedy of the past five years. . . . It is still a nightmare for me."

Noel well understood that his siblings would never have the heart to make a clean break. And even if they did, his family's anguish was a minor consideration. "You speak of your wish," he wrote Hermann, "that 'the case of the errant Fields may at last pass from the news and that we all can once more become private individuals and lead our own lives as we choose.' . . . In saying that you seem to assume that we *wish* to do so. Yet you know that my life has always been a political life, and that for me there is no such thing as a separation between private life and political life. . . . Because of the interference," he wrote Hermann, "not in the East but in the West . . . because of the attitude of the American authorities . . . I shall not be permitted to retire into private life, even if I should wish to do so."

★

At this point in the narrative, my own family's saga intersects with the Fields'. A top-secret Ministry of the Interior memorandum dated January 5, 1955, with the subject "The Case of Noel H. Field," notes that "Endre and Ilona Marton of the Associated Press and United Press, have several times submitted official requests to the Ministry of Foreign Affairs, and have, through their own connections attempted to interview Mr. and Mrs. Field." The American authorities were no longer guarding the Fields' privacy nor their address. My parents were known to be close friends of Ambassador Ravndal. A Marton-Field meeting now became a real threat to the state working hard to keep him under wraps. In another top secret memorandum, dated February 2, 1955, from AVO officer Mrs. Ferenc Kuhari to the minster of the interior, she states, "I have informed Field that the Comrades *do not think* he should telephone the Martons. The Fields felt this might be the best solution. The Martons have repeatedly asked Ravndal for the Fields' telephone number and address. Until now, Ravndal has withheld this information from them. Now, he has let the Fields know he will no longer keep their address a secret, and if they themselves do not get in touch with the journalists, he will let them know where to find the Fields."

On February 24, following a night of bridge at the home of the American military attaché, a swarm of AVO agents surrounded our family car, grabbed my father, and drove him to the Fő Utca maximum-security political prison on the Buda side of the Danube. The jailer who led my father to his cell congratulated him on his "VIP cell," "recently vacated by the American agent Noel Field."

My mother was allowed three more months of freedom, to make arrangements for her young children, before they arrested her as well, in June 1955. She was incarcerated in the same prison, but my parents saw each other only once, during their pretrial hearing.

My parents—who had covered the Rajk trial, as well as the Fields' disappearance and its abrupt finale—were unable to cover the story of Noel Field's next chapter as Communist propagandist. Inmates themselves, they awaited their own trial on fake charges of spying for the CIA. After my parents' arrest, no Western journalist located the Fields until December 1956. Then, during the chaos of the Hungarian Revolution, my mother and father—newly freed from prison—found the Fields, and finally conducted the only known press interview with Noel and Herta Field.

★

By the summer of 1956, Hungarian officials had found a "suitable" job for Noel as an editor/translator at the *New Hungarian Quarterly*—a state-sanctioned literary and political journal. In cramped and smoke-filled offices above a women's dress shop at 12 Váci Utca (today an H&M department store and an Estée Lauder boutique flank the building), Noel groomed English translations of censored articles and short stories meant to showcase the best of Hungarian culture and the arts for the English-speaking world. Not much actual censorship was required, however. Everybody at the *NHQ* practiced self-censorship and had assimilated unwritten taboos. The Communist Party and the Soviet Union were beyond criticism. All references to the West, "the capitalist/imperialists," must always be accompanied by a verbal sneer.

A certain wariness about getting too close to the American Communist in their midst prevailed in the editorial offices of the *NHQ* and Corvina Publishing, where Noel also worked. Noel's colleagues—cultured, English-speaking survivors of multiple political storms—were not fiercely dogmatic. They were, to a man, bewildered by someone who had willingly forsaken the near-mystical protection of an American passport. But they ended up liking this stranger in their midst. "Goodness radiated from him," Corvina editor Ferenc Aczél recalled, "and an eagerness to be helpful. Noel had the appearance of an ascetic—very tall, hollow cheeked, wide eyed. He mixed English and German. But he never spoke of himself, or of prison," Aczél said, adding, "There was another former inmate on our staff, Paul Justus. Noel and Paul were quite close, and they would argue. Justus had no fingernails, nor teeth left—as a result of torture. Noel told Justus he forgave the torture and the terror—as acceptable 'mistakes' on the road toward the perfect Workers' State. Well, Justus did not buy this. So they argued. Neither convinced the other."

In the words of *NHQ* colleague Miklos Vajda, Noel was "the only pure Communist" in the office. "We did not know if he was informing on the rest of us." The records reveal that indeed he was. When a colleague criticized *Szapad Nep*, the party organ, for being "content free," Noel reported him to the authorities. The man was promptly fired.

Aczél, a still-dapper octogenarian, recalled Noel and Herta as "an extraordinarily close couple. They held hands when they walked together," Aczél said. "Of course people noticed Noel in the street. He was so tall and still elegant and did not look at all Hungarian." Noel, however, never fully recovered from the trauma he sustained in the torture chambers of the villa. A slow-moving man who breathed heavily, he seemed decades older than his years. At his death, his colleagues were shocked to learn that when they first met him, he was in his early fifties.

★

With the only independent journalists—my parents—in jail and the Americans keeping their distance, Noel settled into his new life. He was well rewarded for his cooperation. The state paid him one hundred thousand forints compensation for his five years of prison, and ten thousand forints a month for his expenses. At a time when the average Hungarian earned twelve thousand forints a year, this was a princely sum. Each morning, an agent/chauffeur drove him to his Váci Utca office.

A secret State Department cable from the Budapest embassy, dated April 26, 1956, notes that "on Sunday April 21, the drafting officer [Donald Downs] attended a concert by Hungary's famed pianist Annie Fischer, and discovered that the Fields were sitting directly behind him, two rows away. It was clear that [Downs] was also recognized by the Fields as they rose hurriedly at intermission and, averting his gaze, left the auditorium, returning just before the second part of the program started. Both [Fields] looked in much better health than when last seen by [Downs] in December 1954. Mrs. Field in particular looked as if she had put on considerable weight. Noel still retained his long, shaggy hair and although a little heavier, carried himself in a very stooped manner. Whatever they have been doing, it would not appear that they have been suffering financially as both were considerably better and more smartly dressed than even the higher up government officials and their wives who were also in attendance."

Still missing from the Fields' new lives was final and total certification as Communists. On January 13, 1956, Noel Field wrote to the

Hungarian Communist Party, stating, "My wife and I herewith declare our desire to become members of the Hungarian Workers' Party, and we request permission to make formal application for admission, taking into account our status as non-Hungarian political refugees. We are, of course, ready to take whatever preliminary steps are required, and to undergo the necessary political and ideological examinations." Field sounds like a man preparing to take holy orders. "By conviction, we have been communists for over twenty years and have endeavored to act as such in our life and work."

Field's timing was absurdly off. A few weeks later, the cause for which Noel had sacrificed his life was shaken by its roots. Three years after his death, Stalin's own disciples suddenly dislodged the Father of the Peoples from his pedestal. On February 25, 1956, in the Kremlin, at the Twentieth Congress of the Communist Party of the Soviet Union, Nikita Khrushchev, first secretary of the party, broke with Stalin. Denouncing his crimes, errors, and "cult of the personality," Khrushchev declared, "It is impermissible and foreign to the spirit of Marxism-Leninism to elevate one person . . . to transform him into a superman possessing supernatural characteristics akin to those of a god"—precisely Noel Field's crime.

It was a confusing time for Stalinism's remaining fervent adherents. The Communist god's decapitation sent shock waves of fear and euphoria through the Soviet empire—perhaps nowhere more so than in Hungary. Rákosi, Stalin's self-proclaimed "best pupil," was still in power. In Budapest, the excitement of a measure of free speech and the thrilling prospect of reform were in the air. In classrooms and cafés, Rákosi's sadistic rule and senseless forced industrialization were now openly discussed. Rage—controlled by fear until now—was building. So was revulsion as the details of the past were more openly discussed.

In June, the most haunting symbol of the terrible decade emerged from prison. Julia, the widow of László Rajk, her six-year-old son gripping her hand, faced hundreds of Communists. "Let me tell you this," the forty-four-year-old Mrs. Rajk said, "Horthy's jails were better—even for Communists—than Rákosi's prisons. Not only was my husband killed, but my little baby was torn from me," she told the hushed audience. "These criminals have trampled underfoot all sentiment and honesty in this country. Murderers should be criticized. They should be punished." No one could have delivered that message with greater power and urgency than this woman, with her sunken cheeks and dark, burning eyes.

By the summer of 1956, the population's long-banked fury was as hard to tame as a roaring river. In August 1956, one man tried. "It is not for us," Field wrote in the Communist Party organ, "but for the enemies of progress to doubt and regret. . . . They thought the ship was rotting and would founder, and abandoned it to its fate. . . . Who can doubt that the clouds are dispersing and that the ship, though still undergoing necessary repairs, was and is fundamentally sound?" Field proclaimed, as if from a planet far, far away.

The vast majority of Hungarians did not share Field's delusions. In October, revolution was sparked by László Rajk's reburial. In a solemn ceremony in Hungary's pantheon of Communist heroes, one hundred thousand people, including Rajk's widow and young son, lined up to pay their respects. Oblivious to the icy rain that did not let up during the entire service, hatred and a grim determination to avenge their comrades' pointless murders etched the mourners' faces. Noel Field, whose forced testimony helped to convict Rajk and his "accomplices," was not among the mourners.

Two weeks later, on October 23, a spontaneous street demonstration by university students shouted its demands for the withdrawal of Soviet troops, for free elections, and for students' right *not* to join the mandatory Communist Youth League. Thousands of citizens joined the students in the streets of Budapest—and soon in the provinces. Rákosi fled to Moscow. Along with the loathed man, fear itself disappeared. By nightfall, the demonstrators hacked away at the giant statue of Stalin near Heroes' Square. When it finally tumbled, the crowd roared, and the revolution had its symbol. The Hungarian tricolor, with a large hole where the hammer and sickle had been cut, became the uprising's second icon.

Caught off guard, Soviet forces retreated. The revolution seemed miraculously triumphant. (I remember those exhilarating days of October 1956 as my childhood's most dramatic—and hopeful. I saw those days through my parents' eyes—and read on their faces expressions I had never seen. Suddenly everything seemed possible. Change was coming. I was a child, but it was in the air and on my newly freed-from-prison parents' faces.) "*Ruszkik Haza!*" "Russians Go Home!" read the graffiti on every factory wall. The revolution's newly appointed prime minister, Imre Nagy, tried his best to keep up with the population's spiraling demands for free elections, for multiparty rule, free press, and, of course, for "*Ruszkik Haza.*" Schools were closed, workers laid down their tools, and my parents covered the story of their lives.

(I have an unforgettable personal memory of the man who would soon become the revolution's martyred leader. My mother—recently freed from prison, my father still an inmate—and my sister and I had climbed aboard a Budapest streetcar. Nagy, a very ordinary-looking man, balding, with a brush mustache, in a raincoat and holding an umbrella, rose from his seat and signaled for my mother to take it. "What happened to you," Nagy said to my mother as she sat down, taking me on her lap, "it should never have happened." My mother, visibly moved, smiled in silent acknowledgment. Later, she told us who the gentleman was.)

*

Noel Field missed the moment. As Budapest steelworkers, miners, and, soon, Hungarian soldiers joined demonstrators in spontaneous countrywide rallies, Field was in a hospital being treated for a bleeding ulcer.

The "free world" missed it too. Great Britain, France, and Israel launched a war against Egypt during that same week. President Dwight D. Eisenhower was campaigning for reelection.

At daybreak, November 4—Election Day in the United States—Soviet tanks and armored battalions poured into Hungary from points north, south, and east. "My little family must have been a pathetic sight," my father said, recalling that dawn, "doddering about in pajamas. It was dark outside, the streets around the house were empty and peaceful but the sound of tank fire came from all directions. I switched on the radio. It played the anthem and then Nagy's familiar voice, now tinged with heartache. 'Today at daybreak,' Nagy told his countrymen, 'Soviet troops attacked our capital with the intention of overthrowing the legal Hungarian democratic government. Our troops are in combat. The government is at its post.' "

My father pounded out the heartbreaking story of the Soviets' return. Looking up from his typewriter, he noticed my sister and me, "like two little soldiers, waiting for orders. What should the orders be?" My parents decided we had to move fast. Soon we were speeding across the Danube in our Volkswagen Beetle—one step ahead of Soviet tanks, which occupied the bridges minutes later. We requested and were granted sanctuary at the American embassy.

It took heavily armed Soviet forces a mere seventy-two hours to extinguish the uprising. The ragtag army of students, workers, and soldiers kept up a hopeless guerrilla war for weeks, however. More than twenty thousand Hungarians died fighting for their country's independence, and another two hundred thousand fled across the suddenly opened Iron Curtain.

In the long run, the victor lost more than the vanquished. It would take three more decades for the bankrupt system to collapse under its own weight. Budapest, the first battle in a long war, had become a twentieth-century David that tried and failed to defeat the Soviet Goliath. After the crushing of the Hungarian uprising, even most of its loyal adherents realized that Soviet power was based not on ideas but on tanks and troops.

The following year, Noel Field visited Tonia Lechtman in Warsaw. "I don't want to hear this!" Field said, trying to silence Tonia when she condemned Soviet brutality in Budapest. Noel was also upset by the sight of candles on Warsaw's streets lit in memory of the Hungarian freedom fighters.

★

During the chaos of the revolution, my parents located the Fields' closely guarded address. On a bone-chilling December evening, in the gloomy winter of 1956, with Soviet troops patrolling the city, my mother and father arrived unannounced at the Fields' villa. Why did Noel and Herta open the door to them? After all, though Hungarian nationals, my parents were employed by the enemy, correspondents of the Associated Press and the United Press, and had repeatedly tried and failed to interview the Fields—before and after their own jailing—for nearly two years in my father's case, shy of a year in my mother's.

Curiosity, on the Fields' part, was my mother's explanation for why they scored the only interview the Fields ever granted Western press. The two couples had shared a similar fate as inmates of the Fő Utca Prison. For a while Field and my father were both "Prisoner 410," inmates of the same corner cell, Noel until October 1954, my father until August 1955. And in yet another bizarre coincidence, Major Arpad Kretschmer, in charge of Field's "rehabilitation" prior to release, had been my father's interrogator. "It was easy to make Kretschmer talk," my father said, "with unmistakable pride about the role he played in the 'rehabilitation' process of Noel Field." Thus, my father learned from Kretschmer the outlines of Field's strange trajectory, his early conversion to Communism, and his friend Alger Hiss's attempt to recruit him into Soviet military espionage when Noel was already spying for the KGB.

During the revolution's fevered early days, vigilantes dispensed mob "justice," capturing and lynching agents of the reviled AVO. Kretschmer feared for his life and sought shelter in our apartment. My father—appalled to see the popular uprising descend into mob rule—allowed his former interrogator to stay until the violence subsided. Major Kretschmer, according to my father, was "a simple, but friendly little man, with thin, reddish hair and pale blue eyes, who looked uncomfortable on the rare occasions when he wore his uniform, which hung on his frame in a rather unmilitary fashion." The major had shown my father compassion when Papa was at his lowest point as an inmate.

"What happened to the little girls?" was Herta's first question to my mother. My sister and I had been part of the news coverage of our parents' arrest. The *New York Times* featured a photograph of our family in its front-page coverage of my parents' conviction for espionage, on January 15, 1956. The two couples who faced each other were a study in contrasts. I can picture my stylish mother, carefully coiffed, wearing one of her signature silk scarves, fascinated by this austere American couple who had chosen to live in the country we were desperately trying to escape. My father wore his tweed sports coat, crisp shirt, and silk tie, his dark hair—threaded with gray since prison—brushed straight back. The Fields, according to my father's description, wore matching dark blue overalls. "He looks like an old man now," my father said of Noel. "He still has a dignity," he added, "and seems a gentle, quiet man, very cultured and well read. . . . He said he wanted to watch how it would develop after the Stalin Era." Of the newly empowered Soviet puppet, János Kádár, who betrayed the revolution, Field said, 'He saved Hungary from 'White Terror.' " When my father protested that Field was in a hospital during the Revolution's duration, how could he judge its character, Noel answered, "Oh, even there I felt it . . . and my wife told me so." Then, to my parents' astonishment, Field said, "Any plans I had of returning to the

United States are now farther off than ever, because life is exciting here after the Hungarian Revolution."

The couples exchanged prison anecdotes, such as the fact that all four had read *Anthony Adverse*, a twelve-hundred-page potboiler found in the prison library, which, my mother told them, she had used to "press" her blouse. My father asked Noel about Erica, but Field seemed reluctant to talk about the disappointing foster daughter who had chosen West over East. My parents felt that of the two, Herta was the stronger, more determined personality at this stage. Prison had been a slightly less brutal experience for her. She told my parents that she spent many hours making elaborate figurines out of bread, which she then painted—something her jailers encouraged her to do. Field, my father said, "seemed to believe what he said about Communism— as the wave of the future."

Despite this seemingly pleasant visit, in a letter to Alger Hiss dated July 21, 1957, Field (who, of course, writes for many eyes on both sides of the divide) savages my father. "Marton," Field fumes, "did not have the decency to arrange for an interview in advance," he wrote Hiss, "but broke in on Herta and myself unannounced one evening." He also calls my father a "barefaced liar" for reporting that Field was a Communist—something Noel had still not officially acknowledged at that point.

# CHAPTER 22

# THE AGE OF SUSPICION

*I would not realize until thirty years later . . . how wonderfully mirror-like the reflection of paranoia was on the other side of the world.*

—Arthur Miller

*Have you no sense of decency, sir?*

—Joseph N. Welch to Senator Joseph R. McCarthy

O N OCTOBER 26, 1955, Erica's taxi circled around the Brandenburg Gate, the great demarcation between East and West. Crossing the Tiergarten—ablaze with fall colors—she arrived at the place where she had started her journey, five years and two months earlier. The recent inmate of Vorkuta's twilight world was blinded by the bright lights of the Kurfürstendamm, Berlin's showiest boulevard. Where were the haunted, hungry Berliners she remembered from 1950? Well-dressed, well-fed people now idled in the cafés along the Ku'damm. Sleek glass and steel buildings had sprung up in place of the mountains of rubble. But Erica, age thirty-two, emerged from the Gulag steady on her feet, and with the vitality to restart her interrupted

life. Every ounce of her remarkable spirit would be required for the
road back.

Appraising her out-of-fashion summer suit and frayed pumps—
the outfit in which she had been arrested in East Berlin—her battered suitcase by her side, the manager of Berlin's opulent Kempinski
Hotel did not deem her a suitable guest. So Erica dragged her bag to
the less-desirable hotel from where she left on that long-ago August
day, the Hotel am Zoo. There, she was reunited with her mother.
Two resilient German women who had suffered the century's harsh-
est blows now wept tears of joy mixed with sadness. Of the Glaser
family of Pomerania, neither Erica's father nor brother were alive to
share the family reunion.

Almost immediately, a bellman delivered an impressive bouquet
of flowers to Erica's room. "Welcome back," the accompanying note
said. It was signed "R. Hill." The mysterious Mr. Hill himself soon
arrived and identified himself as the CIA's Berlin station chief. So,
after the brief reunion with her mother, "Mr. Hill"—for that was not
his real name—drove Erica to a safe house in Dahlem, Berlin's leafy
diplomatic district. And so began days of debriefing—a milder form
of interrogation—but covering every detail of her arrest, trial, and imprisonment. The names of your interrogating officers? The exact location of those prisons? And always: to the best of your knowledge, was
Noel Field a Russian spy? The setting was comfortable and Mr. Hill
was polite—courtly, even—but there was no doubt in Erica's mind
that in the CIA's eyes, she had to prove her innocence. This was not
the long-dreamed-of homecoming. "When will I see my husband and
children?" Erica kept asking. "As soon as we are through," Mr. Hill
assured her, "you may leave."

A far tougher interrogator named Sig Hoechster, whom Erica remembered from the OSS, soon replaced "Mr. Hill." "His tone," she
recalled, "his threats, everything about him reminded me of my interrogation by Russian officers. Two and a half years of it. It all came

back. And I surprised myself with the same reaction I had shown then: stubbornness and a will to fight back." "What makes you think you can intimidate me?" Erica asked the CIA agent. "I've had far too much experience in Soviet prisons," she assured him. "Those methods will not work with me."

Back at her hotel, Erica cabled her husband, asking him to come to Berlin as her own departure had been delayed. Bob cabled back, "Permission Berlin unlikely." Following Erica's abduction, Bob's passport had been invalidated—for his own safety, he was told. In protest, Erica staged a strike of her own. She refused to answer any more questions unless her husband was allowed to join her.

"Two days later," she recalled, "Bob arrived . . . mystified at all those changes in plans. I had not been allowed to tell him about any CIA involvement . . . and he had imagined all sorts of crazy reasons for my refusal to come to England [where he had awaited her]. Perhaps I did not want to see him at all? Perhaps I was too ill? Perhaps there was another man to hold me back?" She promised him, " 'No more mysteries' . . . and for the next few hours we frantically tried to catch up with our different pasts. So much to tell, so many questions. . . . How can you make up for five years? But it was wonderful to be together, to share," she said. "I wanted it to last forever."

Erica was a stranger to her children. "I was only six months old," Robert Wallach Jr. recalled, "when she disappeared. The only picture we had of her looked like some sort of a mug shot. My first memory of her is in Europe when my father and sister and I visited her for a few days while she was waiting for her U.S. visa." Their reunion was inauspicious. "I was six years old," Robert said. "We went to some sort of a beach resort which turned out to be a nudist colony. No clothes were allowed! It was very cold, and people wore sweaters—but nothing below the sweaters. So this experience just reinforced in my mind the image of a strange foreigner—my mother."

An entirely unexpected hurdle now blocked Erica's passage to a new life in the country where her husband and children lived. In 1955, the United States was an anxious and suspicious place, rich soil for the Wisconsin demagogue Senator Joseph R. McCarthy. His party, out of power for twenty years, soon managed to conflate FDR's New Deal with Communism. Someone had to be held to account for the Cold War and Soviet "penetration." Richard M. Nixon—a more subtle and intelligent politician than Joe McCarthy—skillfully exploited the climate of suspicion. Fear always spreads faster than good sense, and soon even war hero and Secretary of State George C. Marshall was suspect.

Democrats—tarred with having been soft on Communism and gulled by Stalin under Roosevelt—spent the next decades proving their anti-Communist zeal. Forgotten suddenly was America's wartime alliance with the Soviets in the common campaign against Hitler. Forgotten, too, was that the German Communist Party was licensed and approved by the American military government, and recognized by them as one of the four postwar democratic parties.

Erica and her family were among those caught in Senator McCarthy's poisonous wake. America was not the land to open its arms to a self-confessed former Communist—no matter the ordeal she had barely survived. As a former member of the German Communist Party (from 1946 to 1948) Erica was now prevented from entering the United States, under the McCarran-Walter Act of 1952, which barred Communists and other "undesirables." The only way Erica could gain entry was by providing evidence of five years of "anti-Communist activity." For a woman who had spent the preceding five years as a Soviet inmate, that condition seemed preposterous, to put it mildly.

But such were the times that three powerful institutions—the CIA, the State Department, and the Justice Department—all seemed determined to prevent Erica from joining her family. Now, every detail of the thirty-two-year-old woman's life was minutely scrutinized, combed for signs that she might represent a danger to the country, for any evidence that five years of hard labor in the Gulag had not cured her of her former Communist sympathies.

Erica, biding her time in West Germany, put on a brave face. "She pulls herself together," her mother wrote Bob on December 1, 1956, "but she hides a fearful mind. Sometimes she looks very sad and worn out. I know day and night she worries about the future. She wishes to be with her children, to do things for them, then there she is, waiting."

Erica's total cooperation with the CIA in Berlin proved insufficient evidence of good faith. It did not help her case that she was prone to bluntness and chemically incapable of pretense. She refused to be a tool of Capitol Hill propagandists who wanted her to shout her anti-Communism from the rooftops. "I cannot understand," she said, "that it should be so difficult to comprehend my desire for peace, and my dislike for exhibitionism and sensation. What I went through . . . is too serious and too complicated a matter for me to talk about superficially in public."

*

Her former association with Noel Field was the greatest barrier to Erica's US entry. "If Noel does want to help Erica," Bob wrote Kate Field in December 1954, "it is obvious that her future life in the West would be a lot easier if he behaved in a manner less likely to be criticized in this country." After Noel announced his plan to stay in the East, Bob was far more blunt. "I'm tempted to insist," he wrote Elsie Field on November 30, 1955, "you tell Noel to stop bothering my wife."

But Noel did not see his interests in Erica's reunion with her American family. He still hoped she would join him in the East, and continued to cast a giant shadow over Erica's hopes for a new beginning. His pro-Soviet interviews in the French Communist *Libération* prompted her to write Elsie, "Every time he opens his mouth I have to pay for it." She did not often mention Noel to her children, and rarely criticized him in public. But in her letters to Noel's siblings, she expressed her anger. His siblings, however, continued to give their brother every benefit of the doubt. On February 14, 1956, Elsie wrote Erica: "We cannot actually know . . . what his real feelings are, nor how much is written for a possible censor at the one or the other end. Moreover though we expect him to understand, we have to remember that he has been out of touch with the West for a long time now and that he understands things from one side only. . . . From none of his letters have I ever felt that he appreciated what a provocative act his asylum decision was. One can only hope that there will be a time in the future when all this will be cleared up." That day would never arrive.

Six months after her release, Erica was still barred from entering the United States. "I am writing more or less in desperation," Bob Wallach wrote a "Mr. Valenza" of the State Department's visa division on April 17, 1956. "As you know, [my wife] was released from 5 years of imprisonment by the Russians early last Fall and during the intervening six months has been under examination by various authorities. She now has no place to live and is forced to wander across Europe, with no idea of what is to happen to her." He was near the end of his patience. "After all she has been through I very truthfully say that I believe her nerves are incapable much longer of withstanding the uncertainty, fear and delay with respect to her future."

Mr. Valenza was unmoved and silent. On June 11, 1956, Bob again wrote to him that "I have heard unofficially that your office has decided to recommend to the Consul General in London that my wife's visa application be disapproved. As it would be too expensive for me to go to England," the desperate man added, "I wonder if you would be good enough to tell me here and now the reasons for the recommendation." Valenza did not answer this plea either.

In October 1956—the month revolution flared in Hungary— Erica, still barred from the United States, visited Noel's sister Elsie in Geneva. "In no time," Elsie wrote her brother Hermann, "she was part of our family, the children hanging on to her with very real af-

fection. She may belittle her maternal instincts, but she has a wonderful rapport with children. We certainly managed little sleep while
she was here. She seemed glad to be able to talk about her five years'
experiences. What that girl went through! And with what courage
she stood up to her tormentors. Of course, we discussed her future
at length and it looks gloomy. This kind of aimless and rootless life
is absolutely no good for her. Unless Bob's present efforts through a
lawyer produce speedy results he had better plan to make his home
in Europe or he is likely to lose her. . . . Money is also fast running
out. . . . She cannot face starting life anew in a strange place without
her friends, without something which she can call home, without
Bob to help with the children and without absolute assurance that it
will be permanent."

Erica even offered to divorce Bob so that he and the children could
get on with their lives, while she waited in agonizing limbo for her
American visa. But Bob—who had waited so long and fought so hard
for Erica—would hear none of this. "As you can see," Elsie wrote Hermann on February 5, 1957, "it's really a ghastly situation. I wish Erica
could consider other possibilities, even emigrating to New Zealand or
Australia."

After two years of futile and frustrating effort, the Wallachs finally
engaged a prominent immigration attorney, Martin J. McNamara Jr.,
to cut through the thicket of legal obstacles with which the Immigration and Naturalization Service continued to bar her entry.

"Ever since 1950, after my arrest," Erica wrote her new lawyer on
March 18, 1957, "until this very day, I have continuously been humil-
iated: first by the East Germans and Russians, now by the American
authorities. I am not blaming them. . . . I am just trying to explain why
I resent so deeply every attempt to deprive me of the last little bit of
dignity and self-respect that has been left to me. I am not asking the
US authorities for any favors. If they consider that I am a danger to US
security, it is their right to keep me out. The only thing I do believe to

be entitled to is to be told about it openly and at once. . . . I consider it cruel not to have told me so from the very beginning."

In her effort to "prove" to Washington what she suffered in captivity, and because she despised exploiting her personal ordeal, Erica tracked down a former cellmate in an East German prison, and asked her to submit an affidavit to the Immigration and Naturalization Service in Washington. On January 10, 1956, Helga Taunzer submitted this testimony of routine Soviet brutality. "About the middle of April 1951, Erica Wallach came into the cell which I shared with a Ukrainian," her cellmate wrote. "Mrs. Wallach . . . looked very bad. She told me that she had come from a punishment cell where there was only a wooden cot, the window pane broken and no mattress or blanket were given her. In addition, she had been questioned night after night from 10pm to 6am—exactly during the sleeping hours—and had not been allowed to sleep during the beginning of July 1951. The Soviet authorities demanded of her exact information on the alleged espionage activities of her foster father Noel Field and herself. Since she refused to admit things which were not true, the methods of interrogation became increasingly severe. . . . Mrs. Wallach had been beaten black and blue, her face badly swollen. In addition, she was completely filthy, not having been allowed to wash for sixteen days. Her wrists were badly swollen from handcuffs."

Not even this heartbreaking description moved bureaucrats who continued to refuse her visa request. In their way, these "public servants" were as unworthy of that title as the American consular officers who regarded the sea of human misery flooding their Marseille office in the 1940s as a nuisance.

In the soul-crushing jargon that should be prohibited between human beings, US Frankfurt vice consul Lois Unger wrote Erica on July 31, 1957, "This office has been instructed that your application for admission to the United States under Section 212 (a) (28) (9ii) of the Immigration and Nationality Act has been denied. *It has been held that you have failed to establish that you have been actively opposed to the doctrine, program, principles and ideology of the Communist cause and that you have, in fact, failed to establish that you have terminated your affiliation with the Communist cause for at least five years."*

Instead of recognition as a living symbol of Soviet cruelty, Erica was considered a security threat to the United States. "Never in my life," Erica wrote her husband on March 17, 1957, "have I encountered so much ill will. That is, I have: when I was a prisoner of the Russians. But then one accepts it more easily and naturally to be considered an enemy than when one is called a 'free person.' "

Erica closed her letter with a note of bitter irony: "If the intentions of the US authorities were to force me back into the arms of the Communists, they could not have acted more consistently."

She was ready to quit, but her lawyer had one more card to play: Allen W. Dulles, director of Central Intelligence, the man with whom Erica and Noel Field were linked in show trials across the Soviet empire. "As your office may be aware," McNamara wrote Dulles on August 21, 1957, "Mrs. Wallach has been encountering difficulty in obtaining a visa. . . . She believes she has extended the utmost courtesy and cooperation to your agents and would appreciate reciprocal assistance in her case with the Immigration authorities. . . . Mrs. Wallach has two small American children born of her marriage to Mr. Wallach, a native-born American and Army veteran. She has been separated from her husband and children for over seven years. Certainly it would appear that such a person, whose presence in the United States represents no threat to the security of the nation, should not be denied admittance."

Whether it was at Dulles's behest or something else, Erica's case suddenly became an urgent matter for Congress. Gwendolyn Lewis, an aide on the House Un-American Activities Committee, made Erica's case her own, and moved to end the family's two-year ordeal. Gwen, as Erica was soon calling her new friend, flew to Frankfurt and within days had tape-recorded Erica's entire story. "She understood what I was saying," Erica recalled, "and she had a human attitude that had been utterly lacking in all the bureaucrats I had dealt with before."

On October 8, 1957, Congressman Francis E. Walter, sponsor of the McCarran-Walter Act that had barred her entry, wrote to General Joseph M. Swing, head of the Immigration and Naturalization Service. Between the mind-numbing, jargon-filled lines is an indictment of the absurd machinations of a cruel system during a shameful period in American democracy. "That Erica Wallach would not make dramatic speeches or lead some organized movement against the Communists in the course of the last several years is attributed directly to the shocking experiences which she endured at their hand," Walter said. "I earnestly request that the waiver on Mrs. Wallach's case be granted as soon as possible."

In America—even in the worst of times—constitutional safeguards eventually limit the human damage. But these were truly the worst of times.

# CHAPTER 23

# TWILIGHT YEARS

*Many a family has to put up with a black sheep, in your case it is a red one.*

—Noel Field in a letter to his brother, Hermann

*Lying to ourselves is more deeply ingrained in us than lying to others.*

—Fyodor Dostoyevsky

IN JUNE 1957, after six months of investigation and hundreds of interviews, a United Nations Special Committee on Hungary (made up of the ambassadors of the neutral states of Denmark, Australia, Ceylon, Tunisia, and Uruguay) reported that "what took place in Hungary was a spontaneous uprising caused by long standing grievances . . . led by students, workers, soldiers and intellectuals, many of them Communists or former Communists. Those who took part in it insisted that democratic socialism should be the basis of the Hungarian political structure. *It is untrue that the uprising was fomented by reactionary circles in Hungary or that it drew its strength from 'Imperialist circles' in the West."*

On Radio Budapest, Noel still defended Soviet repression, and now attacked the UN. "Neither 400 nor 4,000 pages of dubious testimony," Field said of the report he admitted he had not yet read, "by a hundred or ten times that number of defectors can hamper the forward march of Hungary and other countries of the Socialist camp along the high road toward communism, which all other nations will ultimately follow in their own manner and their own good time." Mere *facts* never much mattered to this fanatic, who had spent the revolution in a hospital.

"It makes me so depressed," Noel's sister Elsie wrote Hermann on March 7, 1957. "I just want to cry and cry." Hermann, however, was still unwilling to give up on their brother. "Don't forget," he chides Elsie, "you and I always loved in Noel his sense of dedication, and his strong character and feel of participation in the world he lives in. It has led him . . . to what to us seems indefensible and irrational . . . but it is still the same Noel."

For a full year, however, his siblings stopped writing Noel. Then, on December 26, 1957, Hermann broke his silence. "[Your radio report on the UN] was a double blow for me, both in injecting the Noel Field controversy back into the public arena, and in a manner bound to destroy the last shred of sympathy [for you]," Hermann wrote. "It will be better to drop all correspondence. I feel sad about this as I had originally hoped that you would find enough fulfillment and satisfaction within the new life you have chosen, and allow the Field name to leave the international scene once and for all."

Hermann still could not reconcile himself to the loss of his beloved brother. Noel was as adept as ever at manipulating him. "Feeling utterly torn," Hermann laments to Elsie. "After Noel's UN utterance I decided to continue the silence that existed since the Uprising. Then came his very brotherly, affectionate letter of last September with its note of yearning to keep in touch. . . . Oh, if only Noel . . . had his eyes opened and had humility in face of the crimes of the past . . .

the deceit and dishonesty that has all but choked the original concepts [of Communism]. But instead everything points to a blind, irrational fanaticism with him. . . . Am I and my family," he asks plaintively, "doomed to live on the receiving end of Noel's activities for the rest of our lives?" The answer was obviously yes.

"It's damnable," Elsie wrote back. "I'm through doing his dirty work. He considers his value not in propagandizing in Hungary, as much as in propagandizing to the West."

★

On December 27, 1957, Hermann matter-of-factly informed his brother that he and his wife, Kate, were "introducing two Hungarian refugees to the New England countryside." For Noel, those refugees were traitors, deserving of the same fate as Ignaz Reiss and Walter Krivitsky.

Yet Hermann still clung to the faint hope of reconciliation. "Nothing is permanent at present," he wrote his sister on November 28, 1959. "We as a family don't want to cut the last ground under Noel if time came and he changed his mind and wished to return."

★

In the aftermath of the revolution, János Kádár ordered mass arrests of striking workers and hunted down those freedom fighters who had not managed to escape to the West. Twenty-two thousand Hungarians were sentenced to long prison terms as "counterrevolutionaries." In 1958, Imre Nagy and his "coconspirators"—briefly granted safe passage to Rumania—were abducted and returned to Hungary. Marshal Tito, now back in the Kremlin's favor, played his treacherous part in this tragic affair—promising the revolution's leaders safe passage, only to lure them into a Soviet trap. After a secret trial, Nagy and his two top aides, Pál Maléter and Miklós Gimes, were executed by hanging at dawn on June 16, 1958.

The shattered country retreated into sullen resignation. Now, even Noel's colleagues at the journal—nominally Communists—distanced themselves from Field and his relentless defense of the Soviet invasion. "He used to say that the Soviets saved Hungary," his colleague at the *NHQ*, Miklos Vajda, said, "and that rescue comes with sacrifice. Noel believed the Soviet propaganda about 'counter revolution' when almost no one else did. I liked to provoke him by pointing out the contrast between theory and practice in Marxism. But Noel always had an answer. 'These are just temporary hardships,' he would say." Vajda recalled that when a Western journalist visited the journal, Noel would quickly scurry to his office, closing the door behind him.

If anyone still doubted Noel Field's fanatical devotion to Communism, he himself erased that last shred of ambiguity in 1960. In an article meant to preempt a biography by *New York Times* correspondent Flora Lewis, Noel wrote a long autobiographical narrative in *Mainstream*, an American Communist Party publication. Field forgives Stalin's crimes as "essential on the road to a Communism." "They hate the same things and the same people I hate. . . ." he writes of those who abducted, jailed, and tortured him, his wife, brother, and foster daughter. "Given their belief in my guilt, I cannot blame them," he said, adding, "I approve their detestation." Like a monk justifying the atrocities of the Spanish Inquisition, he writes of Stalin's rule, "Whatever mistakes . . . have been committed, they cannot affect the fundamental truths that began to dawn on me a quarter of a century ago. These truths will inevitably win out over temporary aberrations."

Of the crushed revolution, Field writes, "Soviet troops have come in defense of socialism, the next stage in Man's evolution towards greater freedom and happiness for all. Soviet troops—and not those *poor, misled youngsters throwing away their lives in a hopeless struggle against them*—are the real freedom fighters." Field seemed to have forgotten that once he, too, was a "misled youngster throwing away [his life] in a hopeless struggle."

Finally, and astonishingly given the bloody "justice" meted out to the revolution's leader, Field claimed, "The wrongs . . . have been righted, the wrong-doers punished, our innocence recognized. . . . In the plain speaking of Khrushchev," Field said, "we sense the consciousness of physical and moral strength—the prevalence, as the Chinese put it—of the East wind over the West wind."

As usual, Noel had given his family no warning before the article hit newsstands. "I'm really sore about this," Hermann fumed to Elsie, who had given up her practice as a doctor to focus on her brothers' case. "Especially in view of our assumption all along of silence about his past. Now, it will look like a connivance—or that we were fools. . . . I'm not prepared to play along one further inch in a subterfuge or cover-up for Noel. . . . Surely, he knows . . . that I and my family will be the main victims." Noel knew, but he didn't much care.

Their brother was a Communist and, far worse, a traitor to his own country, and they had played a part of his cover-up. "Noel can't tell all the truth," Elsie wrote Hermann, "because he can't admit to espionage. Some of this could have been prevented . . . by you and me and E[rica] but we chose a different path . . . mistakenly judging Noel's intentions and capacity. . . . I know it sounds brutal . . . when I say that you must accept part of the responsibility."

Now, after their public embarrassment, Elsie declared, "We would be damn fools to cover up for Noel, damn fools if we don't make our disagreement clear," Elsie wrote Hermann on December 28, 1960. "Noel writes well, sounds so reasonable, he will ensnare dopes and well-meaning liberals. . . . I suggest that you state your disagreement publicly." Noel, unmoved by his family's pain, blandly informed Hermann on December 26, 1960, "As you know, I have my convictions, and whenever these require me to speak out, I shall do so, however great the pain of causing unpleasantness to relatives I continue to hold dear."

★

In the midsixties, Kádár tried to appease his disgruntled population by launching "goulash Communism"—a brand of consumer Communism that allowed a degree of free enterprise and private ownership. Shops suddenly offered unheard-of "luxury" goods such as oranges and bananas, and the choke hold of total surveillance was lifted. Arrests eased up as Kádár's unofficial slogan became "If you are not [actively] against us, you are for us."

Noel's blind support of the Soviet armed intervention was now rewarded. In a rare personal appearance, in 1964, Kádár turned up to celebrate Noel's sixtieth birthday at his office. "Comrade Field," the Hungarian Communist Party chief addressed him, "what would you like for your birthday?" That's easy, the American replied. "More office space for the magazine." Within days, workmen from the Ministry of the Interior arrived, took measurements, counted heads, and set to work transforming a suite of rooms on Rákóczy Boulevard into spacious new editorial offices for the *NHQ*. The regime's gesture was noted by the power elite of Budapest. For Noel, who had yearned for full acceptance for so long, it was the ultimate sign that he was finally a comrade.

*

With the passage of time, however, Noel's dreams of life as a revolutionary evaporated into an illusion. He was of little use to Moscow as it experimented with a policy of détente with the West in the sixties. As the absurd language of "class enemy" was discarded, he increasingly seemed a relic of a reviled system, an embarrassing reminder of Stalin's worst crimes.

Hermann's story was dramatically different. After prison he, like Erica, achieved a remarkable serenity. "My experience taught me a great deal," he said. "That one can survive if one preserves the will to survive, that a negative experience can have positive effects." Hermann channeled his idealism into nonpolitical causes. Father of three children, internationally known as the director of Tufts University's graduate program in Urban, Social and Environmental Policy, Hermann was an environmental pioneer. His autobiographical note in the Harvard Class of 1932 alumni report reveals his role in an embryonic field. "[After prison] I decided to return to my original career and dig myself out of the ruins. . . . Increasingly, I was appalled by the mindless despoiling of the physical environment essential to any quality of life. . . . I asked myself: to be good, must not architecture be environmentally sound? My focus was increasingly toward the central issues of preservation based on . . . sustainable resources whether at the local, regional, or the global scale. With travel to Senegal, Costa Rica, New Zealand and China. . . . My greatest satisfaction," Hermann concludes, "comes at being able to live with Kate in our valley, thirty-five miles from Boston in our eighteenth-century farmhouse, converting the 200 acres gradually into a wildlife sanctuary . . . opening its fields once more to agricultural use and providing open house for our children and grandchildren."

Hermann, the low-key environmental visionary—and not Noel, the delusional and devious Stalinist—became the real change agent in the Field family, "thanks to the search for meaning in that battle for survival," Hermann said, "that cut across the middle of my life." For his sons Hugh and Alan—who spent five years uncertain as to whether their father was dead or alive—the scars never completely healed. Even now, in their late sixties, their eyes can fill when the subject of their father's missing years comes up. The sons still wonder at their father's decision in 1949 to search for his older brother, over his own family's welfare. Their sister, Alison, born after their parents were reunited, is blessedly free of those painful memories of a time when no one would discuss what happened to their father.

★

The next four years were among the most peaceful in Noel Field's troubled life. His colleagues shrugged off his insistence that Marxism-Leninism was the wave of the future. "Very few people in Hungary had those illusions by the sixties," Ferenc Aczél said. "There was a general cynicism about the whole fake system, which was so obviously unworkable." The man who once marched down Pennsylvania Avenue arm in arm with the Bonus Army was now one of the privileged members of the Communist Party. The Fields vacationed in Hungary's exclusive spas reserved for party bigwigs, and benefited from unlimited free medical care. This was of paramount importance for both Fields, plagued by endless post-prison health problems. Their consolation was no longer having to conceal their true beliefs, nor spy against their own country. Noel Field lived a quiet if diminished life as one of the last apologists of a decomposing orthodoxy.

*

An ocean away, Noel's friend Alger Hiss's life was far more complicated. Hiss had risen much higher in his nation's service than Noel, thus his tumble from grace was more spectacular. An April 1945 photograph captures Hiss's stunning reversal of fortune. The scene is the San Francisco conference that gave birth to the United Nations. President Harry S. Truman—beaming and triumphant—has just stepped off the podium after a rousing speech to delegates from around the world. The president is shown reaching out to clasp the hand of a smiling, handsome young man, sleek in a double-breasted suit. Proudly gripping the president's hand is the chief organizer of the UN's founding conference—Soviet spy Alger Hiss.

Hiss's jail time coincided almost perfectly with his friend Noel's. But Alger's time at Lewisburg Penitentiary was dramatically different from Field's. Routine visits from his wife and son, as well as a steady stream of correspondence, connected Hiss to the outside world. Hiss also enjoyed lively interaction with his fellow inmates and was admired by many of them. Still, prison is prison, and, later, Hiss said he wouldn't wish it on anybody—not even his nemesis, Richard M. Nixon.

Alger Hiss strode out of Lewisburg on November 27, 1954, healthy and determined to "prove" his innocence. In an astonishing coincidence, Noel Field was released from Fő Utca Prison the very same day. Field, however, was a man broken in body and spirit.

The times, however, proved inauspicious for Hiss's quest. Republicans, out of power for nearly twenty years, were back, and McCarthy was calling the Roosevelt-Truman era "twenty years of treason." Hiss, former bright star of the New Deal—handy symbol of an era—was now barred from practicing law. Alternating periods of unemployment with low-paying jobs as a salesman, his marriage to Priscilla suffered and, in 1984, ended in divorce.

Richard M. Nixon, the man who helped to expose Hiss, gave Alger an unintended shot of new life in the midseventies. The multiple scandals of Watergate, which unmasked the president as corrupt, power-obsessed, and reckless with the Constitution, helped to revive Hiss's fortunes. Journalists who recently revealed the abuses of Nixon and his thuggish inner circle of "plumbers" now rediscovered his early victim Alger Hiss. The two cases were conflated, and brilliantly served Hiss's decades-long campaign of self-exoneration. To a new generation, Nixon embodied the McCarthy era's shameful excesses, while Hiss became the symbol of endangered liberals and New Dealers. Speaking on campuses and in the media, ever persuasive in his insistence that he was the sacrifice of a fevered time, Hiss became a prominent public figure. There were those who simply refused to believe that Alger Hiss could betray his country. "Even if Hiss himself were to confess his guilt," said a Columbia University professor, and neighbor of Hiss, "I wouldn't believe it."

Hiss continued to deny that he had ever been a Communist—much less Moscow's spy—even as he praised Stalin. In 1986, he told a journalist, "In spite of knowledge of [Stalin's] crimes, he was very impressive . . . decisive, soft spoken, very clearheaded. He almost always spoke without notes." Occasionally, with a flash of irritation, Hiss revealed himself. When told that Irving Howe, a lifelong democratic socialist

who had attacked both Stalin and McCarthy, considered Hiss to be
a liar, Alger's knife-edge politeness slipped. "Howe? I don't consider
him to be of the left." Which is precisely how a Stalinist would dismiss
a mere socialist.

*

Ambiguity shadowed Hiss's case—but that was better than the stamp
of "traitor." In 1992, a lifetime of stony denial of his real affiliation
nearly paid off. A former Soviet general, Dmitri A. Volkogonov, announced that he had not found "a single document that substantiates
the allegation that Hiss collaborated with the intelligence sources of
the Soviet Union." No sooner did Hiss and his supporters begin cele-
brating than the general backpedaled. "What I said," he corrected himself, "gives no basis to claim a full clarification." Volkogonov admitted
he felt great pressure from Hiss and his friends to clear the American's
record, so the eighty-eight-year-old could "die peacefully." The Soviet
archives are famously labyrinthine, and Volkogonov now confessed he
had spent only two days searching, and only in the KGB files, not the
archives of the Soviet military long held to be Hiss's outfit.

In 1993, Alger Hiss and Noel Field's narratives again intersected.
That year, a Hungarian historian named Maria Schmidt found Noel
Field's "rehabilitation" file in the Budapest secret police archives. Field
named Hiss as a fellow Soviet agent with whom he stayed in touch.
Noel had nothing to gain by lying about this in 1954 to Major Arpad
Kretschmer, who had access to all Soviet intelligence files. Moreover,
in 1996, the Venona files—thousands of decoded Soviet intelligence
cables from World War II—added further proof of Hiss's treason. In
these files, Hiss is mostly referred to by his code name "ALES." But
in a number of cables released *subsequently*, due to the efforts of scholars Allen Weinstein, Alexander Vassiliev, John Haynes, and Eduard
Mark, Hiss is referred to by his full name. The Soviet secret services
were not an integrated unit. The tight compartmentalization of the

two branches—military and political—ultimately shattered the cone of secrecy surrounding GRU agent Hiss. Agents of the NKVD—the KGB's predecessor—did not know the GRU's code for its agent Hiss, so they repeatedly referred to him as Alger Hiss.

It is not the purpose of this narrative to re-litigate the Hiss case. For a shrinking but still-determined handful of people, the affair has ceased to be about evidence and a great deal to do with the liberal-conservative culture wars it ignited. Those political and media skirmishes continue. Nor is this the place to sort through the mountain of evidence—some of it circumstantial, a great deal of it factual—attesting to Alger Hiss's service to Stalin.

One startling coda to the convoluted history is worth noting. It occurred during a conversation between Secretary of State Edward R. Stettinius Jr. and Andrei Gromyko, Soviet envoy to the United Nations, on September 7, 1945. Postwar international organizations were the agenda item between Stettinius and Gromyko. For a number of reasons, the Soviet diplomat urged that the UN be located in New York, not Europe. The secretary of state inquired if Moscow had "given any thought to a person who would take the position of first UN secretary general," Stettitnius wrote in his diary. "[Gromyko] said he would be very happy to see Alger Hiss appointed temporary secretary general, as he had a very high regard for Alger Hiss, particularly for his fairness and impartiality." On its own, the Soviet endorsement of an American official would not be proof of Hiss's espionage. In the annals of the Cold War, Gromyko's recommendation of an American to head the world's most important international organization is, however, without precedent.

★

In some ways, Noel lived a freer life in Budapest than his friend Alger in New York. Field lived life as a Communist, while Hiss spent the rest of his life attempting to prove he had never been one in the first place.

Field's freedom, however, came at a great price. Cut off from friends and family, and sidelined from the most dramatic—political, social, and cultural—events of the day, whatever contentment Noel found had to be within the borders of a small country, with its unique culture and impenetrable language. In the editorial offices of the *New Hungarian Quarterly*, Noel had the company of English-speaking Hungarian intellectuals, who preferred discussions about William Faulkner and Philip Roth, the shocking new talent in the American literary firmament, to politics. They considered Noel an eccentric from a time when believing the holy writs of Communism was not a sign of intellectual backwardness. "Once," Ferenc Aczél said, "we counted the collected prison time served by our editorial board. It was thirty years." Their boss, *NHQ*'s founder and editor in chief, Ivan Boldizsár, a shrewd survivor, somehow kept them all safe from the occasional party enforcers.

In yet another strange intersection between the Fields' story and my own, I recall Boldizsár as an occasional presence in my childhood home in Budapest, and as a bemused witness to my swimming lessons in one of Budapest's Turkish baths, the Lukács, where Ivan was a regular. I can still evoke his image in the steamy waters, like some ancient (to my child's eyes) crocodile, spreading the water with his enormous hands and arms, a mysterious smile on his lips. He was a man, so my parents later told me, privy to all the state's secrets, having survived the last days of the Austro-Hungarian Empire, the first communist revolution, the fascists, the Communists, and the failed 1956 revolution—still serenely enjoying his daily Turkish bath. Later, when we were settled in suburban Washington, DC, Ivan occasionally visited my parents. Over tiny cups of espresso, Ivan entertained them with a steady stream of the latest Budapest jokes. "Ivan has not been a true believer," my father told me, "for many years. If he ever was." That tepid faith was Communism in Hungary in the sixties and seventies.

Noel Field could never abandon the faith, which imbued his life with meaning. Where would he turn if his fatal choice proved to be a mistake after all? Captured early by a fantasy that no reality—however cruel—could ever shake, facts were the enemy of his beliefs. But reality kept intruding.

The deep schism between China and the Soviet Union—revealed at the CPSU Congress in 1961—shattered yet another of Noel's fantasies about the united Communist front. The East wind, he had predicted in 1960, would prevail over the West, and now it hadn't. But the following year, Noel took pleasure in the publication of a slim volume by an unknown Russian schoolteacher, Aleksandr Solzhenitsyn. *One Day in the Life of Ivan Denisovich* is a searing portrait of a prisoner's life in the Gulag Archipelago. For Noel, its publication was further proof that the "mistakes" of Stalinism were being corrected. Solzhenitsyn's next, even more critical tome, however, and the one after that, were banned.

Noel's brother and sister visited him twice. In their many hours together in Budapest, there was one subject that Hermann and Noel never broached: prison. Nor did they speak of the terrible ordeal the rest of the family suffered. Hermann still longed for such a conversation. "Kate's account of the five years as it looked from her and Elsie's end," he wrote Noel, "their battle, their unbounded devotion, their hopes and despair. . . . Well, next time I'll make an agenda of all the forgotten bits." But the "forgotten bits" were left forgotten.

In Hermann's view, Noel was still Noel: an idealist with a big heart. "Our days with you," Hermann wrote Noel on July 21, 1964, "will stand out as something to be treasured for their tenderness and simple joy."

The family member Noel most longed to see, however, never visited him in Hungary. Hermann tried to explain to his brother why Erica refused to come. "Erica," he wrote on July 21, 1964, "has an overwhelming responsibility to do nothing which can in any way harm her children (and for that matter Bob). Her natural keenness to see you, and yours to have her come, must be kept secondary to this, after all the hurt that has been done. As painful as any such restraint may be, I can't help feeling that any other yardstick would be ruthless and immoral. . . . I think you forget on what thin ice the present stabilization of her life rests, and how vulnerable she and her family are. . . . Meanwhile, let's all hope that eventually your hope will be fulfilled and that she and you will have the reunion you long for."

Noel never abandoned that hope. On May 18, 1964, in a chatty letter to "Dear Kid," he describes his pleasant routine, interrupted only by trips to the hospital for endless health problems, including trips to Lake Balaton for weeks of spa treatment. In the margin, he scribbled, "And when will we be seeing you?"

# CHAPTER 24

# PRAGUE

*It is a grave error to call upon foreign troops to teach one's people a lesson.*

—Josip Broz Tito

THE SIXTIES ENDED badly for Communism and terribly for Noel Field. In 1968, Moscow violently reversed the "corrected mistakes" and the "forward march." As in 1956, Soviet tanks were the instrument of the reversal. The Prague Spring, as it came to be known, was begun by Czech Communists fed up with Moscow's stranglehold on their lives. Alexander Dubček, the newly elected head of the Czech Communist Party, was a Soviet-trained apparatchik. Like Imre Nagy in 1950s Hungary, Dubček wanted to reform the party from *within*. For a while, the Kremlin, now under Leonid Brezhnev's collective leadership, saw no need for alarm.

But as in Budapest, so in Prague the talk of reform proved as intoxicating as champagne to a population dying of thirst. The gruesome truth about the Slánský trial—in which Noel's name had been used to convict loyal Communists—had recently been publicly exposed.

In its aftermath, Czech Communists were calling for a more general cleansing, including a reexamination of the 1948 "suicide" of Foreign Minister Jan Masaryk. Suppressed atrocities and abuses of Soviet power in the name of the "the people" suddenly exploded in public and in the press. Exuberant mass rallies supporting the party's call for "socialism with a human face" were in flamboyant contrast to the stolid, obligatory May Day marches. The idea—launched by Dubček and his party—of Communism with free elections, a free media, and, eventually, over a ten-year period, a multiparty system—was heady indeed. The Prague Spring was about the power of words and ideas, not guns and Molotov cocktails. To the Kremlin, both were equally dangerous.

From Budapest, Noel followed reports of students massed on Wenceslas Square—their banners proclaiming "Free Speech! Free Elections!" Prague was a city Field knew intimately, so these scenes surely stirred deep emotions. Then, too, as a youth at Harvard and later in Washington, he had marched for similar rights for the disenfranchised and powerless. These were not "counterrevolutionaries" but students with backpacks, housewives carrying string bags of groceries, workers in their soft caps. Wenceslas Square—the heart of the Prague Spring—was the historic neighborhood from where Field himself was kidnapped in 1949.

\*

"I have a hard time," Noel wrote his brother on March 24, 1968, "not giving way to depression and alienation most of the time, and this, to a lesser extent applies to Herta as well." As always, America, not the Soviet Union, was to blame for all the world's ills. "While we have the advantage of living in a society whose aims we basically approve of, we are profoundly affected by what goes on in the rest of the world, especially in America. Sometimes I feel that if I were in America now, I'd have little choice but to set fire to myself in the White House grounds. I realize this may be over pessimistic. I follow positive developments with close interest—from the hippies through the Black Power [movement] to [Eugene] McCarthy and [Robert] Kennedy. But is there any real hope in the face of the forces of evil?"

★

Evil showed its face on August 21, 1968. Its features, however, were not American. Five hundred thousand Warsaw Pact troops from Poland, Hungary, Bulgaria, and East Germany, under Soviet command, poured into Czechoslovakia and crushed Prague's Spring. Soviet tanks rumbled down Prague's narrow, cobblestoned streets as they had in Budapest twelve years before. The demonstrators did not disperse, however. Armed only with clenched fists and rage, they blocked the "fraternal" army of occupation. Graffiti became another of the Czechs' weapons of choice.

Students drew swastikas on Soviet tanks and scrawled *"Rusove Tahnete Domo!"*—"Russians Go Home!"—on walls. Surrounded by faces tight with hate, the soldiers, under orders not to shoot, were prisoners in their own tanks. For weeks the population continued to surge against the occupiers. The Czechs' passive resistance was brave and deeply moving, but ultimately futile. The Kremlin had demonstrated that Czechoslovakia was just another province of the Soviet empire, whose power to determine its own fate was nil. Times had changed in one regard. Alexander Dubček was not executed at dawn, merely dispatched to oblivion in the provinces, and later made ambassador to Turkey. In the eighties, Dubček lived to see a real Prague Spring under Václav Havel. He stood beside Havel and cheered when Warsaw Pact troops withdrew—permanently.

After the Soviets' violent crushing of Czechoslovakia's experiment in reform, perhaps not even Noel Field could delude himself about Communism's true nature.

This time, Noel made no statements supporting the repression. His colleague at the magazine, Rudi Fischer, remembers Noel as withdrawn and tight-lipped after Prague's suppression. That year, Field stopped paying his Communist Party dues.

# CHAPTER 25

# HOME AT LAST

*I left Communism as one clambers out of a poisoned river strewn with the wreckage of flooded cities and the corpses of the drowned.*

—Arthur Koestler

THE GENTLE, ROLLING green hills of the Virginia hunt country preened for Erica Glaser Wallach on a fall afternoon in 1957, as she and her husband drove to Warrenton, Virginia. No sign marked the entrance to "Hopefield," her new home. Erica and Bob arrived at a winding gravel driveway flanked by time-worn, low stone walls on each side, where cows lazily munched grass in the fading autumn light, a vista of paddocks and fields as far as the eye travels. The sight of the house must have taken the weary traveler's breath away. Of faded rosy brick, with a white-columned entrance, Hopefield is a place of simple elegance, burnished by the years, and not much altered since the Civil War.

But now Erica's entire attention was on the two small sentries who stood waiting for their mother, with their aunt and their grandmother, at the front door.

With children who needed their mother, and a husband who had spent the past five years waging a campaign for his wife's freedom, in a setting of calm and unostentatious beauty, Erica healed. The simple meals served on antique china, polished silver, and crystal glasses, in a dining room hung with family oil portraits dating from the Civil War and earlier, soon blurred her memories of the past terrible decade. She, who had started life in an equally refined setting in her native Germany, thrived in the genteel world of the Virginia hunt country. Walking the dogs across the fallow fields, she inhaled farm smells familiar from her childhood. Hopefield seemed created for this survivor of a lost world. Before long, Erica, Bob, Madeleine, and Bobby had forged a close family. Perhaps because even in the Gulag, under the circumstances, Erica had lived an astonishingly full human existence—interacting with her fellow inmates and jailers, actually forming relationships—her transition to freedom was not particularly traumatic. "She loved America," Hope Porter, her sister-in-law, recalled. "She thought Communism was a failed system. But she had not a shred of bitterness about what she had been through—not even toward Noel."

"After just a week at home," her son Robert Wallach Jr. recalled, "I felt I had my mother back. Some of my friends, however," he added, "were terrified of her. She'd grab kids by the scruff of the neck and say things like 'Don't be an ass!' which we never heard from grownups. Mother was not a cozy, cuddly sort."

Erica soon embarked on a new career as a Virginia private school teacher of French and Latin. Her students at the Highland Day School found her blunt style and occasional salty language a thrilling change from other teachers. The story of Mrs. Wallach's summons to the headmaster's office for a scolding was school legend. "Goddamnit," she reportedly answered her frustrated superior, "Why should anybody give a damn if I curse?" Before long the school installed speed bumps on the driveway, in a futile attempt to slow down Mrs. Wallach. Erica was in a hurry. She had been robbed of seven years.

"She had a mischievous gleam in her eye," recalls Stevenson McIlvaine, whose writer mother, Jane McIlvaine, was one of Erica's closest friends. "She talked to us children about how she kept her mind alive in captivity. We were spellbound. We had never heard such things! She never patronized us kids. And she was so clearly not of the riding, hunting world of teas and horse shows. Erica—good looking, tall, with a very deep, Marlene Dietrich voice—made you think of cafés, not horse shows. But," McIlvaine marveled, "somehow, she fit in."

The children took to her faster than some of their parents. The local gentry was wary of this vivid, outspoken woman in the heart of the tweedy, tradition-bound hunt country. Moreover, in the post-McCarthy era, she was suspected of being slightly "pink." Then, too, she had a habit of turning down invitations with almost brutal candor. "You have to give an excuse, Erica," Hope Porter tried to explain. "You can't just say you don't feel like going."

J. Edgar Hoover was not quite done with Erica. During the year following her arrival, twice a week, two of Hoover's agents called on her. "The same question, the same answers," she said, "one more time. They were polite and correct, but ignorant of European politics, and I had to spell everything out and explain the simplest things. . . . The day came," she said, "when they informed me that their investigation was terminated."

Three years earlier, Erica had turned down the offer of financial compensation for the years stolen from her by the Soviet Union. In 1958, however, she accepted a check from the House Un-American Activities Committee. "I enclose a check in the amount of $31.16 to reimburse you for your expenses in connection with your appearance before this Committee. Signed, Richard Arens, Staff Director." In her busy new life, she rarely thought and almost never talked about Noel Field. Now she was truly free.

Her niece, Feroline Higginson, recalls only one incident when

Erica's painful past shattered her composure. "In the spring of 1974, Erica came down to Charlottesville," Feroline recalled. "I was attending the University of Virginia and Aleksandr Solzhenitsyn was our guest speaker. After the lecture, a few of us attended a reception for him in the UVa Rotunda. Solzhenitsyn had his back to us when Erica addressed him in Russian as 'Citizen Solzhenitsyn.' He spun around and said angrily, in Russian, 'No one addresses someone as "Citizen," unless speaking to a prisoner.' Erica, taken aback and quite shaken, replied, 'That is the capacity in which I was in your country.' It was the only time I ever saw Erica, a very formidable person, intimidated. They were both shaken. Solzhenitsyn never relaxed after that." For a brief moment, two former inmates were plunged back in the ice-cold world of the Gulag Archipelago.

✳

Ten years after her ordeal, Erica finally wrote her prison memoir. Characteristically, she flipped Koestler's *Darkness at Noon* to a title better suited to her own temperament, *Light at Midnight.* Plainly written and unheroic, it is, nonetheless, a scorching account of her time in Soviet custody. Erica, however, dwells on the humanity of her fellow inmates, and pities some (not all) of her jailers—themselves victims of the system. *Light at Midnight* is a powerful indictment of a system based on cruelty and the degradation of the human spirit— which, in her youth, she admired. "There is no doubt in my mind," she concludes, "that the five years [of prison] added something to my life."

Not even the publication of her memoir was free from intrigue, however. In those precomputer days, her publisher had only one copy of Erica's finished manuscript. One day, the book disappeared from Doubleday's New York offices. In panic, her editor searched for the missing tome, sending the editorial staff into a tailspin. Fortunately, Erica had made a copy of her unedited manuscript, and the editing process could restart. Several months later, at a Washington garden party, Erica had a chance encounter with the man whose name had been intertwined with Noel Field's and her own. A smiling Allen W. Dulles, head of the CIA, approached her, cocktail in hand. "How is your book coming, Erica?" Dulles asked. Surprised he knew about her memoir, Erica answered that it was soon to be published. "I'm glad," Dulles answered, "I told them it was good, and that it should be published." She asked, "You've read it?" The master spy had given himself away. "I guess I shouldn't have said that," he answered sheepishly. "Made a mistake. Never mind. I really did enjoy it, and I'm glad it's being published."

For Noel Field, reading Erica's book was a more painful experience. Even this practiced denier of reality could not deny that he was the cause of her ordeal. On February 2, 1968, a full year after she sent him her book, he finally wrote to her. "There are passages which I find debatable," he wrote, in a lawyerlike, detached tone. "Not so much as regards the facts, as from the *political point of view*, I mean the wisdom of publishing them at this time (or at all). I have in mind notably your— to my mind *exaggerated*—comments on the East German regime and its representatives."

Then, having fulfilled his role as party propagandist, Noel's letter reveals genuine emotion. What follows is the most revealing account of Field's own life in solitary confinement.

"The thing that overwhelms us is your detailed memory of those five years," he wrote Erica. "In our case—especially in mine—most of the details have—purposely no doubt—become submerged in the subconscious, and only return in sudden disconnected flashes, for instance, when we talk with friends who went through the same experiences, and now, in reading your book. There are numerous paragraphs—whole pages indeed—which I might have written myself with just a few words changed. . . . I could practically repeat every line." Field admits for the first time his own nightmare as Soviet prisoner. "I also played chess against myself, but only in imagination. And I developed a whole system of thought mathematics, including the square and ambic roots of all numbers up to a thousand. I not merely listened to symphonies, but conducted them too. My great annoyance in this connection was that, in the Beethoven symphonies, I know all the movements, but in the case of the scherzos was uncertain which belonged to which symphony!

"A vital difference," Noel wrote Erica, "was your contact by tapping. Neither Herta nor I had any part in it—again because we did not know a word of Hungarian," again underscoring just how isolated he and Herta were in their Budapest prisons, and then adding bizarrely, "In looking back, I'm glad our five years of solitary were uninterrupted by this kind of 'conversation.' In this way, I remained ignorant of Herta's presence, only three cells from mine. I would have gone mad if I'd known it," Noel admits. "Like you, both of us sought to forget the existence, the very names of those we loved," adding the most devastating indictment of an inhuman system. "Once—it must have been in the third year—I heard Herta sneeze. I spent the rest of my stay convincing myself that of course it wasn't she: it was simply the first woman's voice I had heard in three years, so I had jumped to the ridiculous conclusion that it was Herta's!" Indeed, it was Herta's, three cells away.

Within days of receiving Noel's letter, Erica fired off her reply. Hers is as revealing of her passionate humanity as his of his effort to sublimate his. "Thank you for your letter, Noel," she wrote. "I had sort of given up. It had been almost a year since I sent you the book and I assumed that was that. But as far as East Germany is concerned . . . if you think I exaggerated, let me tell you, on the contrary, I toned it down. In fact, I cut out entire passages that made the Germans look a lot worse. And all of it was the exact truth. . . . Debatable as to the wisdom of publication?" she asks. "Surely, it is always debatable, at any period in history. Silence is also debatable," she pointedly concludes. "It has enabled many crimes."

Despite Noel's determined efforts to erase the past, Erica's prison memories summoned his own and he kept returning to her memoir. "In glancing through your book again," in a later, undated letter, Noel wrote, "I was struck by another amusing parallel. I, too, spent my time [in prison] listing the (at the time) 48 States of the Union. For weeks, I tried to systematize them—up and down—I mean North and South, South to North—and left and right—East and West; right of the Mississippi and left of it; etc. Then, for weeks—maybe months—I 'amused' myself by trying to list the capitals and principal cities of each State. Again and again," he relates, "I switched town from one State to another. As I recall, I was completely stumped by North and South Dakota. The closest I came to providing a capital for either one of them was 'Tapioca'!" America, it seems, was still deeply embedded in Noel Field's DNA.

★

In 1993, Erica was unable to deliver her annual witty Christmas toast to a festive gathering of friends and neighbors at Hopefield. She lay ill with cancer in a nearby hospital. Characteristically, she insisted the party proceed. From her sickbed in Warrenton's Fauquier Hospital, she dictated words her son, Robert, read on her behalf. Erica was saying good-bye.

"It took me ten years to get to this country," her son said, reading his mother's words, "and when I came, I came from a totally different world. From the moment I stepped into Hopefield, with Grandma standing at the front door with open arms, and welcoming me home, it has been the most incredible miracle for me. I didn't realize I was walking into the most wonderful family, who gave me loyalty, support, friendship and love. I've had the most wonderful, happy thirty-six years of my life. And I want to especially mention my children, who, by all the laws of psychology, should be the most miserable creatures, but have been my greatest joy, help and love, and I thank them for everything they have done."

Erica Glaser Wallach, age seventy-one, valiant survivor of the terrible past century, died the next day.

# CHAPTER 26

# THE STRANGER

*Two vast and trunkless legs of stone*
*Stand in the desert. Near them, on the sand,*
*Half sunk, a shattered visage lies . . .*
*And on the pedestal these words appear:*
*"My name is Ozymandias, King of Kings;*
*Look on my works, ye Mighty, and despair!"*
*Nothing beside remains. Round the decay*
*Of that colossal Wreck, boundless and bare*
*The lone and level sands stretch far away.*

—Percy Bysshe Shelley

THE TALL, HAGGARD man waits for the number 21 bus at the Freedom Hill stop. A small cluster of commuters hangs nearby, not people to waste smiles or conversation on strangers. Nor are the Hungarians any longer surprised by the American in their midst. Though Noel Field does his best to blend in, murmurs *"jo reggelt,"* good morning, to his fellow commuters, he will never be one of them. His great height; long, ashen hair; high, domed forehead; and elongated features are too obviously Anglo-Saxon, his accent too American, to ever pass unnoticed in Budapest. What precisely brought this man to their bus stop on a hillside in Buda, in this forlorn corner of Central Europe, they do not know. There are too many human wrecks in Hungary in the late sixties. Curiosity can be dangerous.

If the Hungarians searched Noel Field's features more closely, they would see a face haunted by unacknowledged regret. They would also be surprised to learn that he is not so very old at all. In his early sixties, Field, slow of movement and stooped, looks much older. All his fellow commuters know is that—though they see him nearly every morning—he remains a stranger, *the American.*

Yet Noel Field has done everything to distance himself from the faraway country where his family settled over three hundred years earlier. The America he identifies with—a utopia where property and income are equitably distributed among workers—does not exist, and never has. Neither does it exist in those countries calling themselves workers' states, including the one he has chosen as his home. But this Noel Field will not acknowledge. He has spent a decade and a half here without ever once criticizing a system much of its own population reviles. Human aberrations—not the faith itself—were to blame for millions of lives wrecked by mass arrests, fake trials, torture, and executions. Nor has Field ever expressed regret for abetting one of history's most murderous experiments.

Inside the lumbering bus, wheezing its way down Freedom Hill toward the Danube and Pest, Noel daily admires the shimmering panorama, the play of light on the Danube reflecting the architectural fantasies lining the riverbank. This man, who passionately loved mountains—the Alps in particular—is locked in a country of gentler hills, without an outlet to the sea. Noel, however, survives by avoiding the trap of self-examination and self-reproach. He prefers to focus on the beauty of the ancient city he calls home.

★

Budapest in the late sixties is somber and wounded, with much to forget. The city cleaned up the postrevolution rubble fast. Nobody wanted reminders of that failed uprising, not the people and not those who extinguished their hopes. Resignation replaced hope. The Soviets will never leave; János Kádár, who assumed power on the back of Soviet tanks, may not be such a bad man—*we have seen far worse here*—Stalinist terror is in the past. Pleasures are small, but people no longer live in fear. A popular television thriller even features a dog named Stalin. Those who could not accommodate themselves to Kádár's "goulash Communism" have fled or are in jail. The state practices soft repression. The people—like so many agnostics forced to worship—dream of passports and cars, not revolution. Hungary—indeed, the Soviet empire—inches toward a petit-bourgeois, consumer society. The espresso is good. A dozen Turkish baths scattered around the city offer a range of relief. Not even the KGB has figured out how to bug steam baths, so in those watery intellectual cafés there is outlet for dissent. An InterContinental Hotel has risen on the Danube Corso, a source of hope and excitement. Lake Balaton beckons in the summer. Like the rest of the population, Field takes his modest pleasures where he can find them.

The Fields and J. Peters—a relic of Noel's days as a young Soviet agent in Washington—share some convivial evenings at the Matyas Pince, a wine cellar where Gypsy fiddlers scrape out old Hungarian folk tunes and the chicken paprika is the best in town. "Pete," as Whittaker Chambers and Alger Hiss knew him, never fully approved of Field. "Naïve," Pete said of Noel. "Like all the other Quaker communists." In truth, Noel was not much of a spy—he tried his best to serve Moscow, but he lacked the smooth, hard veneer of pros like Pete. There was always a touch of the romantic idealist about Field. Nor was he reluctant to betray his country, however. When called upon to assist in the assassination of a good Communist who disagreed with

Stalin, Field was willing to do his part. Others may have hatched the plot against Ignaz Reiss, and still others pulled the trigger, but Field was prepared to help.

Pete added another notch to his belt in 1972. The famed American film director Joseph Losey was in Budapest to film *The Assassination of Trotsky*. Starring the legendary British actor Richard Burton as the Soviet revolutionary leader and Stalin's nemesis, with scores of other international stars, it was a lavish production, and Losey, a former Communist himself, hired Pete as consultant. The film is a sympathetic portrait of Stalin's archrival. But Moscow's former agent now served Hollywood, and Pete's reward was an invitation to Budapest's most glamorous postwar social event: a birthday party hosted by Richard Burton in honor of his wife, Elizabeth Taylor. Held in the capital's gleaming new InterContinental Hotel, on February 9, 1972, Burton and Taylor—the most celebrated couple of the day—were joined by Princess Grace of Monaco, Ringo Starr, Michael Caine, and Raquel Welch, among other members of the international glitterati. Sipping champagne imported for the occasion from France, Pete, his Hungarian-accented English still shaded by his years in Brooklyn, mingled easily with Hollywood royalty. Who remembered that four decades earlier, the jovial little man with the Harpo Marx mustache tracked Trotsky's supporters in the streets of New York and Washington, DC? Times had changed. J. Peters survived.

The man who sobbed, "All gone, all gone," during the long night of his torment in the Villa must surely have occasionally wept over his life's misbegotten trajectory. There was no one but Herta with whom Noel might share his anguish at the way his life turned out, and she was really an extension of himself. The once-sparkling intellect who dashed through a four-year Harvard curriculum in two years, and of whom one of his State Department chiefs had written, "Mr. Field is one of the most brilliant men we have ever had in the [West European] Division," the man who had drafted speeches for two secretaries of state (Stimson and Hull) now spent his days proofreading the rough English translations of Hungarian writers. Asthma, lumbago, heart trouble, ulcers, and, finally and fatally, cancer were his postprison companions. His final consolation was not Marx, but music. In the land of Liszt and Bartók, there was plenty of that.

"That last day," Herta wrote to his family of Noel's quiet passing on September 12, 1970, "was particularly lovely. Noel slept most of the time, but in the evening we listened to a beautiful performance of [Beethoven's] *Fidelio*—in each other's arms." How ironic that the last piece of music Field heard was Beethoven's ode to freedom, whose hero, Fidelio, languishes in a dungeon, the prisoner of a ruthless dictator.

At the very end, as he was drifting in and out of consciousness, Noel asked for Erica one final time. "I made a big mistake not to visit him. I utterly regret that," Erica said when she heard this of the man who cost her five years of freedom and untold distress. Once, decades before, however, Field had been a loving surrogate father to a lost girl. "I wonder now," she said, still confused by a man of so many parts, "who was he?"

He died with only the faithful Herta by his side. An exile his whole life—not quite Swiss, not quite American, certainly not Hungarian—the deepest roots he planted were in a toxic soil. How could he bring himself to admit such a tragic mistake? Without his faith, who was he?

In death, however, Noel Field realized his cherished dream. Accorded a funeral fit for a Communist hero, Field was hailed in the Hungarian press as "the courageous fighter of the international workers' movement" and, with unintended irony, as "the true son of the American people." He lay in state in the pantheon of Hungary's Communist notables, at the Kerepesi Cemetery. (After many purges, there were too few Communist heroes to fill the many planned crypts, so, over the years, philosophers, physicists, and a celebrated chef, Károly

Gundel, joined them). László Rajk—another of Stalin's "rehabilitated" victims—rests in their midst.

An honor guard of blue-uniformed Workers' Militia, brandishing AK-47s, flanked Field's coffin. At the request of the deceased, they sang long-out-of-fashion revolutionary marching songs. Among the mourners was a motley assemblage of the country's surviving old-time Communists, and Noel's colleagues from the *New Hungarian Quarterly*. Respecting Noel's final request, they joined together in singing the "Internationale." Decades before, the words of this nineteenth-century French anthem to the workers' movement had so stirred Noel he memorized it in Russian, and belted it out in front of the Lincoln Memorial—to the consternation of his Soviet handler, Héde Massing. "This is the final struggle," the Hungarians now sang. "Let us group together, and tomorrow the 'Internationale' will be the human race." Their voices, however, lacked all conviction.

"Frankly," Noel's colleague Rudi Fischer, one of the mourners, recalled, "most of us didn't even know the words anymore. So we just kind of mumbled it. It was pretty embarrassing." Even Moscow had long since discarded the "Internationale," the musical expression of the ideals of the October Revolution, in favor a nationalistic "Hymn of the Soviet Union." But on September 18, 1970, they buried one of the "Internationale's" last true believers.

Herta lived a decade longer. When she died, her ashes were placed in a small marble urn next to her husband's at the Farkasréti Cemetery, a far less exclusive burial ground than the Kerepesi, where Noel's remains were moved shortly after his brief stay in the Communist pantheon. Their ashes remain there, united in death, as they had been in their strange life.

Noel was spared the 1989 funeral of the empire he served. Nor was he was alive when the heroic sculptures of striding, muscular workers, and the demigods Lenin and Stalin preaching to the masses, were hauled from their pedestals, heaved on trucks, and deposited in a park in the outskirts of Budapest. There they still stand in Statue Park, a popular tourist attraction for generations with dimming memories of these bronze giants. Of Noel's empire, far fewer reminders remain than of the Ottomans, who left Budapest scores of magnificent public baths.

Noel Field began life with the best intentions, embracing Communism as the way to prevent another calamity on the scale of World War I. The most powerful figure in his formation—his father—might have guided the passionate youth toward a gentler cause. There was no one else who exercised that moderating influence—and there were so many in the thirties preaching the opposite message. But as Marxism curdled into Leninism, then hardened into Stalinism, Field failed utterly in his youthful ambition to help build a classless society. He never criticized the system he served, never showed regret for his role in abetting a murderous dictatorship. At the beginning, his deception was motivated by idealism. Life changes all of us, of course. Field's remorselessness in inflicting pain on his family and excusing mass murder as "the mistake of a few" points, however, to a more fundamental alteration. Years of deception and self-deception had soaked into his character, washing away the humanity his father tried to implant.

At the end, Noel Field was still a willing prisoner of an ideology that captured him when his youthful ardor ran highest. A man who set out to change the world ended up a stranger in a strange land.

# ACKNOWLEDGMENTS

T HIS BOOK owes its start to stories told by my parents of meeting the mysterious American spy Noel Field during the Hungarian Revolution, when they became the only Western journalists to locate and interview Field and his wife, Herta, in exile. Many years later, my friend the historian Arthur Schlesinger Jr. also spoke to me of meeting Noel Field during World War II. Schlesinger was immediately suspicious of Field's loyalties and discouraged OSS chief "Wild Bill" Donovan from collaborating with the American.

I could not have written this account without the support of Alison, Hugh, and Alan Field, the children of Noel's brother, Hermann. I thank them for their hospitality and for sharing their memories of their uncle Noel and their parents, Hermann and Kate Field. Thanks to them, I also gained access to the Field Family Papers, archived in Boston University's Howard Gotlieb Archival Research Center.

Erica Wallach's family—her children Robert Wallach Jr. and Madeleine Wallach de Heller, and her cousins by marriage Feroline Higginson and Hope Porter—all shared their own stories of this remarkable woman with me. They also allowed me access to Erica's private papers, letters, and other invaluable materials never before available to researchers or historians. I am deeply grateful for their generosity in helping me to bring Erica Glaser Wallach and her astonishing journey to vivid life.

The legendary journalist Flora Lewis, a friend and colleague of my parents, interviewed many of the key figures in this narrative four decades ago. Many of those interviews are published here for the first time, as Ms. Lewis did not use a great many of them in *Red Pawn*, her account of the Field saga. I thank her son Lindsey Gruson for allowing me to use his mother's archives.

Hungarian historian Dr. Ilona Kiss provided invaluable help in navigating both the Hungarian Secret Police Archives in Budapest and the KGB Archives in Moscow. Also in Budapest, my friend John Shattuck, Rector of

Central European University, greatly facilitated my research with a fellowship at CEU's Institute of Advanced Studies. Laszlo Kunos, my Hungarian publisher, introduced me to surviving colleagues of Noel Field's at the *New Hungarian Quarterly* and Corvina Publishers.

I thank Marc Pressman, my resourceful Boston-based researcher, who helped me retrieve documents on the Fields from Boston University's Howard Gotlieb Center. Hungarian historian and archivist Istvan Rev made helpful suggestions, for which I thank him. I must also acknowledge Maria Schmidt, who did early and important research on this subject. The book has also benefitted enormously from many hours of conversation with László Rajk Jr.

My assistant, Loryn Hatch, kept me and the project smoothly rolling; her patience with my many technical challenges was boundless. There is no fact she cannot unearth, no crisis that shakes her always-calm presence.

I am grateful to David Remnick for pointing me toward some important sources. I thank Nader Mousavizedeh for helping me find the right title. Cass Sunstein encouraged me to focus on the lasting impact Noel Field's friend Alger Hiss has made on the ongoing American culture wars. My friend and much-admired writer Larissa MacFarquhar read and improved on an early draft, as did Richard Bernstein and Anne Nelson. Leon Wieseltier supplied insights on history and human behavior—Noel Field's and other True Believers'. The book is vastly better for their generous contributions, even as they worked on their own books.

Anthony Marx, the president of the New York Public Library, provided the sanctuary of the Allen Room, which enabled me to access the Library's unsurpassed collections and gave me a perfect place to work in the company of other writers.

Once again, my gifted editor Alice Mayhew shared my excitement for this project and kept me on the right track throughout. I cannot imagine this work without her guiding presence.

Amanda Urban, my indispensible friend and agent for this and seven prior books, is at the core of my writing life. I am forever in her debt for her unflagging editorial and personal support.

My family—Julia, Andrew, Mathieu, Sabine, Nicolas, Lilli, and, of course, my children Lizzie and Chris—cheered me on and provided love, laughter, and lively conversation. I deeply regret that my parents did not live to see this work—in which, once again, they played their part.

# BIBLIOGRAPHY

Ali, Tariq. *Fear of Mirrors*. Calcutta: Seagull Books, 2010.

Alter, Jonathan. *The Defining Moment: FDR's Hundred Days and the Triumph of Hope*. New York: Simon & Schuster, 2006.

Applebaum, Anne. *Iron Curtain: The Crushing of Eastern Europe, 1944–1956*. New York: Doubleday, 2012.

Berlin, Isaiah. *The Soviet Mind: Russian Culture under Communism*. Washington, DC: Brookings Institution Press, 2004.

Bernd-Rainer Barth, Werner Schweitzer, and Thomas Grimm. *Der Fall Noel Field*. Berlin: Basis Druck, 2005.

Bethell, John T. *Harvard Observed: An Illustrated History of the University in the Twentieth century*. Cambridge, MA: Harvard University Press, 1998.

Billinger, Karl (pseudonym of Paul Massing). *Fatherland*. New York: Farrar & Rinehart, 1935.

Brooks, Howard Lee. *Prisoners of Hope: Report on a Mission*. New York: Fischer, 1942.

Caute, David. *Joseph Losey: A Revenge on Life*. New York: Oxford University Press, 1994.

Cesarani, David. *Arthur Koestler: The Homeless Mind*. New York: Free Press, 1998.

Chambers, Whittaker. *Witness*. Washington, DC: Gateway Editions, 2002.

Checiński, Michał. *Poland: Communism, Nationalism, Anti-Semitism*. New York: Karz-Cohl Publishers, 1982.

Crossman, Richard, ed. *The God That Failed*. New York: Columbia University Press, 2001.

Dandelion, Pink. *The Quakers: A Very Short Introduction*. New York: Oxford University Press, 2008.

Davis, Hope Hale. *Great Day Coming: A Memoir of the 1930s*. South Royalton, VT: Steerforth Press, 1994.

Dobbs, Michael. *Six Months in 1945: FDR, Stalin, Churchill, and Truman: From World War to Cold War*. New York: Vintage Books, 2013.

Dreisziger, Nándor F., ed. *Hungary in the Age of Total War, 1938–1948*. Bradenton, FL: East European Monographs, 1998.

Dulles, Allen. *The Craft of Intelligence*. New York: New American Library, 1965.

Duplan, Christian, and Vencent Giret. *La vie en rouge*. Paris: Éditions du Seuil, 1994.

Duranty, Walter. *I Write as I Please*. New York: Halycon House, 1935.

Faber, David. *Munich, 1938: Appeasement and World War II*. New York: Simon & Schuster, 2009.

Field, Hermann and Kate. *Trapped in the Cold War*. Stanford, CA: Stanford University Press, 2000.

Field, Noel. "Hitching Our Wagon to a Star." *Mainstream*, January 1961.

Fry, Varian. *Surrender on Demand*. Boulder, CO: Johnson Books, 1995.

———. "Our Consuls at Work." *The Nation*, May 2, 1942, 507–9.

Gaddis, J. *George F. Kennan: An American Life*. New York: Penguin, 2011.

Gellately, Robert. *Stalin's Curse: Battling for Communism in War and Cold War*. New York: Knopf, 2013.

Goldman, Eric Frederick. *The Crucial Decade: America, 1945–1955*. New York: Knopf, 1956.

Grose, Peter. *Gentleman Spy: The Life of Allen Dulles*. Boston: Houghton Mifflin, 1994.

Gunther, John. *Behind the Curtain*. New York: Harper, 1949.

Halberstam, David. *The Fifties*. New York: Ballantine Books, 1994.

Halperin, Ernst. *The Triumphant Heretic: Tito's Struggle against Stalin*. London: Heinemann, 1958.

Haynes, John Earl, and Harvey Klehr. *Venona: Decoding Soviet Espionage in America*. New Haven, CT: Yale University Press, 1999.

"Hermann Field Arrives in Zurich for Reunion with Wife and Sister," *New York Times*, November 20, 1954.

Hitchens, Christopher. *Hitch-22: A Memoir*. New York: Twelve, 2010.

Hodos, George H. *Show Trials: Stalinist Purges in Eastern Europe, 1948–1954*. New York: Praeger, 1987.

Ignotus, Paul. *Political Prisoner*. London: Routledge and Kegan Paul, 1959.

Jacoby, Susan. *Alger Hiss and the Battle for History*. New Haven, CT: Yale University Press, 2009.

Jordan, Henry. "Where Is Noel Field?" *Argosy*, November 1958.

Judt, Tony. *Past Imperfect: French Intellectuals, 1944–1956*. New York: New York University Press, 2011.

———. *The Memory Chalet*. New York: Penguin, 2010.

———. *Postwar: A History of Europe Since 1945*. New York: Penguin, 2005.

Kempton, Murray. *Part of Our Time: Some Ruins and Monuments of the Thirties*. New York: New York Review of Books, 2012.

Kinzer, Stephen. *The Brothers: John Foster Dulles, Allen Dulles, and Their Secret World War*. New York: Times Books, 2013.

Klehr, Harvey, John Earl Haynes, and Fridrikh Igorevich Firsov. *The Secret World of American Communism*. New Haven, CT: Yale University Press, 1995.

Klima, Ivan. *My Crazy Century: A Memoir*. New York: Grove Press, 2013.

Koch, Stephen. *Double Lives: Spies and Writers in the Secret Soviet War of Ideas Against the West*. New York: Enigma Books, 2004.

Koestler, Arthur. *Arrival and Departure*. New York: Random House, 2011.
———. *Darkness at Noon*. New York: Bantam, 1968.
———. *Dialogue with Death*. Chicago: University of Chicago Press, 2011.
———. *The Invisible Writing*. New York: Macmillan, 1978.
———. *Scum of the Earth*. London: Eland, 2006.
Koltai, Ferenc, ed. *László Rajk and His Accomplices before the People's Court*. Budapest: Budapest Printing Press, 1949.
Koudelka, Josef. *Invasion 68: Prague*. Paris: Tana Éditions, 2008.
Krivitsky, Walter G. *In Stalin's Secret Service: Memoirs of the First Soviet Master Spy to Defect*. New York: Enigma, 2000.
Latham, Earl. *The Communist Controversy in Washington: From the New Deal to McCarthy*. Cambridge, MA: Harvard University Press, 1966.
*Laurence Duggan, 1905–1948: In Memoriam*. Stamford, CT: Overbrook Press, 1949.
Lendvai, Paul. *The Hungarians: A Thousand Years of Victory in Defeat*. Princeton, NJ: Princeton University Press, 2004.
Lewis, Flora. *Red Pawn: The Story of Noel Field*. Garden City, NY: Doubleday, 1965.
———. "Who Killed Krivitsky?" *Washington Post*, February 13, 1966.
Lukes, Igor. "The Rudolf Slansky Affair: New Evidence." *Slavic Review* 58, no. 1 (Spring 1999): 160–87.
Manchester, William. *The Glory and the Dream: A Narrative History of America, 1932–1972*. New York: Bantam, 1975.
Mark, Eduard. "In Re Alger Hiss: A Final Verdict from the Archives of the KGB." *Journal of Cold War Studies* 11, no. 3 (Summer 2009): 26–67.
Marton, Endre. *The Forbidden Sky*. Boston: Little, Brown, 1971.
Massing, Hede. *This Deception*. New York: Ivy/Ballantine, 1987.
Mastny, Vojtech. *The Cold War and Soviet Insecurity*. New York: Oxford University Press, 1996.
Miller, Arthur. *Timebends: A Life*. New York: Grove, 2013.
Milosz, Czeslaw. *The Captive Mind*. New York: Vintage, 1990.
Mindszenty, J. *Memoirs*, London: Weidenfeld & Nicolson, 1974.
Moorehead, Caroline, ed. *Selected Letters of Martha Gellhorn*. New York: Macmillan, 2007.
Mosley, Leonard. *Dulles: A Biography of Eleanor, Allen and John Foster Dulles and Their Family Network*. New York: Dial Press, 1978.
Murphy, Robert Daniel. *Diplomat among Warriors*. Garden City, NY: Doubleday, 1964.
Orwell, George. *Homage to Catalonia*. London: Penguin, 2013.
Paloczi-Horvath, George. *The Undefeated*. London: Eland, 1959.
Paxton, Robert O. *Vichy France: Old Guard and New Order, 1940–1944*. New York: Knopf, 1972.
Pelikan, Jiri. *The Czechoslovak Political Trials, 1950–1954*. Stanford, CA: Stanford University Press, 1971.
Petersen, Neal H. *From Hitler's Doorstep: The Wartime Intelligence Reports of Allen Dulles, 1942–1945*. University Park: Pennsylvania State University Press, 2010.
Pipes, Richard. *Russia under the Bolshevik Regime*. New York: Knopf, 1994.
Plokhy, Serhii M. *Yalta: The Price of Peace*. New York: Viking, 2010.

"Polish Defector Bares Data on Missing Field Family," *New York Times*, September 29, 1954.

Pollack, Andy. "The Unitarian Who Shook Europe." *Oscailit: Cork & Dublin Unitarian Magazine*, December 2009.

Poretsky, Elisabeth K. *Our Own People: A Memoir of "Ignace Reiss" and His Friends*. Ann Arbor: University of Michigan Press, 1969.

Reed, John. *Ten Days That Shook the World*. Harmondsworth, UK: Penguin, 1977.

Remnick, David. *The Devil Problem: And Other True Stories*. New York: Vintage, 1997.

Rhodes, Richard. *Hell and Good Company: The Spanish Civil War and the World It Made*. New York: Simon & Schuster, 2015.

Sakmyster, Thomas L. *Red Conspirator: J. Peters and the American Communist Underground*. Chicago: University of Illinois Press, 2011.

Sharp, Tony. *Stalin's American Spy: Noel Field, Allen Dulles and the East European Show Trials*. London: Hurst & Company, 2014.

Scammell, Michael. *Koestler: The Literary and Political Odyssey of a Twentieth-Century Skeptic*. New York: Random House, 2009.

Schlesinger, Arthur M., Jr. *The Age of Roosevelt*. 3 vols. Boston: Houghton Mifflin, 1957–1960; 1967, 2002, 2003.

———. *A Life in the Twentieth Century: Innocent Beginnings, 1917–1950*. Boston: Houghton Mifflin, 2000.

Schmidt, Mária. *Battle of Wits: Beliefs, Ideologies and Secret Agents in the 20th Century*. Budapest: Század Int., 2007.

Sebestyen, Victor. *Revolution 1989: The Fall of the Soviet Empire*. New York: Pantheon, 2009.

Shuster, George. *In Silence I Speak: The Story of Cardinal Mindszenty Today and of Hungary's "New Order"*. London: V. Gollancz, 1956.

Sinclair, Upton. *Boston: A Novel*. Cambridge, MA: Linneaean Press, 1978.

Smith, Richard Harris. *OSS: The Secret History of America's First Central Intelligence Agency*. Guilford, CT: Lyons Press, 2005.

Snyder, Timothy. *Bloodlands: Europe between Hitler and Stalin*. New York: Basic Books, 2010.

Solzhenitsyn, Aleksandr. *In the First Circle*, trans. Harry T. Willets. New York: Harper Perennial, 2009.

Spender, Stephen. *World Within World*. London: Hamish Hamilton, 1951.

Stettinius, Edward, Jr. *The Diaries of Edward R. Stettinius, Jr., 1943–1946*. New York: New Viewpoints, 1975.

Straight, Michael. *After Long Silence: A Memoir*. New York: W. W. Norton & Company, 1983.

Subak, Susan Elisabeth. *Rescue and Flight: American Relief Workers Who Defied the Nazis*. Lincoln: University of Nebraska Press, 2010.

Sullivan, Rosemary. *Villa Air-Bel: The Second World War, Escape, and a House in France*. London: Harper, 2007.

Sulzberger, C. L. *A Long Row of Candles: Memoirs and Diaries 1934–1954*. Toronto: Macmillan, 1969.

Szász, Béla. *Volunteers for the Gallows: Anatomy of a Show-Trial*. London: Chatto & Windus, 1971.

Tanenhaus, Sam. *Whittaker Chambers: A Biography*. New York: Modern Library, 1997.

Thompson, Craig. "What Has Stalin Done with Noel Field?" *Saturday Evening Post*, December 15, 1951.

Troy, Thomas F. *Donovan and the CIA*. Frederick, MD: University Publications of America, 1981.

Ulam, Adam B. *Titoism and the Cominform*. Cambridge, MA: Harvard University Press, 1952.

Ungváry, Krisztián. *The Siege of Budapest: One Hundred Days in World War II*. New Haven, CT: Yale University Press, 2005.

United States Congress, House Special Committee on Un-American Activities. *Investigation of Un-American Propaganda Activities in the United States*. Vol. 3. Washington, DC: US Government Printing Office, 1938.

Wallach, Erica. *Light at Midnight*. Garden City, NY: Doubleday, 1967.

"Warsaw Releases Hermann Field," *New York Times*, October 25, 1954.

Weill, Joseph. *Le Combat d'un Juste*. Saumur, France: Éditions Cheminements, 2002.

Weinstein, Allen. *Perjury: The Hiss-Chambers Case*. Stanford, CA: Hoover Press, 2013.

Weinstein, Allen, and Alexander Vassiliev. *The Haunted Wood: Soviet Espionage in America—the Stalin Era*. New York: Modern Library, 2000.

West, Richard. *Tito and the Rise and Fall of Yugoslavia*. London: Sinclair-Stevenson, 1994.

Weyl, Nathaniel. "I Was in a Communist Unit with Hiss." *U.S. News & World Report*, January 9, 1953.

———. *Treason: The Story of Disloyalty and Betrayal in American History*. Washington, DC: Public Affairs Press, 1950.

White, G. Edward. *Alger Hiss's Looking-Glass Wars: The Covert Life of a Soviet Spy*. New York: Oxford University Press, 2005.

Wilson, Edmund. "An Appeal to Progressives." *New Republic*, January 14, 1931.

———. *The Thirties: From Notebooks and Diaries of the Period*. New York: Farrar, Straus & Giroux, 1980.

———. *To the Finland Station: A Study in the Writing and Acting of History*. New York: New York Review of Books, 2003.

Wilson, Hugh Robert. *Diplomat between Wars*. New York: Longmans, Green, 1941.

## INTERNET SOURCES

Rev, Istvan. "Indicting Rajk." Accessed November 13, 2015. http://ccat.sas.upenn.edu/slavic/events/slavic_symposium/Comrades_Please_Shoot_Me/Rev_Rajk.pdf.

Haynes, John Earle, and Harvey Klehr. "Introduction: Alexander Vassiliev's Notebooks: Provenance and Documentation of Soviet Intelligence Activities in the United States." Wilson Center. Accessed November 13, 2015. http://digitalarchive.wilsoncenter.org/document/112855.pdf.

Vassilev, Alexander. Black Notebook, Wilson Center. Accessed November 13, 2015. http://digitalarchive.wilsoncenter.org/document/112860.pdf.

————. White Notebook 2, Wilson Center. Accessed November 13, 2015. http://digitalarchive.wilsoncenter.org/document/112565.pdf.

————. White Notebook 3, Wilson Center. Accessed November 13, 2015. http://digitalarchive.wilsoncenter.org/document/112566.pdf.

## FILM

Schweizer, Werner. *Noel Field: The Fictitious Spy.* Dschoint Ventschr Filmproduktion, 1997.

# NOTES

Abbreviations: The Soviet and Russian security organs have been re-organized and renamed several times since 1918, originally named the OGPU, then the NKVD, then the KGB, and today the FSB. For the sake of simplicity I use KGB as my shorthand reference, since the purpose and the techniques of all these security apparatuses remain the same.

For the description of Noel Field's days in Prague prior to his abduction, I relied on Field's letters to his wife, Herta, as well as Czech and Hungarian secret police records (as below). Also, Flora Lewis's *Red Pawn: The Story of Noel Field* (Garden City, NY: Doubleday, 1965), Tony Sharp's *Stalin's American Spy: Noel Field, Allen Dulles and the East European Show Trials* (London: Hurst & Company, 2014), and Jiri Pelikan's *Czechoslovak Political Trials, 1950–1954* (Stanford, CA: Stanford University Press, 1971).

## CHAPTER 1: A SWISS CHILDHOOD

Interviews with Alan Field, Hugh Field, and Alison Field, as well as their father, Hermann Field's, unpublished collection of letters to his family, entitled *Letters from Krakow* (Field family private papers).
See also Lewis, *Red Pawn*, 1–50.
Noel's self-description is in the Field Files, Hungarian Institute of Political History Archives (HIA), Budapest.
August 4, 1954, letter to his interrogating officer, Major Arpad Kretschmer, op. cit.

13  " 'A Call to the Young . . . ' " Field Papers, Howard Gotlieb Archival Research Center, Boston University.
14  "Dr. Field, who straddled . . ." Leonard Mosley, *Dulles: A Biography of Eleanor, Allen and John Foster Dulles and Their Family Network* (New York: Dial Press, 1978), 47–49.
14  "In early 1918, Allen Dulles joined . . ." Peter Grose, *Gentleman Spy: The Life of Allen Dulles* (Boston: Houghton Mifflin, 1994), 32.

15   "On the morning of . . ." Noel Field to Hermann Field, December 29, 1963, Field
     Papers, Gotlieb Center.

## CHAPTER 2: AMERICA

Robin Carlaw of Harvard University Archives, Pusey Library, provided back-
ground information for this chapter.
Noel's letters are in the Field Papers, Gotlieb Center.
Noel's term papers, op. cit.
For Sacco and Vanzetti: Upton Sinclair, *Boston: A Novel* (Cambridge, MA: Lin-
naean Press, 1978).
Stephen Koch, *Double Lives: Spies and Writers in the Secret Soviet War of Ideas Against
the West* (New York: Enigma, 2004), 16–17, 39–48, 53, 373–74.
Sam Tanenhaus, *Whittaker Chambers: A Biography* (New York: Modern Library, 1997), 67.
On Münzenberg: Richard Crossman, ed., *The God That Failed* (New York: Colum-
bia University Press, 2001), 64.
Michael Scammell, *Koestler: The Literary and Political Odyssey of a Twentieth-Century
Skeptic* (New York: Random House, 2009), 80, 93, 104–5.

## CHAPTER 3: THE MAKING OF A RADICAL

23   "Graduating from Harvard . . ." Lewis, *Red Pawn*, 33–50.
23   "Lacking in social experience . . ." Lewis, *Red Pawn.*
26   "I have been a pacifist . . ." Field's letter to his mother is found in Field Papers,
     Gotlieb Center.

Noel at the State Department:

Bernd-Rainer Barth, Werner Schweitzer, and Thomas Grimm, *Der Fall Noel Field*
(Berlin: Basis Druck, 2005), 162, 285–86.
For George Kennan's experience as a Foreign Service entrant during the same pe-
riod, useful description can be found in John Gaddis's *George F. Kennan: An
American Life* (New York: Penguin, 2011).

For background:

Edmund Wilson, *The Thirties* (New York: Farrar, Straus & Giroux, 1980).
William Manchester, *The Glory and the Dream: A Narrative History of America* (New
York: Bantam, 1975), 3–57 for vivid portraits of the Depression, the Bonus
Army, and the presidency of Herbert Hoover.
Mosley, *Dulles*, 73.
Ben Gerig interview, Flora Lewis Papers, Howard Gotlieb Archival Research Center, Boston University.
26   "The race problem . . ." Field letter, Field Papers, Gotlieb Center.
27   "Allen Dulles . . ." Mosley, *Dulles*, 73.
27   "I was different . . ." Letter to Nina Field, January 8, 1927, Field Papers, Gotlieb Center.
28   "Lucky Lindy . . ." Noel to Nina Field, June 23, 1927, Field Papers, Gotlieb Center.

29  "My real life . . ." Noel to Hermann, October 23, 1928, Field Papers, Gotlieb Center.

32  "I have lying before me . . ." Op. cit.

32  "They were called Hoovervilles . . ." Manchester, *The Glory and the Dream*, 3–20.

35  "The whole scene was . . ." Op. cit., 16.

Murray Kempton, *Part of Our Time: Some Ruins and Monuments of the Thirties* (New York: New York Review of Books, 2012).

35  "Moneymaking . . ." Edmund Wilson, "An Appeal to Progressives," *New Republic*, January 14, 1931.

J. B. Matthews testimony is from the HUAC Files, Investigating Section Series 4, Box 107 Field Files, National Archives.

36  "The nation . . ." Jonathan Alter, *The Defining Moment* (New York: Simon & Schuster, 2006) and Arthur M. Schlesinger Jr., *The Age of Roosevelt*, vols. 1 and 2 (Boston: Houghton Mifflin, 2002, 2003).

37  "When I came to the State Department . . ." Alger Hiss to Flora Lewis, Flora Lewis Papers, Gotlieb Center.

## CHAPTER 4: THE CONVERT

For background: Crossman, *The God That Failed*.

Nathaniel Weyl, *Treason: The Story of Disloyalty and Betrayal in American History* (Washington, DC: Public Affairs Press, 1950).

Hope Hale Davis, *Great Day Coming: A Memoir of the 1930s* (South Royalton, VT: Steerforth Press, 1994).

Thomas Sakmyster, *Red Conspirator: J. Peters and the American Communist Underground* (Chicago: University of Illinois Press, 2011).

42  "Hal Ware . . ." Davis, *Great Day Coming*, 101.

Weyl, *Treason*, 417–23, 426, 429–30; see also:

Harvey Klehr, John Earl Haynes, and Fridrikh Igorevich Firsov, *The Secret World of American Communism* (New Haven, CT: Yale University Press, 1995), 81, 87, 96–97.

43  "Membership in the underground . . ." Davis, *Great Day Coming*, 98–105, 256, 330–31, 336.

43  "Ware provided . . ." Sakmyster, *Red Conspirator*, chapters 5 and 6.

44  "Even in Germany . . ." Whittaker Chambers, *Witness* (Washington, DC: Gateway Editions, 2002), 338.

44  "Recently declassified . . ." Op. cit.

44  "The secret apparatus . . ." Op. cit., 77.

44  "a test and a binder . . ." Op. cit.

44  "Hiss paid more . . ." Chambers, *Witness*, 572.

45  "Actual truth . . ." Arthur Koestler, *The Invisible Writing* (New York: Macmillan, 1978), 26, 31.

46  "Similar Communist cells . . ." Op. cit., 26.

For a description of spy craft as taught to Hede Massing by Ignaz Reiss, see Hede Massing, *This Deception* (New York: Ivy/Ballantine, 1987), 67–70.

49  "Much of the still . . ." Chambers, *Witness*, 281.
49  "Hiss began an intensive campaign . . ." Noel Field interrogation record, Field Files, HIA, September 23, 1954; Chambers, *Witness*, 381.
Recruiting Duggan: Massing, *This Deception*, 176–79.
Massing's and Bazarov's cables to Moscow Center, and Moscow's replies, throughout the book are from the Vassilev Notebooks: Translations from the KGB files by Alexander Vassiliev (the KGB files were opened in the early 1990s and then closed again in 1996, by which time Vassiliev had done his important work accessing and then translating the files relevant for this period). They are filed in the Wilson Center's Cold War International History Project digital archive: http://digitalarchive.wilsoncenter.org/collection/86/vassiliev-notebooks.
Also: Allen Weinstein and Alexander Vassiliev, *The Haunted Wood: Soviet Espionage in America—the Stalin Era* (New York: Modern Library, 2000) and from "In Re Alger Hiss: A Final Verdict from the Archives of the KGB," *Journal of Cold War Studies* 11, no. 3 (Summer 2009).
See also: John Earl Haynes and Harvey Klehr, *Venona: Decoding Soviet Espionage in America* (New Haven, CT: Yale University Press, 1999) and Klehr et al., *The Secret World of American Communism*.
Roger Baldwin's interview is filed in the Flora Lewis Papers, Gotlieb Center.
Alger Hiss interview: op. cit.
50  "In 1935 . . ." Davis, *Great Day Coming*, 108.

## CHAPTER 5: SPY GAMES

51  "Noel was a worrier . . ." Interview with Flora Lewis in the Flora Lewis Papers, Gotlieb Center.
51  "In 1934 . . ." Massing, *This Deception*, 140–52.
52  "Hede was beguiled . . ." Op. cit., p. 142.
55  "The three unlikely . . ." Op. cit., and see also Chambers, *Witness*, 381–82. See also Noel Field interrogation record of September 23, 1954, Field Files, HIA, Budapest. This section on the Massings is based on their interviews with Flora Lewis, Flora Lewis Papers, Gotlieb Center.
56  "The mentality of the State . . ." Field's lengthy autobiographical narrative is in the Field Files, HIA, Budapest (which contains the secret police files), and is dated June 23, 1954. Field's spying at the Naval Conference is described in his handwritten German-language statement to the Hungarian secret police, June 23, 1954, Field Files, HIA, Budapest.
57  "Our friend [Field] . . ." From the KGB Files as transcribed by Vassiliev, Yellow Notebook #2, April 26, 1936, http://digitalarchive.wilsoncenter.org/collection/86/vassiliev-notebooks.
59  "Moscow was not pleased . . ." Op. cit. and March 5, 1936.
60  "Actual damage . . ." Tanenhaus, *Whittaker Chambers*, 314.
61  "In Geneva . . ." Massing interview with Flora Lewis, Flora Lewis Papers, Gotlieb Center.

61  "Reiss was the real thing . . ." See Massing, *This Deception*, and Walter G. Krivitsky, *In Stalin's Secret Service: Memoirs of the First Soviet Master Spy to Defect* (New York: Enigma, 2000), 218–23, 225–29, 233, 250, 252, 298.

62  "Personal affections . . ." Noel Field, "Hitching Our Wagon to a Star," *Mainstream*, January 1961.

62  "The more irrational . . ." Paul Massing interview, Flora Lewis Papers, Gotlieb Center.

## CHAPTER 6: SPIES IN FLIGHT

64  "Ruddy faced . . ." Wallace Carroll interview, Flora Lewis Papers, Gotlieb Center.

64  "Paul Massing . . ." Interview with Flora Lewis, Flora Lewis Papers, Gotlieb Center.

65  "In late 1936 . . ." Noel Field testimony, September 23, 24, and 29, 1954, Field Files, HIA, Budapest.

66  "The man whom . . ." Op. cit., and see also Massing, *This Deception*, 188–90, 198–201.

67  "Now, finally . . ." Yellow Notebook #2, cables from agent "Jung" to Moscow, August 15, 1937; September 11, 1937; Massing, *This Deception*, 189–201; Noel Field testimony of September 23, 1954, Field Files, HIA, Budapest.

68  "[Reiss] is liquidated . . ." Yellow Notebook #2, September 11, 1954.

68  "For the time being . . ." Op. cit.

68  "He was a traitor . . ." Noel Field to Paul Massing, Flora Lewis Papers, Gotlieb Center.

69  "In Washington . . ." Yellow Notebook #2, Jung's cables to Moscow, September 28, 1937; January 1, 1938; February 2 and 8, 1938; March 1, 1938; June 28, 1938; July 1, 1938; August 4, 1938; February 10, 1939; March 6, 1939; May 10, 1939; April 11, 1940; February 25, 1942, http://digitalarchive.wilsoncenter.org/collection/86/vassiliev-notebooks.

73  "Noel's new contact . . ." Noel Field testimony of September 23 and 29, 1954, Field Files, HIA, Budapest.

73  "Krivitsky's defection . . ." Noel Field statement, September 29, 1954, Field Files, HIA, Budapest.

## CHAPTER 7: DESPERATE COMRADES

77  "In a book-crammed . . ." Chambers, *Witness*, 459–63; Krivitsky, *In Stalin's Secret Service*, 218–22.
Flora Lewis, "Who Killed Krivitsky?" *Washington Post*, February 13, 1966.
FBI Memorandum to Director J. Edgar Hoover from Agent A. Rosen, February 11, 1941, FBI Krivitsky File via FOIA.

80  "Once in Moscow . . ." Massing, *This Deception*, 203–35.

81  "Bazarov shot . . ." Moscow to agent "Mer" Vassiliev, Yellow Notebook #2, February 25, 1939, http://digitalarchive.wilsoncenter.org/collection/86/vassiliev-notebooks.

81  "My trip to Moscow . . ." Noel Field statement, September 29, 1954, Field Files, HIA, Budapest.

## CHAPTER 8: SPAIN

For background: Stephen Spender, *World Within World* (London: Hamish Hamilton, 1951).
George Orwell, *Homage to Catalonia* (London: Penguin, 2013).
Arthur Koestler's memoirs: *Scum of the Earth* (London: Eland, 2006); *Arrival and Departure* (New York: Random House, 2011); *The Invisible Writing*; *Dialogue with Death* (Chicago: University of Chicago Press, 2011).

85  "Spain was to be . . ." Kempton, *Part of Our Time*.
85  "Steadfast . . ." Noel Field, "Hitching Our Wagon to a Star."
85  "I think the happiest . . ." Paul Massing interview, Flora Lewis Papers, Gotlieb Center.
86  "This charge . . ." Orwell, *Homage to Catalonia*, 241.
86  "I know you will forgive . . ." Noel Field letter to family, January 29, 1939, Field Papers, Gotlieb Center.
89  "The Glaser family . . ." Erica Wallach, *Light at Midnight* (Garden City, NY: Doubleday, 1967).
89  "Everything changed . . ." Op. cit., 144–47.
91  "My long blond . . ." Op. cit., 272.
92  "For the young girl . . ." Op. cit., 28–31.
93  "I repeat in writing . . ." Noel Field letter of February 18, 1942, Field Papers, Gotlieb Center.

## CHAPTER 9: WAR

96  "For many Europeans . . ." Koestler, *Scum of the Earth*, 244.
97  "What went through Noel Field's . . ." Flora Lewis interview with Dr. Zina Minor, Flora Lewis Papers, Gotlieb Center.
98  "Arriving at Kraków . . ." Hermann Field, *Letters from Krakow*, Field family private papers.
98  "On May 13 . . ." Op. cit.
99  "On September 2, 1939 . . ." Tanenhaus, *Whittaker Chambers*, 204, and also Chambers, *Witness*, 470.

## CHAPTER 10: MARSEILLE

102  "The Fields' earnest manner . . ." Susan Elisabeth Subak, *Rescue and Flight: American Relief Workers Who Defied the Nazis* (Lincoln: University of Nebraska Press, 2010), 84, 88, 109–110, 121–22, 146, 148–49, 179–82, 202, 204, 219, 223.
102  "Among those in flight . . ." Koch, *Double Lives*, 332–34.
103  "Until the Fields' . . ." Varian Fry, *Surrender on Demand* (Boulder, CO: Johnson Books, 1995).
Howard Lee Brooks, *Prisoners of Hope: Report on a Mission* (New York: Fischer, 1942).
104  "This government . . ." Subak, *Rescue and Flight*; and also Long to Berle, June 26, Breckinridge Long Papers, US Library of Congress.

104 "Fry fired back . . ." Varian Fry, "Our Consuls at Work," *The Nation*, May 2, 1942, 507–9.

104 "Within a year . . ." Fry, *Surrender on Demand*, 236–37.

105 "Through Fry . . ." Michel Gordey to Flora Lewis, Flora Lewis Papers, Gotlieb Center.

107 "Anyone who . . ." Noel Field Report, USC Records, March 6, 1942.

107 "At Rivesaltes . . ." USC Records, March 6, 1942; also Noel Field Report in Subak, *Rescue and Flight*, 88.

107 "I lived and worked . . ." Noel Field statement, June 23, 1954, Field Files, HIA, Budapest; and Noel Field, "Hitching Our Wagon to a Star," 6–7.

108 "Dr. Joseph Weil . . ." Joseph Weil, *Le Combat d'un Juste* (Saumur, France: Éditions Cheminements, 2002), 242.

108 "When I tried to timidly insert . . ." Op. cit.

109 "In March 1945 . . ." Subak, *Rescue and Flight*, 209; Fry Papers, March 26, 1945.

109 "Bénédite already had . . ." Lewis, *Red Pawn*, 152.

109 "You are too noisy . . ." Op. cit.

110 "Noel loved . . ." Zina Minor interview, Flora Lewis Papers, Gotlieb Center.

110 "Noel soon hired . . ." Paul Massing interview, op. cit.

111 "Minutes ahead . . ." Andy Pollak, "The Unitarian Who Shook Europe," *Oscailit: Cork & Dublin Unitarian Magazine*, December 2009; also Field Project, USC records, Andover-Harvard Theological Library, Harvard University.

## CHAPTER 11: THE SPY IN WARTIME

113 "It's not quite the thing . . ." Subak, *Rescue and Flight*, 153.

113 "I think of the past . . ." Noel Field to mother, op. cit., 179.

114 "To Dr. Joseph Weil . . ." Op. cit., 204.

114 "Surrounded by Axis troops . . ." Richard Harris Smith, *OSS: The Secret History of America's First Central Intelligence Agency* (Guilford, CT: The Lyons Press, 2005), 187–94; and Stephen Kinzer, *The Brothers: John Foster Dulles, Allen Dulles, and Their Secret World War* (New York: Times Books, 2013), 66–70.

114 "I'd put Stalin . . ." Op. cit., 9.

115 "The first chance . . ." Op. cit., 24.

115 "Dulles soon settled . . ." Grose, *Gentleman Spy*; and Mosely, *Dulles*, 44–49, 73, 129–32, 147–48, 172, 275–77, 505.

115 "In 1941 . . ." Elizabeth Dexter interview with Flora Lewis, Flora Lewis Papers, Gotlieb Center.

116 "In a secret internal . . ." Allen Dulles telegram 1687 to Paris, November 30, 1944, as cited in Neal H. Petersen, *From Hitler's Doorstep: The Wartime Intelligence Reports of Allen Dulles, 1942–1945* (University Park: Pennsylvania State University Press, 2010), 403–4, 431, 628.

116 "Soft spoken . . ." Arthur M. Schlesinger Jr. to the author; and Arthur M. Schlesinger Jr., *A Life in the Twentieth Century: Innocent Beginnings, 1917–1950* (Boston: Houghton Mifflin, 2000), 334.

117   "After years of silence . . ." Noel Field statement, September 23, 1954, Field Files, HIA, Budapest.

## CHAPTER 12: CHILD OF THE CENTURY

All quotes in this chapter are from Erica Wallach's memoir *Light at Midnight*, as well as "The Erica Wallach Story: Report by HUAC," March 21, 1958, from the long interview Erica gave Flora Lewis, among the Flora Lewis Papers, Gotlieb Center, and from the German documentary film *Noel Field: The Fictitious Spy* by Werner Schweizer (Dschoint Ventschr Filmproduktion, 1997), and, where indicated, from Erica's private correspondence, for which the author thanks Robert Wallach Jr.

120   "I was perfectly willing . . ." To Flora Lewis, Flora Lewis Papers, Gotlieb Center; also HUAC Investigative Section series 4, Box 107, National Archives.

120   "He arrived at everything . . ." Flora Lewis interview, Flora Lewis Papers, Gotlieb Center.

122   "All these things . . ." Op. cit.

## CHAPTER 13: COLD PEACE

For background: Tony Judt, *Postwar: A History of Europe since 1945* (New York: Penguin, 2005); Anne Applebaum, *Iron Curtain: The Crushing of Eastern Europe, 1944–1956* (Garden City, NY: Doubleday, 2012); Krisztáin Ungváry, *The Siege of Budapest: One Hundred Days in World War II* (New Haven, CT: Yale University Press, 2005).

124   "We must be firm . . ." Schlesinger, *A Life in the Twentieth Century*, 477.

124   "I saw Noel in 1945 . . ." Weill, *Le Combat d'un Juste*, 243.

124   "Later in 1945 . . ." Subak, *Rescue and Flight*, 202; see also USC Field Files Box 2, 1945–1947, Andover-Harvard Theological Library, Harvard University.

125   "He was the hero . . ." Rev. Ray Bragg interview with Flora Lewis, Flora Lewis Papers, Gotlieb Center.

125   "It is so utterly . . ." Noel Field to Erica Wallach, December 6, 1945, Field Papers, Gotlieb Center.

125   "We have met . . ." Op. cit.

125   "We really . . ." Op. cit.

126   "By 1946 . . ." "Confidential Memo to the USC," August 6, 1946, USC Files, Andover-Harvard Theological Library; "Harvard Divinity School Transcript of the Meeting with Mr. Henson," September 10, 1946, USC Files; Noel Field correspondence with Dr. William Emerson and Francis Henson, USC Files; and also Rev. Bragg interview with Flora Lewis, Flora Lewis Papers, Gotlieb Center.

127   "Noel's blazing . . ." Elizabeth Dexter to Flora Lewis, Flora Lewis Papers, Gotlieb Center.

127   "She perceives . . ." Charles Joy, "She Has Known Terror," *Christian Register*, April 1946; and also Subak, *Rescue and Flight*, 202.

128 "The disaster . . ." Judt, *Postwar*, 19.

130 "I told Noel . . ." Bragg to Flora Lewis, Flora Lewis Papers, Gotlieb Center.

132 "I should have . . ." USC Files, April 1957, Frank GZ Glick Memorandum for Files, Box 3.

132 "Dear Kid . . ." Noel Field to Erica Wallach, Field Papers, Gotlieb Center.

132 "For a decade . . ." Sakmyster, *Red Conspirator*, chapter 9 and epilogue.

## CHAPTER 14: MAN WITHOUT A COUNTRY—1948

134 "We slept . . ." Arthur Miller, *Timebends: A Life* (New York: Grove, 2013), 258.

134 "In the long run . . ." Noel Field to Erica Wallach, February 29, 1948, Wallach family private papers.

135 "Going West to East . . ." Robert Gellately, *Stalin's Curse: Battling for Communism in War and Cold War* (New York: Knopf, 2013), 300.

136 "This would make you . . ." Craig Thompson, "What Has Stalin Done with Noel Field?" *Saturday Evening Post*, December 15, 1951.

137 "The national mood . . ." Some of the best studies of the Chambers case that provided background for this chapter are: Tanenhaus, *Whittaker Chambers*; Allen Weinstein, *Perjury: The Hiss-Chambers Case* (Stanford, CA: Hoover Press, 2013); Chambers, *Witness*; Susan Jacoby, *Alger Hiss and the Battle for History* (New Haven, CT: Yale University Press, 2009); G. Edward White, *Alger Hiss's Looking-Glass Wars: The Covert Life of a Soviet Spy* (New York: Oxford University Press, 2005).

138 " 'Hiss,' his former control . . ." "Interview with J. Peters by Allen Weinstein," Allen Weinstein Papers, Hoover Institution; "Letter to Comrade Berman," Field Files, HIA, Budapest.

## CHAPTER 15: THE END OF THE LINE

141 "On October 15 . . ." "Ex State Department Aide Called Red by Chambers—Noel Field Named in House Inquiry," *New York Herald Tribune*, October 15, 1948.

142 "Herta asked . . ." Testimony of Herta Field, undated, Field Files, HIA, Budapest.

142 "His colleagues . . ." Paul Massing to Flora Lewis, Flora Lewis Papers, Gotlieb Center.

142 "I was afraid . . ." Noel Field testimony of March 1954, Field Files, HIA, Budapest. The Alger Hiss letter of October 19, 1948, is in the Field Files, HIA, Budapest.

143 "On Capitol Hill . . ." *Laurence Duggan, 1905–1948: In Memoriam* (Stamford, CT: Overbrook Press, 1949).

144 "Shaushkin . . ." Alexander Vassilev, Yellow Notebook #2, March 1938–December 1948, http://digitalarchive.wilsoncenter.org/collection/86/vassiliev-notebooks. Also, Weinstein and Vassiliev, *The Haunted Wood*, part 1, "Communist Romantics, the Reluctant Laurence Duggan"; "Investigations: The Man in the Window" (obituary of Laurence Duggan), *Time*, January 3, 1949; Nathaniel Weyl, "I was in a Communist Unit with Hiss," *U.S. News & World Report*, January 9, 1953; Massing, *This Deception*, 176–77; Venona File 36857, 19s.

144  "Increasingly, the Fields . . ." Michel Gordey to Flora Lewis, Flora Lewis Papers, Gotlieb Center.

145  "One of my greatest . . ." Noel Field testimony of March 1954, Field Files, HIA, Budapest.

145  "As to ourselves . . ." Noel Field to Erica Wallach, Field Papers, Gotlieb Center.

## CHAPTER 16: BLOODLUST AGAIN

147  "An epic . . ." Adam B. Ulam, *Titoism and the Cominform* (Cambridge, MA: Harvard University Press, 1952).

148  "On the ottoman . . ." Aleksandr Solzhenitsyn, *In the First Circle*, trans. Harry T. Willets (New York: Harper Perennial, 2009), 96–98.

151  "Stalin chose Budapest . . ." Béla Szász, *Volunteers for the Gallows: Anatomy of a Show-Trial* (London: Chatto & Windus, 1971); George H. Hodos, *Show Trials: Stalinist Purges in Eastern Europe* (New York: Praeger, 1987); and George Paloczi-Horvath, *The Undefeated* (London: Eland, 1959).

151  "Happily for Stalin . . ." This section was tremendously enhanced by the author's many hours of conversation with Endre and Ilona Marton and László Rajk Jr.

151  "I need hardly tell you . . ." Noel Field letter to Oskar Kosta, undated, Field Files, HIA, Budapest.

152  "I went to Moscow . . ." Gellately, *Stalin's Curse*, 311.

152  "Today I'm sticking close . . ." Noel Field to Herta Field, May 9, 1949, Field Papers, Gotlieb Center.

For a description of Noel Field's interrogation at the Villa, the author relied on the first-person experiences related by her parents, Endre and Ilona Marton, as well as the vivid published accounts of Field's "coconspirators," Béla Szász, George Hodos, and George Paloczi-Horvath.

## CHAPTER 17: KIDNAPPED

155  "The sessions always . . ." The testimony of secret police (AVO/AVH) officer Gyula Décsi, one of Field's interrogators, is in the HIA Field "Rehabilitation" File of May 16, 1954, Field Files, HIA, Budapest.

155  "I stood for nine days . . ." Szász, *Volunteers for the Gallows*, 52.

156  "When did you . . ." Op. cit., 45–49

157  "On July 7, 1949 . . ." Noel Field letter to the American embassy, Field Files, HIA, Budapest.

158  "Rákosi travelled . . ." Gábor Péter testimony, October 18–23, 1956, Field Files, HIA, Budapest.

158  "On September 16 . . ." This section is based on the author's parents' accounts. As correspondents for the Associated Press and United Press, they were in the courtroom covering the Rajk trial. This account is rounded out by László Rajk Jr.'s personal account, as well as the published Hungarian transcript of the proceedings, "László Rajk and His Accomplices before the People's Court of Budapest."

159  "Everybody performed . . ." Endre Marton, *The Forbidden Sky* (Boston: Little, Brown, 1971), 5, 86–87.

160  "Let us remember . . ." Lewis, *Red Pawn*, 20.

160  "In the Prague trials . . ." Hodos, *Show Trials*, 84; and see also Pelikan, *Czechoslovak Political Trials*.

162  "My arrest . . ." Noel Field testimony, March 18, 1954, Field Files, HIA, Budapest.

162  "My accusers . . ." Field, "Hitching Our Wagon to a Star."

## CHAPTER 18: TWO MORE FIELDS DISAPPEAR

163  "She was very secretive . . ." Hélèné Matthey to Flora Lewis, Flora Lewis Papers, Gotlieb Center.

164  "It's a long time . . ." Herta Field's letter of May 22, 1949, Herta Field Files, Field Files, HIA, Budapest.

164  "Herta asked Hermann . . ." Hermann Field's account of his arrest and imprisonment is contained in his gripping joint biography with his wife, Kate, *Trapped in the Cold War: The Ordeal of an American Family* (Stanford, CA: Stanford University Press, 2000). The author gratefully acknowledges the support Hermann and Kate's three children, Allison, Hugh, and Alan, provided in capturing the human drama of their father's disappearance and its impact on their childhood.

166  "The same day . . ." See Igor Lukes, "The Rudolf Slansky Affair: New Evidence," *Slavic Review 58*, no. 1 (Spring 1999): 160–87; as well as Pelikan, *Czechoslovak Political Trials*.

166  "I heard my husband . . ." Field testimony conducted by AVO Major Gyorgy Szendy, undated but likely from 1954, Field Files, HIA, Budapest.

166  "Around Christmastime in 1953 . . ." Herta Field's "rehabilitation" testimony, undated but from 1954, Field Files, HIA, Budapest.

167  "Arthur M. Schlesinger . . ." Schlesinger, *A Life in the Twentieth Century*, 499–500.

167  "The moment . . ." Hermann and Kate Field, *Trapped in the Cold War*, 39–40.

## CHAPTER 19: ERICA FALLS IN THE NET

This chapter is based on interviews with Erica Wallach's children, Madeleine Wallach de Heller and Robert Wallach Jr., and their cousins Feroline Higginson and Hope Porter.

*Welcome Home* is Erica Wallach's unpublished fourteen-page description of her ordeal and final homecoming; Wallach family private papers. All quotes from Erica are from the following sources:

Erica Wallach interview in Schweizer, *Noel Field*.

Descriptions of Erica's prison ordeal are from her memoir, *Light at Midnight*.

"The Erica Wallach Story: Report by HUAC," HUAC Investigative Section series 4, Box 107, Field Files, March 31, 1958, National Archives.

All correspondence between Robert and Erica and her mother, Marie Therese Glaser, is from the Wallach family private papers.

## CHAPTER 20: THE PRISONS OPEN

182  "After long personal . . ." June 20, 1954, Field Files, HIA, Budapest.

182  "He had also begun a hunger strike . . ." Noel Field sixty-five-page letter, March 18–22, Field Files, HIA, Budapest.

183  "Field's reprieve . . ." "Polish Defector Bares Data on the Missing Field Family," *New York Times*, September 29, 1954.

183  "Josef Swiatlo's own . . ." *News from Behind the Iron Curtain* [Munich] 4, no. 3 (1955).

183  "Even as Swiatlo . . ." "US Notes to Poland and Hungary."

184  "Swiatlo's announcement . . ." Henry Jordan, "Where Is Noel Field?" *Argosy*, November 1958.

The October 2, 1954 transcript (in Hungarian) of Swiatlo's Radio Free Europe broadcast is in the Field Files, HIA, Budapest.

184  "Not a word . . ." Erica Wallach interview, Schweizer, *Noel Field*.

184  "They must guarantee . . ." February 10, 1955, Field Files, HIA, Budapest.

185  "Hermann, also suddenly . . ." "Warsaw Releases Hermann Field," *New York Times*, October 25, 1954.

185  "I first got . . ." Hermann and Kate Field, *Trapped in the Cold War*, 401–3; and "Hermann Field Arrives in Zurich in Reunion with Wife and Sister," *New York Times*, November 20, 1954.

## CHAPTER 21: STILL NOT FREE

The Fields' voluminous surveillance records are catalogued in the Field Files, HIA, Budapest.

189  "A top secret . . ." Op. cit., November 1, 1954.

190  "Only one American . . ." This information is from Ambassador Ravndal's close friends, the author's parents, Endre and Ilona Marton.

191  "Now, Ambassador . . ." January 29 internal memorandum (unsigned), Hungarian Ministry of the Interior, Field Files, HIA, Budapest.

191  "I am authorized . . ." Ravndal's note is in the Field Files, HIA, Budapest.

192  "To my utter amazement . . ." Noel Field letter to Monica Felton, Field Files, HIA, Budapest.

193  "Herta and I love . . ." Noel Field to Hermann and Kate Field, Field Files, HIA, Budapest.

194  "1. His statement . . ." Szalma Jozsef memorandum, January 7, 1955, Field Files, HIA, Budapest.

194  "Field, wrote . . ." Mrs. Ferenc Kuhari, January 30, Field Files, HIA, Budapest.

195  "If you had simply . . ." Hermann Field letter to his brother, May 4, 1955, Field Files, HIA, Budapest.

195  "I just can't bring myself . . ." Elsie Field letter, April 24, 1955, Field Papers, Gotlieb Center.

196  "The Case of Noel H. Field . . ." January 5, 1955, Field Files, HIA, Budapest.

198 "A certain wariness . . ." Author's interview with Noel Field's colleague Ferenc Aczél at Corvina Publishing and the *New Hungarian Quarterly*.
199 "On January 13 . . ." Field letter to the Communist Party, Field Files, HIA, Budapest.
200 "On February 25 . . ." Applebaum, *Iron Curtain*.
200 "Let me tell you this . . ." Author's interview with László Rajk Jr.

## CHAPTER 22: THE AGE OF SUSPICION

Letters between Erica and Robert Wallach and Noel, Hermann, and Elsie Field are also among the Wallach family private papers, as is the letter to Erica from Curt Pohl, Erica's former fellow inmate. All Erica's correspondence to her attorneys and other officials is similarly from the family papers.

## CHAPTER 23: TWILIGHT YEARS

United Nations Special Committee on Hungary Report, June 1957.
218 "On Radio Budapest . . ." *New York Times*, June 27, 1957.
218 "It makes me so . . ." Elsie Field to Hermann Field, Field Papers, Gottlieb Center.
218 "[Your radio report] . . ." Op. cit.
218 "Feeling utterly torn . . ." Op. cit.
219 "It's damnable . . ." Op. cit.
220 "He used to say . . ." Author's interview with Miklos Vajda.
220 "Soviet troops . . ." Noel Field, "Hitching Our Wagon to a Star."
221 "I'm really sore . . ." Hermann Field to Elsie Field, December 21, 1960, Field Files, HIA, Budapest.
221 "As you know . . ." Noel Field to Hermann Field, December 26, 1960, Field Papers, Gotlieb Center.
222 "Comrade Field . . ." Author's interview with Miklos Vajda.
222 "Hermann's story . . ." Harvard Class of 1932 Class Report, Harvard University, Cambridge, MA, 1982.
223 "Very few people . . ." Author's interview with Ferenc Aczél.
225 "Even if Hiss . . ." Weinstein, *Perjury*, 540.
226 "What I said . . ." Op. cit., 596.
226 "That year . . ." Mária Schmidt, *Battle of Wits: Beliefs, Ideologies and Secret Agents in the 20th Century* (Budapest: Század Int., 2007).
226 "Moreover, in 1996 . . ." Haynes and Klehr, *Venona*.
227 "One startling coda . . ." Edward Stettinius Jr., *The Diaries of Edward R. Stettinius, Jr., 1943–1946* (New York: New Viewpoints, 1975), 416.
228 "Once . . ." Author's interview with Ferenc Aczél.
229 "Our days with you . . ." Hermann Field's letter to Noel Field, Field Files, HIA, Budapest.
230 "Dear Kid . . ." May 1964, Field Files, HIA, Budapest.

## CHAPTER 24: PRAGUE

For an excellent visual representation of the Prague Spring, see Josef Koudelka, *Invasion 68: Prague* (Paris: Tana Editions, 2008).

232   "I have a hard time . . ." Noel Field letter, March 24, 1968, Field Papers, Gotlieb Center.

234   "This time . . ." Author's interview with Rudi Fischer.

## CHAPTER 25: HOME AT LAST

235   "The gentle . . ." Author's interviews with Robert Wallach Jr., Madeleine Wallach de Heller, Feroline Higginson, and Hope Porter.

All correspondence—including with Noel Field—in this chapter is from the Wallach family private papers.

The description of Erica as teacher is from the author's interview with Stevenson McIlvaine.

Erica's run-in with Allen Dulles is told in her unpublished memoir, *Welcome Home*, Wallach family private papers.

The text of Erica Wallach's final speech is also in the family papers.

## CHAPTER 26: THE STRANGER

245   "Like all the other Quaker . . ." Sakmyster, *Red Conspirator*, 174.

246   "The famed . . ." David Caute, *Joseph Losey: A Revenge on Life* (New York: Oxford University Press, 1994), 50, 288–89.

246   "Mr. Field is one of . . ." HUAC, Investigative section series, Box 107, Field Files, February 28, 1958, National Archives.

247   "That last day . . ." Herta Field to Hermann Field, September 1970, Field Papers, Gotlieb Center.

247   "I made a big . . ." Erica Wallach interview, Schweizer, *Noel Field*.

247   "He died with only . . ." *New York Times*, September 14, 1970.

247   "In death . . ." Author's interview with Rudi Fischer.

# PHOTO CREDITS

1. Bettmann/Corbis/AP Images.
2. Associated Press.
3. Field Family Collection.
4. Corbis.
5. Corbis.
6. Bettmann/Corbis/AP Images.
7. Courtesy of the author.
8. Three Lions/Stringer.
9. United States Holocaust Memorial Museum, courtesy of Simone Weil Lipman.
10. Audiovisual Collection, Unitarian Universalist Association, Public Information Office, Photographs, ca. 1950–1985, bMS 15033, Andover-Harvard Theological Library, Harvard Divinity School, Cambridge, Massachusetts.
11. Associated Press.
12. Bettmann/Corbis/AP Images.
13. *New York Daily News* Archive.
14. Ben Heinemann.
15. Interfoto/Foto Wilhelm.
16. Keystone-France/Contributor.
17. Bettmann/Corbis.
18. Courtesy of the author.
19. Courtesy of the author.
20. Corbis.
21. Corbis.
22. Wallach Family Collection.
23. Field Family Collection.
24. Field Family Collection.

# INDEX

# ABOUT THE AUTHOR

**Kati Marton** is the author of *Enemies of the People: My Family's Journey to America*, a National Book Critics Circle Award finalist. Her other books include *Paris: A Love Story*; *The Great Escape: Nine Jews Who Fled Hitler and Changed the World*; *Hidden Power: Presidential Marriages That Shaped Our History*; *Wallenberg*; *The Polk Conspiracy*; and *A Death in Jerusalem*. She is an award-winning former NPR and ABC News correspondent. She lives in New York City.

# *More from* KATI MARTON

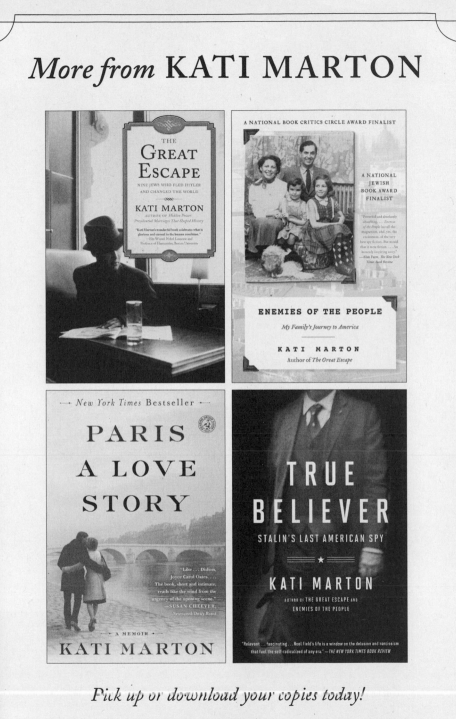

*Pick up or download your copies today!*

56896